CW01084659

About the Author

Born to drive, John worked for many years as a tanker driver. He's clocked up the equivalent miles by truck, car and motor-bike, to travel sixty times around the world.

He is passionate about political, legal and economic injustices, environmental issues, travel, food, drink and good company.

He resides with Christine in tranquil, rural Bulgaria to this day.

Dedication

This book is dedicated to Christine. Without your continual love, support and belief, none of this would have been possible. The journey we began together on a cold January night in Calais has been the most exhilarating time of my life. Thank you!

To Ray and Elaine, Chris's parents, and to my parents, David and Jenny for their faith, encouragement and understanding when informed of our plans. They have had their own adventures coming out to see us and had any preconceptions or doubts swept away.

In memory of Elaine, we miss you very much!

John Mabbs

IT'S ABOUT TIME!

AUSTIN MACAULEY PUBLISHERS™

LONDON • CAMBRIDGE • NEW YORK • SHARJAH

A CIP catalogue record for this title is available from the British Library.

ISBN 9781786931603 (Paperback)
ISBN 9781786931610 (Hardback)
ISBN 9781786931627 (E-Book)
www.austinmacauley.com

First Published (2017)
Austin Macauley Publishers Ltd.
25 Canada Square
Canary Wharf
London
E14 5LQ

Imagine:
You no longer had a mortgage
You willingly packed your job in
You were free of debt
You were free to live life as you pleased
You were free to follow your dreams

Table of Contents

INTRODUCTION

It's About Time…
That you take a step back and look at the bigger picture
That you pursue the life of your dreams
To be true to yourself, what do you really want?
To realise that Time is more precious than money
To liberate yourself from 'time served'

Have you ever thought – is this as good as it gets? Wondered what's in store for you and how you'll ever accomplish some of your lifelong dreams. Even worse have you resigned yourself to never being able to achieve any of them? Maybe you're told by others that's the way it is?

Just because it is, doesn't mean it should be!

A huge percentage of us intensely dislike our jobs, a million of us have full time jobs but live on or below the poverty line and have little or zero work life balance. This is compounded by surveys conducted in care homes revealing a list of death bed regrets lamenting unfulfilled dreams, too much time at work and not enough spent with loved ones. Chief among these regrets was 'I wish I'd lived a life true to myself, not the one others expected of me.'

How many years have you been loyal and hardworking and can you see yourself getting off that treadmill any time soon? If you could bring forward your release date, wouldn't that allow you to have some time really living?

All we have is now! To take control of your life is the ultimate freedom. His Holiness the Dalai Lama summed it up thus:

'Man sacrifices his health in order to make money. Then he sacrifices money to recuperate his health. And then he is so anxious about the future that he does not enjoy the present; the result being that he does not live in the present or the future; he lives as if he is never going to die, and then dies having never really lived.'

A recent survey of the over fifties carried out by the Daily Mail came up with the eye opening biggest regret being; marrying the wrong partner! It did not reveal how many participants were still married to that same partner but, is it fair to anyone to spend your life with someone you secretly don't love anymore? It reveals a substantial number of us are not living the life we wanted, but just putting a brave face on it.

Instead of following your usual Monday morning routine, what if I told you:

You no longer had a mortgage
You willingly packed your job in
You were free of debt
You were free to live life as you pleased
You were free to follow your dreams

Yes, this escape plan involves upping sticks and leaving the UK for sunnier climes but we've found this is the easiest real method of changing your life forever, because it provides many options otherwise not open to you.

The single most important reason I have for writing this book is this; it would be an act of supreme selfishness to keep this information to myself. If it helps one person or family enjoy the freedom and quality of life that my wonderful girlfriend and I do, it is mission accomplished.

You don't need to wait for six numbers to come up on the lottery or be the beneficiary of a large inheritance. If you've always wanted a place in the sun this little book can give you all the help and advice you need to unlock your freedom from the rat race, to live the life you know you deserve and most important of all, live a life true to yourself. All you need is an open mind; to be a home owner with at least £50 to £75 thousand in equity; or a home in the UK you can rent out; along with a keen sense of adventure and the belief that this transformation is possible.

If you are happy in your job, receive a good wage and a good work-life balance, good for you! This book may be of interest to you if you are looking to find an affordable holiday home and you want some handy tips about motoring across Europe.

If as an avid traveller, you've always fancied attempting your own 'Top Gear' challenge, 'Long Way Round', 'Eat, Pray, Love' adventure or to get a taste of the experience portrayed in the hit film '*The Best Exotic Marigold Hotel*' then keep reading!

Summing up then, vast numbers of us hate our jobs, our bosses or both, we marry the wrong person and will end up on our death bed wondering what the hell happened to us and how and why did we let this happen, why didn't we do the things that made us happy? Why?! Why on earth do we do this to ourselves? Doubtlessly, this explains our binge drinking culture, the record number of us who are on anti-depressants, those who self-harm or have eating and other compulsive disorders.

So, if you are of my generation, mid-forties or a little older, you recognize some or all of the situations described, you have a property worth substantially more than the mortgage you took out twenty years ago but the equity is lost to you, or you have a place you can rent out for the average amount, this just might change your life forever!

For those of you that are younger, there are many options for you and by following some of the learnings and principles in this book, you will be able to create a fulfilling life elsewhere. You have time on your side to get it right sooner and live a happier life by manifesting your goals right now!

Turn your imagination into reality. This is your time!

SECTION 1
In search of the truth

JOINING THE DOTS

This first section is looking at the big picture and shines a light on the situations and actions that have brought the world to where it is today. In my mind, it's nothing short of chaotic.

There is a global awakening taking place thanks to the Freedom of Information Act and unauthorised leaked information supplied by well known 'whistle blowers' making available documented evidence of wrong doing. Who knows to what extent we have been misled and how much remains hidden, yet to be disclosed.

My hope is that you will find this section informative, revealing and thought provoking.

I think the following advice from the genius of Bill Hicks sums up exactly how life on this planet could and should be.

'The world is like a ride in an amusement park, and when you choose to go on it you think it's real because that's how powerful our minds are. The ride goes up and down, around and around, it has thrills and chills, and is very brightly coloured, and it's very loud, and it's fun for a while. Many people have been on the ride a long time, and they begin to wonder. "Hey, is this real, or is

this just a ride?" And other people have remembered, and they come back to us and say "Hey, don't worry, don't be afraid ever, because this is just a ride?" And we.......kill those people. "Shut him up! I've got a lot invested in this ride, shut him up!" Look at my furrows of worry, look at my big bank account and my family. This HAS to be real. "It's just a ride".

But we always kill the good guys who try and tell us that, you ever notice that? And let the demons run amok...... But it doesn't matter, because it's just a ride. And we can change it any time we want, it's only a choice. No effort, no work, no job, no savings of money. Just a simple choice right now, between fear and love. The eyes of fear want you to put bigger locks on your doors, buy guns, close yourself off. The eyes of love see all of us as one. Here's what we can do to change the world, right now, to a better ride. Take all that money we spend on nuclear weapons and defences each year and instead spend it feeding and clothing and educating the poor of the world, which it would pay for many times over, not one human being excluded, and we could explore space, both inner and outer, forever, in peace.'

Bill Hicks

Powerful and thought provoking words. The lyrics of John Lennon's *Imagine*, also show the simple steps we could take to achieve a fantastic and rewarding way of life.

"Knowledge makes a man unfit to be a slave."
Frederick Douglass

"Those who control the media, control the mind."
Jim Morrison

What else makes you consider leaving your homeland? Are the newspapers and TV news outlets reporting falling sales of luxury cars, reduced salaries for bank CEOs, and falling orders for private yachts[1]? No, they are not. Are Premier League footballers seeing their wages fall in line with the falling attendances at the grounds they play at? No, they are not. Football fans are being priced out of the game they love, top management at the banks have seen their wages reach a point where they earn 200 times more than the employee behind the reinforced window in the branch[2], this at a time when tens of thousands of staff have been laid off.

There are more than a million people on zero hour contracts in the UK[3]. It may suit some of them if they are already retired and looking for a top up in their pensions but for someone younger, trying to make a meaningful life for themselves it's near impossible. They can't rent anywhere, apart from staying at home with mum and dad indefinitely. They will not get sick pay, holiday entitlement or any pension provision whatsoever and therefore they are little better off than being slaves. Successive governments love to brag about the number of jobs their policies have created. Labour claimed to have created four million and the coalition one million. Most of these have been poorly paid, part time jobs with over eighty percent of them having gone to Eastern European immigrants[4]. It is similar over the pond in

America, obviously without the EU open door immigration policy, though the numbers of Mexicans crossing the border illegally is a serious issue.

If you have teenage sons and daughters what do you see happening for them in the coming decades? Are they going to be better off than your generation? Are they going to be better off than the baby boomer generation? Not a chance of that be honest now. The baby boomer generation will be looked at by historians as the luckiest generation in human history[5]. They had affordable homes which have rocketed in value, jobs for life and excellent pension schemes. The following generations are locked into a race to the bottom for the benefit of the corporate and financial elite whose wealth and power has been increasing for at least thirty years.

It seems to be an un-alterable fact that the general rule in our society and our place in it, is that there are among us the "have's and have not's" or as former Wall Street trader and economist Max Keiser observed, "the have not's and the have yachts". It is also an un-alterable fact that the richest 1% at the top have seen their wealth grow by up to 15% since the height of the economic crash of 2007/ 08. There are now more than a hundred billionaires in the UK for the first time with their average wealth according to Forbes being around £3.2 billion. Oxfam published a report revealing the top eighty-five wealthiest individuals had more money between them than over half the population of the planet[6]. Indeed, the combined wealth of the richest individuals in the UK is put at over five hundred billion pounds. This pales almost into insignificance when in

2010 the BBC reported that £21 trillion belonging to the super rich was stashed away in off shore havens[7]. This is staggering when one considers that the cost of removing everyone from poverty, hunger, disease and homelessness on a global basis would cost according to some estimates around £500 billion. This global elite could literally save the world from utter misery and destitution for little more than a tiny fraction of their cash reserves. It might be argued that I am approaching these conclusions from the politics of envy, that I must be a rabid, dyed in the wool and foaming at the mouth socialist, I just believe it is unacceptable both morally and spiritually for the world's governments to waste so much money on the War Machine when only eight days spending power on it would end hunger, poverty, disease and homelessness. While it is true my father was once a member of the communist party, and took part in the CND march to Aldermaston in 1958, he never pushed his political opinions on me. He mellowed over time, becoming a member of the Labour Party even standing as a candidate in local elections. He left for the SDP after the split in Labour ranks caused by the so called "gang of four" breakaway and ended up supporting the Liberal Democrats. I, on the other hand, voted for Margaret Thatcher in 1987 and John Major in 1992. Work commitments meant I missed my chance to vote in 2001 and 2005. Hardly the archetypal "red under the bed!"

We all know there has always been in existence a class structure in the UK and there always has been rich and poor but the gap has been widening for thirty years and has reached morally indefensible levels today. This is also true in the United States as witnessed by the Occupy Wall Street phenomenon in the autumn of 2011. This movement, like the one in London, began to crumble only after infiltration by the authorities but the "We are the 99%" message entered the mainstream lexicon permanently as a result and anti-establishment political parties made sweeping gains in European elections in 2014[8].

The majority of hard working people have seen stagnant wages and rising living costs for what seems like forever. Throw in austerity measures and the still to be paid for quantitative easing and banker bail out money, the deeply unpopular bedroom tax and the threat of potential interest rate rises to come, it is little wonder that only a third of the electorate bothered to vote at all in the 2010 General Election. It's also little wonder that the country has a binge drinking issue and record numbers of people prescribed anti-depressants[9]. Trying to make sense of it all when you feel like you're constantly running just to stand still is terribly debilitating. We live in a consumer based economy but how can that possibly work if few of us can afford to consume?? If we were earning liveable salaries there would be no such entities as "pay day" loan companies. They are little more than glorified and well-advertised loan sharks. They appear to have the veneer of respectability because they sponsor Premier League and Scottish Premier League football clubs but this doesn't detract from the appalling levels of interest they charge, up to 3,000% or higher. Many thousands of homeowners are using credit cards to keep up with their mortgage or rent payments and the large rise in the number of visitors to food banks is further evidence that while the official figures say Britain has the fastest growing economy in Europe, one that is recording even more growth than the United States, the benefits are still to be felt by most[10]. The so called "trickle down" theory of economics has proven to be utterly fictitious[11].

I bought my first house in 1990 at the age of twenty-three. It was a three bedroom semi-detached house with a garage and cost me the princely sum of thirty-eight thousand pounds. I qualified for a mortgage because I met the three times salary rule which had been the norm forever. I lived in Nottinghamshire and well away from the affluent south east corner of the country which meant when I came to sell my house ten years later I lost six thousand pounds in the process. I was still able to buy a new four bed detached house under the three times salary rule. Even then, I soon found myself with very little expendable income after all my bills and property prices remained flat for most of the following four years.

Fast forward to today and the average house price in London equates to eleven times the average salary. I'm not an economist but this is patently a totally untenable scenario! As stated I was twenty-three and that was the average age of a first time buyer. Now it is nearly forty and with the average monthly rent pushing £700 a month what does this tell you? At what level do house prices become completely unaffordable? Do young people have to stay at home with Mummy and Daddy indefinitely and become increasingly infantilised? Does sharing a home with three or four other people have to become the norm? Why not make it ten, eleven or twelve as many immigrants from Eastern Europe do? The BBC recently had an interview with three young entrepreneurs. One owns a company that rents outfits out to people who can't afford to buy clothes. Another ran an agency which in essence rents out enough space in a house or flat to put down an air bed as an alternative to trying to rent your own flat, and the other managed an online car sharing company that helped bring three or four people together to share a car journey for those who can't afford to own and run their own vehicle. There will be some who will argue that this is a good thing if it cuts down both congestion and pollution but really? Where is the aspiration in this[12]? If you can't afford anything but an air bed space, rent your outfits, share your journeys AND have three decades of university tuition fee repayments to look forward to, what is the incentive here? If this wasn't enough there is the issue of pension provision in the future.

In twenty or thirty years there will be millions of workers who will have to work until they are seventy, as they do in Germany but unlike the Germans they will look forward to their retirement from a position of deprivation and chronic impoverishment. The National Employment Savings Trust announced in May 2014 that a person needs to have an annual pension of £15,000 to be able to pay their bills and a modest amount of expendable income left over. This is now and doesn't take in to account the levels of hidden inflation plus there aren't many people retiring on that level of income. Because of quantitative easing, the value of annuities has fallen off a cliff[13]. In 1990 if you retired with a pension pot of £100,000 you could expect a lump sum of £25,000 and an annual pension of £10,000 for life. Now the annual amount is down to £5,000 so you have lost half your pension from the word go. There has been an attempt to subliminally suggest to the masses that retirement isn't all it's cracked up to be[14]. Missing the buzz of work and the camaraderie of colleagues mixed in with the content of daytime TV might send many reaching for the sleeping pills and a bottle of vodka but only if there is already a deficit in imagination or expectation. Another factor to be considered is if people are staying at work till they are in their late sixties or early seventies, will this not adversely impact on the under 25's trying to get a foot on the employment ladder?

In Japan there are people in their eighties flipping burgers in fast food restaurants because the value of their pensions has crashed in the twenty years since their economy imploded spectacularly[15]. The Nikkei is still not back to half the level it was at after all this time. When the Japanese economy blew up, the population was able to deal with the immediate aftermath better than might have been the case because the workforce had high levels of personal savings and the level of unemployment was very, very low. Twenty years after the meltdown and the Japanese economy is still a basket case. The UK on the other hand has had to contend with the crash from the opposite position to Japan and this explains the rise of payday loan companies. To back up the case I'm making I have drawn on opinions from both the left and right of the political spectrum. Owen Jones, *Guardian* writer and TV commentator, and Noam Chomsky, Professor of Linguistics and Philosophy at *MIT*, are as left of centre as is possible and Ferdinand Mount, Baronet, Old Etonian, the man who ran the Number 10 policy unit under Margaret Thatcher and the Centre for Policy Studies could not be more right of centre if he tried. All three of them have brilliantly agreed in their books (*The Establishment, How the World Works* and *The New Few*) how the top of the pyramid, the elite, oligarchy or Establishment have made sweeping gains in both wealth and unchallenged power at the expense of the rest of society. I have discovered their works relatively recently and after I began writing this book but it is fantastically reassuring to have such academic, philosophic and political clout in my corner.

It does seem that there is more than one elephant in the room for Mr. and Mrs. Average to contend with, but when there is a herd of them rampaging towards you it's understandable to reach for another can of beer or bottle of wine and escape to the safety of watching *Britain's Got Talent.*

(Now former) Prime Minister David Cameron has also stated that the notion of early retirement is no longer an option for the vast majority of us so do we have no choice but to just keep calm and carry on? Do we now have the risk of future interest rate rises to keep us awake at night? There has after all been crash after crash since the South Sea Bubble, recession after recession after depression followed by more recessions but lately, more of us are beginning to see that it is not the banksters or the political classes who feel the pain of these events that have occurred under all political colours, it is the ordinary citizenry who have borne the brunt of these events.

What happened to bring about the crash of 2007/08 was almost a mirror image of what happened on Wall Street in 1929 and to compound this disaster, the legislation brought in in the aftermath to prevent banks from making the same mistakes, the Glass Steagall Act was repealed by President Bill Clinton on his last day in office[16]. Unsurprisingly, this was done at the behest of the big players on Wall Street, and Chancellor Gordon Brown had already let the City of London foxes in to the coop by taking away the regulatory powers of the Bank of England and placing them in the hands of the new Financial Services Authority. Essentially, these powers enabled Nick Leeson to be caught and prosecuted for bringing down Barings Bank in 1994. The FSA have admitted late in the day that they weren't up to the job and investment bankers and traders alike feasted on the rewards available in the futures market without the tedium of complying with capital to lending restrictions. In effect, repealing Glass Steagall and the Bank of England's powers was to remove the firewall that had protected us from the ravages of the Great Depression. The movies *Rogue Trader*, *Wall Street*, *Wall Street 2*, *Margin Call*, *The Wolf of Wall Street* and *The Big Short* give a pretty accurate depiction of what was going on in the run up to the crash. Now we had a situation where so many banks were technically insolvent that the whole global economy was teetering on the brink and a new phrase was heard in the media for the first time: TOO BIG TO FAIL.

In America, Congress was told to vote in favour of an initial $800 billion bail-out paid directly to the same predators that caused the crash. They were told bluntly by the Treasury Secretary and former CEO of Goldman Sachs, Hank Paulson, that if they didn't approve the bailout by Monday morning the skies would fall, the Dow Jones would drop by 2,000 points and there would be martial law in America. In Britain the Royal Bank of Scotland came within two hours of going bust and a Northern Rock style run on the banks would have followed with disastrous consequences for the UK economy. This is where the comparison with the 1929 crash ends. Many bankers were tried and jailed for their activities in the run up to that event but the US Department of Justice decided that the jailing of any Wall Street CEOs would un-nerve the US economy to such an extent that confidence would vanish and the economy would collapse entirely[17]. So, 'too big to fail' also became 'too big to jail' and the whole circus was now free to go back on the road again. The futures and derivatives market is a huge casino, only now the house not only keeps the winnings but gets bailed out by the public when they lose. This may be a simplified version of events but there are experts out there who will try and spin reality using jargon and complicated economics theories to baffle the lay person into shrugging their shoulders and grudgingly moving on, leaving them in peace and plenty to continue with their bomb proof shady dealings.

"It is well enough that the people of the nation do not understand our banking and monetary system, for if they did, I believe there would be a revolution before tomorrow morning."
Henry Ford

Another simpler way to compare what happened is the good old family game of Monopoly. For instance, one of your rivals owns Mayfair with a hotel and you land on it. You owe him £2000 rent. You own the Electric Company and a couple of stations and you only have £300 in cash. You still need £1325 to stay in the game. The rules say you are out. They don't suggest asking for a bail out of £4,000 from the bank and carry on, which is essentially what is happening the world over today.

The world and its assets are valued at around $600 trillion. A rather large amount of money yet the derivatives market is worth between $3-4 quadrillion. Quad what?? Quadrillion. In sheer number of digits it looks like this: $40,000,000,000,000,000. Then there was Libor, the deliberate rigging by the banks, and with the knowledge of the Bank of England, of the inter-bank lending rate. There has been the concept of the quaintly named "mis-selling" of loan protection insurance worth billions of pounds to consumers. Not one person from the banks has been prosecuted for this yet if a till operator at the local super market takes a tenner out of the register and gets caught they are fired, prosecuted, given a criminal record and made unemployable.

In essence everything is rigged or manipulated in favour of the super-rich. It is like a Ponzi or pyramid scheme and it is kept going only by money printing with close to 0% interest rates. When these rates inevitably rise the bubble will burst with nothing short of catastrophic results. This will make the crash of 2007/8 resemble a minor shunt, not the multiple pile up that is coming. To make matters worse, your money, if you have any, will not necessarily be safe in your bank account. A precedent has already been set in Cyprus in March of 2013 for what was quaintly called a "bail in"[18]. A charming way of calling it for what it really was. Robbery of private funds in exchange for worthless shares in the bank.

"Those who cannot remember the past, are condemned to repeat it."
George Santayana.

I believe we are repeating the exact same mistakes that led to the Wall Street Crash of 1929 and the ten years of global financial devastation that followed and was ultimately only reversed after six horrifying years of carnage in World War Two. And the central banks cleaned up, as they always have after a good war particularly when they funded both sides. The house always wins.

In all honesty and in my humble opinion, I don't think they were mistakes, Wall Street has run the United States government since the passing of the Federal

Reserve Act of 1913 and has been pulling the levers of power ever since.

There are plenty of words of warning from luminary figures in the past, not just from a self-proclaimed "barrack room lawyer" such as me.

"Banking was conceived in inequity and was born in sin. The bankers own the Earth. Take it away from them, but leave them the power to create money, and with the flick of a pen they will create enough deposits to buy it back again. However, take it away from them, and all the great fortunes like mine will disappear and they ought to disappear, for this world would be a happier and better world to live in. But if you wish to remain the slaves of the bankers and pay the cost of your own slavery, let them continue to create money."
Sir Josiah Stamp, former Director of the Bank of England, University of Texas speech 1927.

"The real menace of our Republic is the invisible government...the little coterie of powerful, international bankers virtually runs the United States government for their own selfish interests."
John F Hylan, Mayor of New York City, 1935

"The principle of spending money to be paid by posterity, under the name of funding, is but swindling futurity on a large scale."
Thomas Jefferson

"We have in this country one of the most corrupt institutions the world has ever known. I refer to the Federal Reserve Board and the Federal Reserve Banks. This evil institution has impoverished and ruined the people of the United States and has practically bankrupted our government. It has done this through the defects of the law under which it operates, through the mal-administrations of that law by the Federal Reserve Board, and through the corrupt practices of the moneyed vultures who control it."

Congressman Louis T McFadden (who was poisoned before he could begin impeachment proceedings against the Board members in Congress)

"Give me control of a nation's money and I care not who makes its laws."

Mayer Amschel Rothschild

"I believe banking institutions are more dangerous to our liberties than standing armies. If the American people ever allow private banks to control the issue of their currency, first by inflation, then by deflation, the banks and the corporations that will grow up around them will deprive the people of all property until their children wake up homeless on the continent their fathers conquered. The issuing power should be taken away from the banks and restored to the people, to whom it properly belongs."

Thomas Jefferson

"When a government is dependent on bankers for money, they, and not the leaders of the government, control the situation, since the hand that gives is above the hand that takes. Money has no motherland; financiers are without patriotism and without decency; their sole objective is gain."
Napoleon Bonaparte

"Governments don't rule the world; Goldman Sachs rules the world."
Alessio Rastani, independent stock market trader

Economics is made out to be boring, uncool, too complicated and a subject for nerds with equally boring friends. We learn all we know from smart, suit wearing types on the TV who appear to be the font of all wisdom. Well, they didn't see the meltdown of 07/08 coming, did they[19]?! Those who did, like Professor Steve Keen of Kingston University or Peter Schiff, get nothing like the airtime they deserve and when they do, they still get mocked by establishment economists.

There is an excellent and illuminating documentary presented by the former Sky News economics guru, Jeff Randall, called *"Born Bankrupt"* which in less than thirty minutes explains exactly why there is going to be an almighty generational crisis in the next twenty to thirty years. It can be found on YouTube and it backs up exactly the words uttered by Thomas Jefferson about swindling futurity on a large scale. The scale of what Randall reveals is far, far worse than anything Jefferson could have conceived of two hundred years ago.

Another documentary/film which explains everything that has happened is called *"Four Horsemen"* this explains the clash between classical and neo-classical economics with insightful input from former figures at the IMF and World Bank and goes on to suggest how the world can be changed for the better.

The world's mainstream media is also complicit in keeping the masses in total ignorance of the giant fraud perpetrated on them for centuries. It is, in essence, a governmental public relations agency. With some honourable exceptions, most of what is broadcast is a diet of one sided propaganda; endless talent shows, reality TV, cooking, celebrity gossip and pointless game shows, the sole object of which, under the guise of entertainment, is to keep us suitably distracted from the real issues. The press machine does a very successful job of diverting blame at the most vulnerable groups in society. For example: unemployed, elderly, disabled people; along with immigrants and other minorities.

It is hard to accept that we are already living in the dystopian vision of the future predicted by George Orwell in his seminal work of *'1984'*. None the less we are, he describes it quite starkly and accurately in this paragraph where he spoke about the keeping of the masses in their place:

*"If it once became general, wealth would confer no distinction. It was possible, no doubt, to imagine a society in which **wealth**, in the sense of personal possessions and luxuries, should be evenly distributed, while **power** remained in the hands of a small privileged*

caste. But in practice such a society could not long
remain stable. For if leisure and security were enjoyed
by all alike, the great mass of human beings who are
normally stupefied by poverty would become literate and
would learn to think for themselves, and when once they
had done this, they would sooner or later realise that the
privileged minority had no function, and they would
sweep it away. In the long run, a hierarchical society
was only possible on a basis of poverty and ignorance."

Orwell also noted how an everlasting war was "waged by each ruling group against its own subjects… to keep the structure of society intact."

Poverty, ignorance and fear; all of this brings me to thinking about what other ways they are keeping us dumbed down, drugged up and in fear! How many people do you know who are on anti-depressants right now? I know of plenty and many of which are students. How is sinus trouble going to be improved by taking even mild anti-depressants? The philosopher Bertrand Russell said the following in his 1953 book, *The Impact of Science on Society*: "Diet, injections and injunctions will combine, from a very early age, to produce the sort of beliefs that the authorities consider desirable, and any serious criticism of the powers that be, will become psychologically impossible."

The pharmaceutical giants spend hundreds of millions of dollars lobbying politicians and in return, they go on to make hundreds of billions in profits every year. Good business for them, particularly as some governments are considering making vaccinations mandatory.

But is this good for us? Certainly many are and it would be crazy to say that they are not needed generally, but when cases of children with autism worked out at 1 in 10,000 in 1970 to 1 in 50 in 2013, something somewhere has gone seriously wrong[20]. Dr. Andrew Wakefield brought down vitriolic abuse on himself by the medical establishment for suggesting that the MMR vaccine could have been a factor in the increasing number of autism cases. Tony Blair refused to say whether his newborn son Leo, had received the triple vaccination in 1998, stating it was a 'private matter'. Perhaps it was, but he still failed to give a ringing endorsement to the procedure by keeping silent about it which has led many new parents to seek either single vaccinations or abstain from them altogether. An Italian Court ruling did find a link between the MMR vaccination and autism but mainstream media ignored the ruling.

In America four hundred thousand people die every year due to unexpected effects of normal medication, over-prescription or incorrect diagnosis by doctors[21]. This is a terrifying number. The number of German civilians killed by allied bombers during World War Two was one hundred thousand every year for the duration of the war.

What makes this even more outrageous is that the US government has passed legislation protecting the big pharma corporations from lawsuits caused by their products. Monsanto similarly has such protection from the masses and they have the added safeguard of a 'revolving door' policy that has seen former senior employees taking up positions in the Department of Justice while politicians find lucrative opportunities in the opposite direction.

There are many millions of citizens across the world who believe the "War on Terror" is exactly the scenario predicted by Orwell. And these people cannot be dismissed as mere "conspiracy theorists". How on Earth can such a war ever be declared as finished? In 2004, President George W Bush stood on the flight deck of the nuclear powered aircraft carrier USS *Abraham Lincoln,* close to the combat zone off the coast of California and declared to the world's media and the folks back home, "Mission accomplished!" This statement, given the huge numbers of civilians killed since this ridiculous utterance, in sectarian fighting and the fall of several Iraqi cities to so-called insurgents, looks pretty ludicrous. The power vacuums created by the overthrowing of the Iraqi and Libyan governments, has directly brought about the existence of groups like Isis. The definite winners of this ongoing blood bath have been the same winners from the ten year war in Vietnam thirty years before. The military industrial complex made $43 billion in profits from Vietnam, to date, the US taxpayer has been stung for over $3 trillion and counting while back at home whole cities and even entire states are technically bankrupt. Millions of Americans have no idea if they will ever receive their 401K's (the equivalent to our pension pot) and in the UK, a new survey suggests if citizens wish to retire at the age of sixty-three, they will need to pay in £13,512 in to their pension pot every year. Yeah, right! There are few who are able to set aside such amounts of spare cash every year except the likes of former Knight of the Realm, Mr. Fred Goodwin who, far from getting his collar felt after the near collapse of his bank, the Royal Bank of Scotland, walked away into the sunset with a seven figure pay off and a seven hundred thousand pounds annual pension which he will have to soldier on with while reports of another public funded bail out of the bank is rumoured to be on the cards. It must be remembered that while the coalition government has shredded £82 billion in cuts from public spending, banker bonuses since the crash have topped more than £90 billion[22]. This hardly chimes with the claim "We're all in it together". The Chancellor used public money to challenge the EU through the courts when they suggested capping banker bonuses in 2014.

CURRENT STATE OF THE WORLD

There are some who see the current state of the world with the rich growing wealthier and the rest hanging on to what they have with their finger nails as perfectly normal. They believe, somehow, that as a society we are wealthier, healthier, happier, kinder, more humane, more peaceful, more equal and longer lived than any generation in history. They believe in more extensive use of fossil fuels, nuclear power (despite the untold consequences from the melt downs at Fukushima) and lavish praise on genetically modified crops (while pouring scorn on those deeply opposed to messing with the laws of nature) and can't wait for the cost benefits of hydraulic fracturing (fracking) while glossing over the immeasurable environmental damage caused by such activity!

Personally, I don't believe this to be the case. As regards the planet and possible impacts of these activities, there are renewable energy sources not yet fully evaluated with little or no impact on the planet which should be invested in. As an example, the media went very quiet about the impacts of Fukushima as tolerance levels were manipulated to suggest that what was once considered very dangerous is now an acceptable limit of radiation, also denial of meltdowns which later proved untrue[1]. The impacts have been worse than Chernobyl and will be continuing for many years. How safe is the air, the sea and the seafood we eat? The damage to the food chain has not been openly reported on but if you look on the internet you can see the field of radiation and its progress around the planet. It's a huge cause for concern and is far more threatening to life, liberty and the pursuit of happiness than terrorism ever will be. Yet the establishment would have us all believe that events in Syria are more dangerous than the meltdown of six reactors throwing out more radiation than all the previous nuclear detonations carried out since the end of World War Two. This is clearly preposterous.

These individuals do not inhabit the same world as the rest of us and the view from their ivory tower is deeply distorted. Where they are correct is that we are living longer and the state is now trying to subliminally suggest that retirement isn't all it is cracked up to be, and while charities like 'Children in Need' and 'Comic Relief' continue to receive increased donations from the public, it emerged that some of the monies raised were invested in morally challenging portfolios like tobacco, alcohol and the armaments industry[2]. This is all the more reprehensible since 'Comic Relief' has always aimed to help poor children in Africa yet invests in the sectors that have helped decimate the continent for years and kept its people in abject misery. Between them, these commodities kill millions of people around the world every year and even the Church of England had invested millions in the payday loan company, Wonga[3]. It is enough to give you a migraine getting your head around these situations.

There was a recent explosion at an exploratory fracking well in Bobtown, Pennsylvania which left extensive fires burning for five days[4]. Nearby residents were hospitalised with respiratory complaints and a worker at the site was tragically killed in the incident. The owner of the site, multi-national oil giant Chevron, which incidentally made profits in 2013 of over twenty-one billion dollars, offered the affected residents a gift voucher each for a large cheese pizza (no extra toppings) and a two litre bottle of soda in compensation. In a statement the company said it always attempts to operate its sites in an incident free manner but this can't of course be guaranteed. That's not very reassuring if you live nearby to, or wake up finding a drilling well being set up in your neighbourhood. Governments are moving heaven and earth to remove the procedures which may delay the race for shale gas, like public consultations or planning permission. In return, a cash bribe to the local authorities and a 1% share in the profits to the community are offered to try and reduce scenes of local protesters clashing with security guards escorting drilling equipment and the fleets of tankers delivering volatile and carcinogenic chemicals used in the process. There is also the immense amount of water used during the working life of a fracking well, over two million litres and the very real risk of water table contamination.

There is also the rise of traffic accidents with the increased amount of vehicle movements and the reports of seismic activity caused by the high pressure fracturing of the rock strata deep underground. I wonder if the 1% revenue bribe will compensate for the fall in value of homes in and around the area close to fracking sites. Supporters of fracking go to great pains to try and convince sceptical members of the public that there is no evidence of water contamination and therefore no cause for alarm. Many millions of people are far from convinced by their promises including the CEO of Exxon-Mobil who took out a writ against the construction of a well near his mansion in Texas[5], and they are somewhat less vocal about the contamination caused to the drinking water supply in the town of Camelford in 1989 when 20 tons of aluminium sulphate was accidentally pumped into the wrong storage tank. Only now, twenty-five years later are the long term consequences to public health in the town becoming clear[6]. This was caused by one chemical. Hydraulic fracturing involves the use of over six hundred chemicals including mercury, radium, methanol, lead and hydrochloric acid. In surface water areas such as ponds, streams and rivers near to fracking wells, levels of methane, which is one of the most damaging greenhouse gases, are seventeen times higher than non-exposed sites. This is evidenced by the ability to ignite vapour in streams or your household water taps with a match or lighter. In one incident in America, a teenage girl passed out in the shower from methane gas fumes. Does no one remember the movie '*Erin Brockovich*'[7]?

Now we have GMO's to contend with, these are Genetically Modified Organisms which are used in genetically modified foods amongst other things and we have no idea what effect they may have on the human body over time. The idea is to improve and increase crop yield and variety[8].

However, once this genie is out of the bottle you can't put it back! This is interfering with nature and as we know everything needs to be in balance on the planet for it to thrive so what might this process be doing to the balance of other things, for example insects, birds etc.

Monsanto is the corporation most widely known for producing and marketing GM crops. There is Intellectual Property Law on these GM organisms, which is interfering with the livelihood of local farmers around the globe, threatening their use of seeds and certain crops. Under the Trans Pacific Partnership agreement Monsanto can sue any government which refuses to give them access to their markets[9]; currently many countries in Europe are fighting the Monsanto invasion.

The supporters of GMO and geo-engineering also tend to extol the benefits of globalisation and free trade and point to corporations like Nike that grew from a tiny head office in 1972 to a giant global entity merely by contracting with factories in Asia to supplying American shops. Perhaps it might be argued that it is good business to have products made for pennies on the dollar and sold for huge profits to US consumers, but are the workers overseas enjoying the fruits of their labour or are they still living on five or ten dollars a day?

Did the more than nine hundred workers killed in Bangladesh when their factory collapsed[10], feel fulfilled and unexploited knowing their hard work was helping British consumers get cheaper clothes? Then there was the shocking mass shooting of striking platinum miners in South Africa[11]. Thirty-seven of them were mown down and killed in a hail of automatic weapons fire by police officers. If this had happened under white minority rule there would have been demands for economic sanctions to be imposed on such a barbaric government. Their crime was asking for a pay rise and they were killed for it. It is often the way authority deals with the masses, and has done so for centuries.

As far as free speech and being equal, this is the sort of thing that went on. The Peterloo massacre was part of the movement to get the vote. I wonder how much things have changed. If they have changed significantly then why today do we have to be in a 'free speech zone' to speak our views openly?

The Peterloo massacre of August 16th 1819 was a classic example of the fear caused to the ruling classes when 60,000 men, women and children dressed in their Sunday best, came to hear the words of the popular and charismatic reformer and radicalist Henry "Orator" Hunt in St Petersfield, Manchester. Fearing that a French style revolution was about to begin, orders were given by the magistrate William Hulton, for the arrest of Hunt and everyone else on the podium. When cavalry officers and their horses got stuck in the narrow approaches leading to the hustings, they began lashing out with their sabres, cutting people down on all sides. In the following panic

15 people died at the scene or later from their wounds and between 400 to 700 were injured. One of them, John Lees, was a former soldier who fought at Waterloo four years earlier. Before succumbing from his wounds, he told a friend "At Waterloo there was man to man, but there (St Peter's Field) it was downright murder".

In my humble opinion, what happened that sunny day in Manchester was no different from the outcome inflicted on hundreds of thousands of young people demanding reform and freedom from tyranny. This was June, 1989 in Tiananmen Square in Beijing.

Whether it was the chartists of 19th century Britain, pro-democracy protesters in China or the Occupy Wall Street protests, the state has a despicable habit of lashing out violently at those with legitimate grievances.

The bastion of freedom and champion of democracy, the United States isn't exempt from this behaviour either. It sent the cavalry in under General Douglas McArthur to break up protesting veterans from World War One who were demanding full payment of their war bonds early as they and millions of other citizens suffered from the Great Depression[12]. The US government also treated anti-Vietnam War protesters as potential threats to national security. The FBI conducted Operation Minaret in association with the NSA to monitor the activities of not just student activists but also prominent anti-war journalists, sports and movie stars, and politicians[13]. Even the telephones of Senator Frank Church and civil rights leader, Dr. Martin Luther King Jr were illegally tapped[14].

In June of 1971, some members of the activist community took matters into their own hands and performed a break in at the FBI office in Media, Pennsylvania[15]. They got away with thousands of classified documents which revealed how the FBI hoped to create an "atmosphere of paranoia within the anti-war community...that there was an agent behind every mailbox". Files also showed evidence of forgery, blackmail letters and threats of violence to those opposed to the war. Perhaps the worst example to be uncovered was the attempt to blackmail Dr. King into committing suicide[16]!

The then Attorney General John Mitchell, attempted to prevent journalists from publishing the stolen documents, explaining that to do so would put lives at risk (where have we heard this before?). The Washington Post editors were not convinced and published them anyway including evidence that a local police chief, a post master, letter carriers, campus security officers and switch board operators were FBI informants. The Bureau attempted to justify its illegal activities and its Director, Clarence Kelley, announced on NBC news that, "The government would have been derelict in its duty had it not taken measures to protect the fabric of our society".

The break in at the FBI office took place a year after the Ohio National Guard, armed with M1 Garand rifles, complete with bayonets had opened fire on student protesters at Kent State University, killing four and wounding nine[17]. The FBI never found those responsible for the break in despite exhaustive attempts over many years and the anger felt by those in power at attempts to shine a light on them and their illegal activities still resonates today.

The Media Pennsylvania activists were the fore runners of WikiLeaks. Instead of system hacking and back door access to top secret computer systems, they had to stake out the FBI office, learn locksmith skills and physically find and remove files. They were regarded as enemies of the state, just as much as Julian Assange is today. On the subject of WikiLeaks, Chelsea Manning and Edward Snowden are the most high profile of whistleblowers and have received incredibly harsh media and government treatment. This isn't surprising as the media continues to fulfill its role as a government echo chamber.

Over seventy years ago Colonel Claus Von Stauffenberg broke his oath to Hitler by trying to assassinate him. History judges Von Stauffenberg to be a hero and I believe this will be the case for today's high profile whistle blowers.

So what has changed over all of this time really? We are given the illusion of equality and freedom of speech but whenever someone stands up and speaks out with any effect, there are consequences. Each one of us can make a difference, if we want a better world, the truth needs to come out and we must stand up for what is right. If enough people stand up for what is right, positive change will happen.

"We must be the change we want to see in the world."
Gandhi

"Dissent is the greatest form of patriotism"
Thomas Jefferson

"There is little value in insuring the survival of our nation if our traditions do not survive with it. And there is very great danger that an announced need for increased security will be seized upon by those anxious to expand its meaning to the very limits of official censorship and concealment"
John F Kennedy

I have covered many examples of what I think is so very wrong with the world right now. And if this wasn't compelling enough, the revelations coming out of the Palace of Westminster about the existence of a multi-party paedophile ring is another sickening manifestation of a system that is rotten to the core[18]. How on earth did a former Radio One DJ end up with such close connections to royalty and politicians at the very highest levels? Saville gave himself a code name 'Deep Cover' he was the perfect middle man between the Establishment and celebrity culture. Certainly the truth remains concealed behind the Official Secrets Act, undoubtedly police investigations will conclude that there is insufficient evidence for any prosecutions. Why is it that we are learning about these horrendous acts over thirty years after the fact?! Who is responsible for holding this back and for not taking the culprits to task over it?

If you can find this out, I'm sure their reason for non-disclosure would be 'National Security.' In a bid to be seen to be doing something about the Saville scandal, investigations have led to unfortunate celebrities being named and shamed for far less serious acts. This is a convenient decoy to take focus off the 'main event' and is readily accepted by the masses.

So what does the government propose to do to get to the truth of the matter? Appoint an eighty year old grandee of the Establishment to investigate...the Establishment with more than enough obfuscation and whitewash to sweep the report under the table, a tactic used for decades with the same results[19]. Fortunately, public reaction stopped this in its tracks though the next appointee seems to be best friends with one of the most senior figures accused of historic child abuse, a former Home Secretary no less, yet claims to have no links to the Establishment? Now she too, has had the good sense to resign throwing the whole inquiry into chaos. Perhaps that has been the aim all along, and nor is it unique to Great Britain. In the '90s a colossal paedophile ring was uncovered in Belgium involving members of the government, journalists, police officers and judges[20]. Why should we have any loyalty or allegiance to such a monstrously corrupt system or any of its advocates? Most of it seems to be completely connected with the men behind the curtain, those who do pull the levers of power and set the global agenda. Who are these individuals, how are they organised and why do we not hear enough about them in the mainstream media?

Again, some very luminary figures from the past can provide the answers:

"There is something behind the throne greater than the King himself."
William Pitt the Elder, House of Lords 1770

"The world is governed by very different personages from what is imagined by those who are not behind the scenes."
Benjamin Disraeli, Prime Minister, 1844

"Behind the ostensible government sits enthroned an invisible government, owing no allegiance and acknowledging no responsibility to the people"
Theodore Roosevelt, 26th US President

"I am a most unhappy man. I have unwittingly ruined my country. A great industrial nation is controlled by its system of credit. Our system of credit is concentrated. The growth of the nation, therefore, and all our activities are in the hands of a few men. We have come to be one of the worst ruled, one of the most completely controlled and dominated governments in the civilized world. No longer a government by free opinion, no longer a government by conviction and the vote of the majority, but a government by the opinion and duress of a small group of dominant men."
US President Woodrow Wilson

"We shall have world government whether or not we like it. The only question is if world government will be achieved by consent or conquest."
James Paul Warburg-Globalist banker

"In politics, nothing happens by accident. If it happened you can believe it was planned that way"
Franklin Delano Roosevelt, US President
"We are grateful to the Washington Post, NY Times, Time magazine and other great publications whose directors have attended our meetings, and respected their promises of discretion for almost forty years. It would have been impossible to develop our plan for the world if we had been subject to the lights of publicity during those years. The supranational sovereignty of an intellectual elite and world bankers is surely preferable to the national autonomous determination practiced in past centuries."
David Rockefeller, Council on Foreign Relations, founder of the Trilateral Commission and member of the powerful secretive organisation, the Bilderberg Group.

"When the citizens are rendered unable to control their financial affairs, they of course become totally enslaved, a source of cheap labour."
Rockefeller Foundation, 1979

There is enough information to write to write another book on not just the Bilderberg's but their subordinate groups, the Council on Foreign Relations and Trilateral Commission but others like Daniel Estulin, the late Jim

Tucker and Guardian reporter Charlie Skelton have already done great work on the subject[21].

Suffice to say The Bilderberg Group has been around for sixty years now. Its members include royalty, members of the intelligence community, senior press barons, senior bankers, members of the military industrial complex and politicians from both sides of the political spectrum. The list includes former prime ministers, foreign secretaries, secretaries of state and defence, finance ministers and their political opposite numbers, business moguls and even trade union barons make up the numbers. It hosts annual events in June alternating between North America and Europe. Minutes of its meetings are never published and members are sworn to secrecy. The hotels used are turned into fortresses and snarling private security guards patrol the grounds.

Until recently, the BBC denied there was any such group in existence and the lack of coverage on mainstream media is not due entirely to an unaware population, it is more to deal with the quote by Rockefeller. After all every year in Hollywood, gold statues are awarded by multi-millionaires to other multi-millionaires and the world's press fall over themselves in fawning admiration (another example of distraction), yet when 150 of the most powerful and influential figures show up in one place to decide the future of the planet, the world's media becomes conspicuous by its absence.

WEAPONS OF MASS DISTRACTION

One of the main arguments put by supporters of our political system is that everyone has a vote, everyone has a say in who governs our country so there is no need for so called "political protest" or swivel eyed loons jumping from one faddish nonsense to the next. We have a functioning and free democracy. Yeah, right. What is the point of voting for one political party over another? Their agendas are almost indistinguishable, they are members of the same secretive clubs and organisations and they are owned by the same powerful interests behind the scenes. The mainstream media do their best to keep up the illusion but surveys now show that in the UK only 41% of the viewing public believe the news they see on TV, and in America the figure is barely more than a third[1]. This is massively encouraging and the rise in popularity of the "alternative" media will only grow as disillusionment with the system continues to increase. I believe that what is happening in the economy is a kind of financial apartheid. The wealthy are protected while the poor get poorer[2]. The threat of more immigration and the spreading of zero hour contracts will be used to keep wages as low as the business world can get away with. The economy is doing fine, claim many media economic correspondents; the reality is that it is the ordinary people who are not[3]. Twenty years ago two global agreements came into force, the North American Free Trade Agreement and the General Agreement on Tariffs and Trade. Both were planned in secret away from prying public eyes and any involvement from unions only came after it had been passed into law. These agreements have been great for the trans-national corporations and the financial and professional sector. The rest of the workforce has gained nothing and often lost heavily. Now the Trans Pacific Partnership agreement is close to being signed by the world's most powerful, industrialized nations. Again, the negotiations have been conducted in complete and total secrecy, always an ominous sign for the man or woman in the street. What is it that politicians say about snooping on the public? "If you've nothing to hide you have nothing to fear." One snippet of the treaty has leaked out. Corporations of all sizes will be able to sue governments around the world if they believe legislation passed by them is damaging their profit margins. The consequences of this are just staggering. For 50 years or more, particularly in the US, large companies have been able to gain tax rebates and vast subsidies by threatening to move elsewhere within the country or, more is the case today, off shore altogether. Now they are able to be more open about their ambitions as their collective power has increased. It is no coincidence that corporations have the whip hand over politicians, they have after all been handsomely funding their election campaigns for decades and they haven't done this from just a patriotic consideration.

To think that your economic prospects are going to get back to where they should be anytime soon or improve significantly in the near future is completely unrealistic. There is an incredible document that was discovered by accident inside an old IBM photocopier that had been sold for spare parts[4]. Contained within was the blueprint of the future of humanity as it was intended by the likes of Rockefeller and others. It was drawn up in 1979 and the juicy, dot connecting stuff is in the lower half though it is worth taking the time to read it all with a couple of large coffees. It is titled 'Silent weapons for quiet wars' and can be viewed online and I think you will be left completely outraged. Here is a snippet and you can judge for yourself whether it chimes with what is going on today. Remember, it was written thirty-five years ago.

Diversion, the Primary Strategy

Experience has proved that the simplest method of securing a silent weapon and gaining control of the public is to keep the public undisciplined and ignorant of the basic system principles on the one hand, while keeping them confused, disorganized, and distracted with matters of no real importance on the other hand.

This is achieved by:

- *disengaging their minds; sabotaging their mental activities; providing a low-quality program of public education in mathematics, logic, systems design and economics; and discouraging technical creativity.*

- *engaging their emotions, increasing their self-indulgence and their indulgence in emotional and physical activities, by:*

- *unrelenting emotional affrontations and attacks (mental and emotional rape) by way of constant barrage of sex, violence, and wars in the media – especially the T.V. and the newspapers.*

- *giving them what they desire – in excess – "junk food for thought" – and depriving them of what they really need.*

- *rewriting history and law and subjecting the public to the deviant creation, thus being able to shift their thinking from personal needs to highly fabricated outside priorities.*

These preclude their interest in and discovery of the silent weapons of social automation technology.

The general rule is that there is a profit in confusion; the more confusion, the more profit. Therefore, the best approach is to create problems and then offer solutions.

Diversion Summary

Media: Keep the adult public attention diverted away from the real social issues, and captivated by matters of no real importance.

Schools: Keep the young public ignorant of real mathematics, real economics, real law, and real history.

Entertainment: Keep the public entertainment below a sixth-grade level.

Work: Keep the public busy, busy, busy, with no time to think; back on the farm with the other animals...

Since most of the general public will not exercise restraint; there are only two alternatives to reduce the economic inductance of the system.

Let the populace bludgeon each other to death in war, which will only result in a total destruction of the living earth.

Take control of the world by the use of economic "silent weapons" in a form of "quiet warfare" and reduce the economic inductance of the world to a safe level by a process of benevolent slavery and genocide.

The latter option has been taken as the obviously better option. At this point it should be crystal clear to the reader why absolute secrecy about the silent weapons is necessary. The general public refuses to improve its own mentality and its faith in its fellow man. It has become a herd of proliferating barbarians, and, so to speak, a blight upon the face of the earth.

They do not care enough about economic science to learn why they have not been able to avoid war despite religious morality, and their religious or self-gratifying refusal to deal with earthly problems renders the solution of the earthly problem unreachable to them.

It is left to those few who are truly willing to think and survive as the fittest to survive, to solve the problem for themselves as the few who really care. Otherwise, exposure of the silent weapon would destroy our only hope of preserving the seed of the future true humanity.

The rest of this document is nothing short of a revelation. It is surely indicative of the sort of information that is kept under lock and key in government vaults, away from prying eyes under the guise of "national security" and, predictably, the authorities and media will dismiss it as a fake, refuse to comment on an unauthorized document. They'd say that no substance should be drawn from such a document and who'd leave such damning information lying around? Well, they would say that wouldn't they and there have been numerous examples of laptops and ministerial briefings being left in taxis and railway trains by civil servants and politicians[5]. Read it yourself and make your own mind up.

I have saved the best quote till last as it emphasizes everything that is utterly wrong in the world today, why you should feel no guilt for wanting out of such a morally and financially bankrupt system, and a hope that it could be made vastly better by people working together and for a shared future. It also helps explain why the man who uttered it was seen as such a threat by those who believe themselves to be the masters of the entire world.

"The very word secrecy is repugnant in a free and open society, and we are as a people inherently and historically opposed to secret societies, to secret oaths and to secret proceedings. For we are opposed around the world by a monolithic and ruthless conspiracy that

relies primarily on covert means for expanding its
sphere of influence, on infiltration instead of invasion,
on subversion instead of elections, on intimidation
instead of free choice. It is a system which has
conscripted vast human and material resources into the
building of a tightly knit, highly efficient machine that
combines military, diplomatic, intelligence, economic,
scientific and political operations. Its preparations are
concealed not published, its mistakes are buried not
headlined, its dissenters are silenced not praised, no
expenditure is questioned, and no secret is revealed.
That is why the Athenian lawmaker Solon, decreed it a
crime for a citizen to shrink from controversy. I am
asking your help in the tremendous task in informing and
alerting the American people confident that with your
help, man will be what he was born to be- free and
independent"
President John F Kennedy

Kennedy was suggesting we all have an obligation to be Julian Assange, Edward Snowden, Chelsea Manning or any number of other whistle blowers. When you have a system that criminalises those who expose government wrongdoing you are living in a de-facto totalitarian state.

IF VOTING CHANGED
ANYTHING IT'D BE ILLEGAL

Shakespeare said "all the world's a stage" and nothing could be more true than the theatre of global politics. On the stage they play their opposing roles so well, however behind the scenes they all go to the same restaurants, bars, clubs, events, and belong to the same secret societies. Have you ever wondered why the key policies a party is voted in for never seem to get successfully implemented? More often they are actively ignored or altered and this is because behind the scenes there is an overarching plan that is driven by the global elite, who are going to get what they want either way.

Both Ferdinand Mount and Owen Jones travelled the country and spoke to ordinary people about their views on politicians and they both got the same answers: they're in it for themselves; they don't listen to us; there's no difference between any of the parties; all they do is feather their own nests. The Establishment has got us exactly where they want us and with the Labour party promising to be tougher than the Tories in yet more austerity measures if they win power, the message "keep calm and carry on" reveals its real, darker meaning;

"Shut up! Just get on with it because there is no alternative!" It reinforces the message that you have no power in your own life and there is absolutely nothing you can do about it. You can almost hear the delighted slaps on the back within the Establishment as this message, mixed in with a bit of patriotic fervour serves their interests delightfully.

Less than 1 in 8 employees in the private sector are members of a union, the figure is little higher in the often demonized public sector. Collective bargaining is a thing of the past and in the realm of industrial relations the pendulum has swung way too far in favour of the bosses. This has brought about a state of near defeatism which isn't surprising. The staff at Monarch Airlines voted to accept wage cuts, redundancies and diminished pension contributions in exchange for them being allowed to keep their jobs[1]. A situation preceded this at the Grangemouth oil refinery in 2013 when the Unite Union tried to improve workers' pay and conditions. From his £130 million yacht, the CEO of Ineos, the refinery owner and tax exile Jim Ratcliffe demanded complete capitulation from the work force or the whole place would be closed down forever[2]. The largest union in the country could do nothing to prevent it and the staff at Grangemouth set the precedent for Monarch Airlines and doubtless other employers across the UK to hold a gun to the heads of their staff. It is worth noting that the government and the media leapt to the defence of Mr. Ratcliffe and crucified the Union in trying to protect the interests of their members.

The Establishment has successfully managed to focus the blame for the crash of 2007/8 away from themselves and onto the poorest, most disadvantaged members of society. The newspapers reinforce this with furious headlines about "benefits scroungers" leeching off hard working families and TV shows like *Benefit Street* and documentaries about Eastern European immigrants coming over here and taking away our jobs, reinforces this narrative very powerfully. Our membership of the European Union allows for free movement of people, goods and services across the continent. It was the Labour government under Tony Blair who put down the welcome mat and it is impossible to reverse this policy. And honesty is needed here, if you were in the shoes of the immigrants and it was legal and encouraged, wouldn't you be on the first plane to Luton if you could increase your earnings by eight times what you were earning at home? Aren't they following the mantra we were all encouraged to do once, long ago: "Go West young man"?

The Establishment is also content for the media not to comment much on the £25 billion that is annually lost to the Treasury by clever and intricate tax avoidance schemes by its members, the corporate elite. Much is promised through the media by politicians to tackle the issue, but more often than not, celebrities like Jimmy Carr and disability benefit claimants are held up as the villains defrauding the public purse. Once again shielding the real moustache twirling, but all too real, pantomime villains at the top of the pyramid.

The media is less forthcoming about where the £1.2 trillion pounds of taxpayer money given to the banks in 2008 has actually gone. They seldom mention how the number of billionaires has doubled during the era of grinding austerity or how the top 1% has seen its wealth increase by 15% since 2008. They have glossed over the off-shore hideaways that in 2010 contained £21 trillion belonging to the new super rich elite. The BBC reported it briefly and forgot about it pretty soon, but if the union movement had been doing this, it is easy to imagine how it would be spun in the tabloids.

The media has a habit of reporting stories it would rather not cover in the small hours of the morning or last thing at night and then dropping any further coverage altogether. In 2010, on a cold and early winter's morning, I was making my way to work and listening to the BBC World Service. The interviewer was talking to the former Greek Finance minister about Greece's chronic debt problems. He openly admitted that with the help of Wall Street giant, Goldman Sachs, they had totally cooked the books in order to meet the membership criteria needed to join the Euro. What the Greeks didn't realise was that as well as charging them €2 billion euros for their illicit actions, Goldman also bet against them on the futures market effectively being paid twice! Goldman Sachs is a member of what is known as 'The Troika', a group combining other Wall Street giants, the IMF, World Bank and European Central Bank. Since 2008, they have been asset stripping Greece, buying up public utilities for pennies on the dollar and sentencing the ordinary citizens who had no knowledge of the financial scams being perpetrated behind their backs, to decades of debt slavery[3].

The Establishment is also intertwined with its close cousins across the pond and in the European Commission. It shares the same goals and lack of accountability and through secretive forums like the Bilderberg Group and Trilateral Commission it has frequent opportunities away from the public glare to entrench its current and future strategies without challenge. Goldman Sachs, yes them again, are a huge player within the US political Establishment. Every Treasury Secretary for forty years, under Republican or Democrat administrations, has been a senior figure at Goldman. Goldman and the other banks were fully recapitalized and are richer now than before the financial crisis they helped create. The stock markets are close to record levels but based on what? The IMF has again downgraded global growth forecasts so what is driving the markets higher when confidence seems so brittle? The answer could be algorithms. The Pound fell sharply on Asian markets and analysts speculated that a news report triggered automated trading systems to sell the currency heavily. Another explanation could be the record levels of acquisitions and mergers, together with stock buyback programs fuelled by vast amounts of cheap money. Some cynics might suspect these activities would generate more lavish bonuses on top of the $100 billion earned since 2009[4].

Goldman's tentacles are wrapped so tightly around the levers of power on Capitol Hill that it is also known as Government Sachs. The UK Establishment has a similar revolving door policy in all aspects of day to day policy making decisions. To demonstrate the point, the current chief executive at the Bank of England is from

Goldman Sachs, as is the head of the European Central Bank (they are all members of the Bilderberg Group). It is deep, entrenched and cross party in nature. Removing or changing it is going to be a very long, painful and massively difficult process. They hold all the cards and will zealously guard them with everything at their disposal. The police and armed forces are sworn in allegiance to the Crown, not the citizens and their loyalty should be guaranteed if push came to shove.

There was a time when people power caused near panic in government circles[5]. The fuel strikes and blockades in 2000 had huge popular backing. Gordon Brown had increased fuel duty by huge amounts since becoming Chancellor three years earlier. Under the Tories, the cost of petrol and diesel had risen from 37 pence per litre in 1986 to 55 pence per litre in 1997. Brown had raised it from 55 to 85 pence in just three years and ordinary motorists were utterly furious. Hauliers saw their costs surging while suffering the double whammy of increasing foreign competition running on far cheaper French diesel. Refineries the length and breadth of the country were blockaded, supermarket shelves were empty and the motorway networks were clogged in organized go-slows in well-coordinated convoys. It is essential to remember that tankers carrying fuel to hospitals and other key public utilities were allowed out by the blockaders and that the majority of the public supported the actions of the protesters.

For the first time since assuming power, the government was behind in the opinion polls and they set out to blacken the name of the protesters through the media. Tony Blair, at his weekly press conference slammed the protesters for putting innocent lives at risk and threatening the financial well-being of the country. With Gordon Brown offering a few concessions and the suggestion of charging foreign trucks vignettes for using the UK road network, support began to drain away from the blockaders and things started to get back to normal. Within Whitehall, the government was furious at this near uprising by elements of "the enemy within". They brought in new legislation making sure there would never again be a repeat of such actions. Blockaders of fuel refineries would in future be charged under terrorism legislation and any hauliers allowing their vehicles to be involved would lose their operator's licence, putting them out of business immediately.

This is a vivid example of how the Establishment will react to any perceived threat to its position. Any public figures speaking out against it are subject to vilification and humiliation through the full force of the media. I've already used one quote from the 19th Century former slave, abolitionist leader and Afro American social reformer Frederick Douglass; here is another

"Power concedes nothing without a demand. It never did and it never will."

We the People do actually have the power, we're told that we don't and never will and this is why I do not subscribe to the "keep calm and carry on" doctrine. It ultimately acts as a force of defeatism cloaked in the disguise of patriotism, the last refuge of the scoundrel as Thomas Jefferson noted two centuries ago. It also explains why there is so little protest in the street. There is ample evidence, and Owen Jones's book offers examples of it, that people everywhere are just being ground down and take one blow after another. The actions of the Establishment have left many people resigned, without hope and believing that resistance is pointless. This of course, suits the Establishment and only perpetuates their total dominance. This really is the meaning of the often used cliché: 'It doesn't matter who you vote for, the government always gets in'.

Nor is this sense of unfairness restricted to Britain and the United States. Ordinary people across Europe have taken the brunt of destructive social and economic policies for years now. Youth unemployment rates have topped 50% in many countries and this is an utter outrage[6]. The Indignados movement in Spain organized a march from Madrid all the way to Brussels to protest at austerity measures heaped onto them by the Troika, not that the media bothered to cover it. Similar movements exist in Portugal and Italy, and the people of Ireland are seething at the latest round of tax increases, through new water charges as part of the bail-out program dumped onto them by their government at the behest, again of the Troika[7]. The Irish media also tries to play down the levels of support that the protesters have across the country.

Supporters of the Establishment should not be so self-assured that their perceived positions as Masters of the Universe will prevail endlessly. Situations can change very, very quickly and if the disparate movements across Europe and America can coordinate their message, their strategies and ideas with a single, unified voice, then nothing would be impossible. All bets would be off.

The collapse of communism was incredibly rapid across Eastern Europe and those entrenched regimes could not believe what was happening to them[8]. The East German president even ordered his soldiers to open fire on thousands of protesters on the streets of Leipzig. He watched aghast on TV as those same soldiers joined the ranks of the protesters who were, after all, their friends, families and neighbours. Within just two short weeks it was all over for the government. Change for the better can happen. "If just one man could stand tall, there would be hope for us all, somewhere, somewhere in the spirit of Man!"- lyric from Jeff Wayne's musical version of HG Wells' 'The War of the Worlds'.

2015 is the 800th anniversary of the signing of Magna Carta. King John and his Court could never have imagined their dominance would be successfully challenged and that "Due process and trial by your peers" became the rights of everyone, not the few, enshrined in law forever at least until today's politicians brought in the concept of secret courts. In the heart of every person on earth there is a deep resentment at injustice. Logic demands that the needs of the many outweigh the needs of the few and this is why the legend of Robin Hood is so loved around the world. Robin's famous adversary was the Sheriff of Nottingham and his partner in cruelty, Sir Guy of Gisborne. What has really improved since the 13th Century? It would take more than 600 years before the masses had any semblance of an effective voice at Westminster, and this was only a token. Women only got the vote in 1921 and this after years of agitating by the Suffragette movement.

Petitions and public protests are largely ignored and, in the case of the Chartist movement of two centuries ago, a petition of two and a half million people demanding the vote, better working conditions and wages was not even accepted through the doors of Parliament. Getting such a huge number of people to sign required incredible effort and showed the strength of feeling among the masses but resulted with the censure of the newspapers of the day, the jailing of editors and journalists and the Peterloo massacre.

Voting today, using the analogy of Robin Hood, in a supposedly mature democracy gives us the choice of either voting for the Sheriff of Nottingham or Sir Guy, of choosing the lesser of two evils and yet still ending up with evil.

So anyway, now that I've scratched the surface of what's wrong with system, what do we do about it? How do we change it?

We start with ourselves and changing things within our sphere of control.

GENETICALLY MODIFIED THINKING

As a result of everything going on around us, we are being manipulated and led into a way of thinking which is based on fear and ignorance. It is being programmed into our beliefs, through the inputs of, media, TV, schooling, religion, rules and regulations. Even the food products available, prescription medicines and drinking water we are provided have a role to play in our distraction and control. This facilitates the herd mentality conveniently used to keep everyone in the pack and following their lead. Few people want to step out of line and be exposed to the consequences.

The messages of fear and hidden truths continually fed to us, dictate our beliefs and model our behaviour. Unless you can see through the 'smoke and mirrors', take a step back and rationalize, you will never be in control of your destiny. Seek the truth and make your own decisions wisely, this is the only way to be free.

The great Bob Marley's *Redemption Song* comes to mind here...

"Emancipate yourself from mental slavery, none but ourselves can free our minds"

Genetically Modified Thinking – Model of Associated Inputs *(Source: Blue C Therapies)*

This model shows the external factors influencing us through life; these input streams instil in us our values and beliefs, which we take on board unconditionally. What we are essentially doing, is relinquishing control of our life's journey. We don't often question these aspects until we reach an age of maturity, or until we encounter a bad time or a significant issue in our lives. Most people would then call it a 'mid-life crisis' this is in reality a point of awakening! We then begin to analyse certain areas of our lives and why they went so wrong, or not as planned. In doing this we must look into the basic beliefs we have been following and question whether these are our true beliefs or someone else's imposed belief.

Once you begin to explore you find many things that don't make sense, and as you dig deeper, you realise how much we really don't know. You begin to uncover your true self, who you are and what makes you happy and fulfilled. With this as the ultimate goal, you can then start on a new path with your revised beliefs and consequently, revised behaviours. New and better things will start to happen for you with much more becoming possible, even with the smallest of behavioural shifts.

(Source: Blue C Therapies)

MANIFESTING AN ENLIGHTENED WORLD

Consider what it would look like, what criteria would define it and what's most important to you.

Here are my thoughts on key criteria:

- Live in harmony with each other: Do unto others as you would have done to yourself
- Embrace the value in everyone and nurture spiritual (as opposed to materialistic) growth
- Provide everyone with somewhere safe to live
- Create solutions in harmony and balance with the planet
- Revisit our beliefs about health, healing and successful cures
- Eradicate disease
- Express gratitude for what we have and share the joy of living in 'the now'

In essence we need to reflect in our lives 'The 5 Reiki Principles' by Dr. Mikao Usui:

Just for today, do not be angry
Just for today, do not worry

Just for today, be grateful
Just for today, work hard
Just for today, be kind to others

As I see it there are four main component parts to achieving an enlightened world:

Part 1

REPENT AND REFORM

What to do with the 1% at the top of the pyramid? The ones who have lavished upon themselves all the trappings of wealth, privilege, status and unrivalled power? Do we return to the barbarism of the Reign of Terror that followed the French Revolution, or the monstrous and genocidal purges of Stalin, the Khmer Rouge, Chairman Mao and others? I say most emphatically not!!

The answer is to follow the incredible example of the **Truth and Reconciliation Commission** set up by Nelson Mandela and Archbishop Desmond Tutu in South Africa, following the end of the apartheid system of white minority rule[1]. A similar scheme would need to be set up at a reformed United Nations level where everyone involved in the worst excesses of human behaviour, from law enforcement, military, special forces black op teams, intelligence agencies, corporate fat cats, financial oligarchs, and above all the politicians, could all come and clear their consciences without the imminent threat of a trip to the gallows or a firing squad.

The technology to transform the world is there[2]. The needs of the people can be easily met and a bond of common purpose around the globe is there. All that is lacking is the will of our political and financial masters, to put it into action. In essence then, we must find leaders who believe in this reality and have the lack of ego and greed to make them great humanitarian leaders. Can you think of any?

Remember Frederick Douglass's words;

"Power concedes nothing without a demand; it never has and never will."

Plato noted how leaders needed four characteristics in order to have good governance: Courage, wisdom, self-discipline and justice. The absence of any one of these would cause rot and corruption to set in. I suggest that Plato and his contemporaries were Shamans in everything but name[3].

In the revolution against our materially obsessed world we could do with the wisdom of the Native American Indians and the Australian Aborigines. It would be brilliant for reconciliation and healing in regards to the monstrous treatment they have been subjected to in the not too distant past.

Part 2

FUNDING THE CHANGES

Take half the £21 trillion that's sitting in **offshore tax avoidance accounts** - a fraction of this money would clothe, feed, and shelter half the population of the planet that currently has no proper sanitation, no electricity and no easy access to drinking water. Another fraction of this money could be used to implement the technology invented by Nikola Tesla more than a century ago. This could provide unlimited, clean and free electrical power for the whole world. Enabling us to make areas like the Sahara and Kalahari Desert into an oasis. We would also have the ability to tackle our global waste issues, investing in biomass plants in every country to deal with our waste products efficiently and with minimum impact on the environment.

I will be accused of being a communist for suggesting a fifty percent haircut on the funds hidden in the Cayman Islands and other tax havens, but no one accused the banks of this when the people of Cyprus had half of their funds taken away in 2013.

Wealth re-distribution has been going on for centuries, as Voltaire noted in the 17th century and Plato observed in 300BC. What we have here, as so recently experienced by the bailing out of the banks with public money, is socialism for the rich.

The media is owned by the rich for the rich and they have the ability to cover the issues of the day with whatever slant they please. They then keep the masses entertained with soaps, reality TV and sports. A perfect example of what was called 'Bread and Circuses' during the beginning of the decline of the Imperial Roman Empire.

Part 3

SOMEWHERE TO BELONG

Entire cities could be built and **new communities established**. This would relieve the current pressure of refugees fleeing from the chaos and barbarism that western policy makers have unleashed in the last fifteen years. There would be no need for wars over resources, no need for nuclear power generation, fracking or crude oil production. There would be no need for GMO crops either as living in harmony and balance with the planet would be a key objective. The other colossal benefit would be the funds needed to finally eradicate cancer from our lives.

The young and unemployed from all over Europe could get involved in the new developments that will be managed by innovative leaders and current experts in these fields. This would be a true global union of thoughts, ideas, aspirations, purpose, motivation, support, investment and fulfilment – honest collaboration untainted by politics, religion, ego and greed. Tens of millions of us would have work, rebuilding towns and cities, constructing new ones, building desalination plants, creating effective water supply systems, safely dismantling the old power generating plants and replacing them with Tesla Towers, cultivating the land and growing sufficient food organically. To begin with, there are baron parts of Europe where new communities could be built using all the methods that we want to evolve to, as a proof of concept. By the way if you've never heard of Nikola Tesla, search the internet for him you'll be inspired.

"If you want to meet a genius, talk to Mr. Tesla"
Albert Einstein

You will learn how investors like J P Morgan baulked at the idea of 'free energy' - how were they going to make a fortune out of that idea? Tesla's a fool! Well we've seen where that mindset has brought humanity to.

Part 4

PERSONAL REFLECTION

We could have a common purpose across the world, a shared vision of a peaceful planet, a secure and viable future for us all that gives dignity and real freedom to everyone, not just a privileged few. Our possibilities for advancement and evolution would be vast, unlimited and wholly achievable. Or, you can 'keep calm and carry on', reach for the anti-depressants and kid yourself that somehow, someway, everything will work out in the end. We have all played some part in where we are today, even if that is merely acceptance. **If we want change we all must play a part in that too**, even if that is only to state what we want and stand up against what we don't want and not buy into the propaganda and manipulation going on all around us.

Thoughts are energy and they get to their destination, so keep your thoughts positive and focused on what you want to happen. We all have to heal our thoughts and our ways for the changes to occur. The more people thinking about and sending energy to a particular solution, the more power it has.

Having spoken to people across Europe, it's massively reassuring to see what choice most would go for. We only need to believe in ourselves, to stop repeating the same mistakes again and again, and to turn the world into the paradise it could easily be.

Einstein defined insanity as doing the same things over and over again and expecting different results. The reality of our political system reflects this and is proof of why nothing changes. So too does our education system which is in dire need of revision to facilitate the lives and careers of our young people and the industries of the future.

We have to make our voices heard; we have the power to not comply, to peacefully withdraw from the system that has played us for two millennia. But I'm one ordinary person with a few ideas. How about seven billion people talking about it, getting their voices heard, bouncing ideas off each other. The energies created would be electric and we'd soon discover we have far more in common than separates us.

"Imagine all the people living life in peace. You may say I'm a dreamer, but I'm not the only one. I hope someday you'll join us and the world will live as one."

It's about time!

What do you think? Do you agree? What ideas and solutions do you have? It's time to imagineer our future.

PLAYING OUR PART IN THE CHANGE

Until this collective sweeping away of the current Establishment shows itself to be a real, tangible possibility, the unstoppable momentum needed to see it through begins to positively manifest itself. We've taken the only other course open to us, to disconnect ourselves from the current paradigm and escape in the opposite direction to those heading for the UK. Here the ex-pat community is a net contributor to the Bulgarian economy to the tune of hundreds of millions of leva every year. We don't have the right to welfare or the vote but we do have the chance to live a fantastic quality of life free from the burdens of debt, low pay, zero hour contract jobs, mortgages and high rents and swap it for a slower, relaxed lifestyle with the added bonus of Greek summer and autumn weather. We can live, not just exist. Getting away from the situation of living just to work provides a huge feeling of what it must be like to win the lotto, without waiting for the 1 in 45 million chance of success. It has given us the chance to step back and see the bigger picture, put things into context, and make decisions true to ourselves.

One positive action in your life has the potential to change the world or so I read online. I believe that as completely as I do the following quote:

"The planet does not need more successful people. The planet desperately needs more peacemakers, healers, restorers, storytellers and lovers of every kind"
The Dalai Lama.

The Dalai Lama's credibility has gone down in my humble opinion since his recent meeting with George W Bush where he describes some of the former presidents' decisions over Iraq as "not very successful". Seriously? That's like saying Hannibal Lector has questionable menu choices. Understatement aside, I still agree with his quote.

To the reader I wish you love, happiness and a wonderful future. Go and write your own story, you are after all supposed to be the leading lady or leading man in your own life!

SECTION 2
Our Story

THE GREAT ESCAPE... FROM AUSTERITY, CONFORMITY AND THE RAT RACE

The information and events in this book are based on a true and continuing story.

Come with us and enjoy the ride...

CHAPTER 1
ESCAPE THE ILLUSION

*"The trick is to enjoy life, not wish away your days
waiting for better ones ahead."*
Marjorie Pay Hinckley.

*"We are caged by our cultural programming. Culture is
a mass hallucination and when you step outside the mass
hallucination you see it for what it is worth."*
Terence McKenna.

July 2007

The lowest point of my life, I'd just finished loading all
my worldly possessions into the back of a hire van and
was taking a walk around what had been my dream
home one last time just to ensure I hadn't left anything
behind. I'd had to sell following the divorce from my
wife, and was moving to a house less than half the size
and smaller than my first house that I'd bought sixteen
years earlier.

It began after I'd resigned from my comparatively
well paid job as a long distance tanker driver, in an

attempt to spend more time at home with my wife and step-son and was now looking at self-employment as an uncertain but exciting alternative career as a courier. Only weeks after I'd started and I'd moved my life savings into my mortgage account to ease the financial transition, my wife dropped the bombshell on me that she was seeing someone else, and to kick me where it hurt, she demanded half the equity despite the fact that I had bought the house and paid all the bills, council tax, mortgage etc. for the past six years! So there I was just me and the cat, in a big empty house with half the furniture and appliances missing, wondering what the hell I did wrong! To cut a long and torturous story short, ten months later the house finally sold and I could move on.

Within two weeks of moving in to my new house, it was surrounded by flood water and I had the fire brigade at my door, asking if I wanted to evacuate. I declined their offer, put another layer of sandbags around the house and waited for the River Idle to do its worst. Luckily the waters never entered the house but I couldn't help wondering what I'd done to deserve such horrible misfortune. A few nights later, after the waters had receded I was woken up in the small hours of the morning by a wailing alarm. A ferocious storm was battering the town and the strong winds had blown my motorbike off its side stand and caused it a lot of damage. I went out into the garden, heaved the bike back upright and yelled abuse at the top of my lungs, giving the finger to the skies above.

At least my gamble with self-employment seemed to pay off and I earned a similar amount to my full time job in my first year but I had more freedom and fewer threatening memos, no more increased workloads for less pay, and I had the satisfaction of being in charge of my own destiny.

It didn't last and each of the next three years saw my turnover fall by £5000. Increasing prices at the pump, rising insurance premiums, less work and no increase in pay rates to compensate for the increase in fuel costs left me looking at a bleak future. Luckily I caught a break and was offered a job as a sub-contract courier for a major national delivery company. They had received abuse in the press for losing a consignment of government mail with the names and addresses of hundreds of thousands of people as well as their bank details. In order to keep their £1 billion contract they came up with a plan to use sub-contract couriers on dedicated runs to collect and deliver confidential information from HMRC and Job Centre offices the length and breadth of the country.

For the first time in many years I had a job that I actually enjoyed and was reasonably well paid for. At least I was able to keep my head above water as the financial crisis of 2007/8 continued to bite. I wasn't in too much debt and had a steady enough job. At the end of each month though, I hardly had anything left from my wages as there were always bills to pay for keeping the van running and all the other mentioned costs. I even took to sleeping in the back of the van a couple of times a week to keep my fuel costs down including during the very harsh winter of 2010/11. I was the only driver who managed to complete all of my assignments during the worst of the weather. I wasn't best pleased one particularly bad week that, because my colleagues had stayed at home, the company had assumed I had as well, and I wasn't even paid having driven on untreated roads in temperatures of minus eighteen degrees Celsius!

Three months later and having just bought another van to replace my Vauxhall Combo that expired with 200,000 miles on the clock, rumours started flying around that bad news was on its way. Due to austerity measures and reductions in government spending, the company had been told to knock a huge amount off the annual bill or lose the contract in the long term. It was our section under the spotlight and sure enough the rumours turned out to be true. We were in for big changes and individually we were called into the office for the news. "The good news is that you're not going to lose your job; the bad news is that you'll have to work an extra twenty unpaid hours a week AND take a wage cut of five thousand pounds a year" I said I'd have to think about it as I had a great deal to consider. Two seconds later I informed them of just what they could do with that offer and left the office for the last time. I had two weeks to think about what to do until my notice was finished and I was out of work.

I remembered the character Howard Beale from the film 'Network' and his often viewed tirade in the newsroom in front of millions of viewers *"I'm mad as hell and I'm not gonna take it anymore!!"* I'd done everything in life that a good citizen is supposed to do, work hard, vote, obey the law (most of the time), pay my taxes and not rock the boat. Where had it got me? One backwards step, after another, after another. I went for an interview with a local company that involved me driving tankers again but with even more anti-social hours than before and, here was the cherry on top, less than half of what I'd been earning four years previously! Having been phoned up on my walk home to be offered the job I decided to do two things, firstly decline the job offer and secondly to watch the longer 'YouTube' clip of Howard Beale. It went something like this... *"Everyone knows things are bad, it's a depression, everyone's out of work or scared of losing their jobs. The dollar buys a nickel's worth, banks are going bust, shop keepers keep a gun under the counter, punks are running wild in the street and no one seems to know what to do about it and there's no end to it! We know our air's unfit to breathe and our food's not fit to eat, we know things are bad, worse than bad they're crazy, it's like everything is going crazy everywhere so we stay at home, we don't go out anymore and all we say is; "Please, at least leave us alone in our living rooms, let me have my toaster, TV set and my radio and I won't say anything, just leave me alone!" Well, I'm not going to leave you alone – I want you to get mad, I don't want you to riot or protest, I don't want you to write to your congressman cos I wouldn't know what to tell you to write. I don't know what to do about the depression and the inflation or the Russians or the crime in the streets. All I know is that first you've got to get mad! You've got to say I'm a*

*human being God Dammit! My life has value!! I'm as
mad as hell and I'm not going to take it anymore!"*

In the four years I had lived in this modest, little
house in Nottinghamshire I had been predominantly in a
very dark place inside. I still had not properly got over
the heartbreak of my divorce. I was haunted by the loss
of everything I'd worked so hard for, the end of the only
time in my life that I had been genuinely happy and, for
the first time in my life, really in love. I'd read that some
men deal with a broken heart by crying like a baby and
others buy an Uzi 9mm and climb a clock tower. I'd
already wasted enough time doing one of those and I
certainly wasn't going to do the other, I'm not that great
with heights. I made a promise to myself each January
that if things didn't work out for me workwise or in
finding a nice girlfriend that I'd sell the house and
everything I had left in the world. I'd keep what I could
carry on my motorbike and just take off, see a bit of the
world and take what came my way as an opportunity to
start over. I know that society sees examples such as this
as ample evidence of a mid-life crisis but I don't agree.
In ages past it was referred to as a mid-life change. A
realisation that one was not where one wanted to be in
life, that something had to give and the consequences of
being brow beaten back into line would be
catastrophically bad. I'd already tried everything I
possibly could and was now looking at falling into the
final abyss.

"Better the devil you know."
Anon.

No wonder the author of this dreadful cliché never put their name to it. It is the probably the most stifling and inhibiting phrase known to man. I find it as reprehensible as "it's too good to be true" or "choosing the lesser of two evils" because if you follow that pearl of wisdom you will still end up with evil. These clichés pale into insignificance compared with the most damaging, almost Orwellian newspeak slogan of them all:

"Keep calm and carry on"
Ministry of Information, British Government.

I know it was supposed to keep up public morale while the Luftwaffe rained down high explosive bombs on towns and cities across the country, that it still serves to emphasize the good old stiff upper lip mentality but for me at this time it served no valid purpose at all.

My self-esteem had been trashed enough and to just put up with more painful blows was not going to do me any good. What was needed was an alternative, something new that would offer hope, not more of the same. Ok, I faced an uphill struggle to hold on to my house. I tried going back to sub-contract courier work but this turned out to be utterly pointless. The amount of work I was getting was barely enough to cover my fuel costs and the penny dropped that I was in all honesty working for nothing. I could try working two or three part time jobs to keep my head above water and barely have any quality time to enjoy my house and garden or sell up and do a runner.

In June 2010 I was lucky enough to begin a relationship with Christine. We met properly at a friend's house to watch England play America in the World Cup. At least something positive began for us after the shocking match. We became inseparable through the misery of the England vs Algeria match and noted the jeers from England's long suffering fans in South Africa.

She was a friend of a friend and had recently separated from her husband after more than twenty-five years of marriage. She had been given an exit from her senior position at one of the big six energy providers in the country after thirty years of loyal service, and was looking at working for herself as a complementary therapist. She'd trained in the ancient Japanese practice of Reiki, and also NLP (Neuro-Linguistic Programming) and had qualified as a shamanic healer. She had put a lot of effort into setting up her own business however the financial meltdown ensured that people did not have enough spare cash to be able to take adequate advantage of her therapies and therefore she was looking for additional work to supplement the situation she faced.

I became fascinated at the teachings of Reiki and of spiritual healing in general and this brought about a complete reversal of previous opinions I had about so called "New Age" beliefs. I found myself more and more convinced that everything happens for a reason and of the importance of karma in our lives. I read more about shamanism and trained to become a Reiki practitioner.

Through Chris I met some very inspirational new friends including Jon and Helen, a wonderful couple from Lancashire who were also qualified shamanic healers.

What I learnt also confirmed suspicions I'd long held about the nature of global governments and organised religion. The belief structure that I had grown up under was losing its powers of persuasion and I could palpably feel a sense of empowerment rising within me. This has only been strengthened by the knowledge that the CIA, Russian and Chinese intelligence agencies have been using shamanic skills like remote viewing and even tarot cards for the purpose of international espionage since the 1970s[1]. They have had budgets of hundreds of millions of dollars between them and have no difficulty accepting the concept of life on other worlds and dimensions as fact. These skills were never meant to be used for such purposes and have led to the mental breakdowns of many of those involved.

These revelations became the backdrop of the hit TV series Stargate and the government program it was based on was called Operation Sunstreak. Now a new TV series called Ascension also has its basis in fact. There was a project to build a vast nuclear powered space craft on a mission to Barnard's Star. Fifty-seven of the world's top scientists agreed it was possible but would require the entire gross national product of the United States to pay for it. And since these were the days before electronic money was created, when the dollar was still pegged to the price of gold the project never got off the ground.

In my conventional life I could only see Chris at weekends and then I was always tired because of very early morning starts and frequent late finishes. This was an alarmingly familiar scenario for me as it was one of the main reasons for my marriage breaking down and the beginning of a downward spiral of events that almost led me to a total breakdown and thoughts of potential suicide.

After a long walk and bouncing ideas off each other we returned to Chris's flat and decided to hold a crystal divination for our next course of action. She'd trained in this technique as part of her recent shamanic healing course and wanted to try it out. I was considering whether or not to put my house up for sale.

In the cul-de-sac where I lived there were four similar properties on the market. Two hadn't seen any potential buyers in over a year, one for eighteen months and the house two doors down from mine had sold at a loss of over twenty-five thousand pounds on the asking price. This notwithstanding we asked the crystals if my house would sell, the answer was yes. How long would it take – within three months, six to nine months or one year? The answer was within three months. First thing on Monday morning I started the process of selling up and by the end of the second week in July 2010, a For Sale sign was up outside the house.

We did some basic tidying up and repainting, put in a new bath room suite and left it at that. Within the first month I had three prospective buyers interested but eventually they bought other properties. I was still confident it would go and I was still doing courier jobs but was now having to borrow money from Chris until the house sold.

We needed a plan as to where to move to afterwards. We both liked watching the show 'A Place in the Sun' but it often seemed to feature properties that are beyond the reach of most people and the couples involved always seemed fifteen or twenty years older than us. However the show does reveal a tantalizing glimpse of an appealing new way of life. We'd have to do more research on somewhere to live! After a beer and several frustrating online searches looking for somewhere affordable we came across Rightmove Overseas, I mentioned in jest about looking at Bulgaria. "What on earth for? It'll probably be some bombsite of a place in the middle of nowhere!" Was Chris's first thought and as it turned out when I clicked on the link to be pretty accurate. A picture of a derelict barn in the middle of nowhere for a thousand pounds appeared! BUT there were also some nice apartments by the sea starting from £12,000. All ideas of negativity went out of the window at that point. We both took a sharp intake of breath and looked at each other at the same moment. It was our Eureka moment!

A few weeks later we took a holiday break to Albufeira in the Algarve. It is one of Chris's favourite locations and we enjoyed our week there. We have made many friends there, particularly one of the musicians that plays virtually every night during the holiday season, Martin Jonathan, check him out at Steps Bar if you're ever there and enjoy the chilled out atmosphere made possible by the bar crew, Chris, Andre and the girls. We sat on the beach and mused about our options and the events and circumstances that brought us to this moment in our lives.

CHAPTER 2
BREAKING AWAY

Chris was due to either extend the rental period on her flat in Wetherby or give her notice to leave. She chose the latter. We found a storage facility nearby in Leeds and part of their introductory offer included the free use of a transit van for 48 hours. We used this time well and moved all her possessions into storage as soon as we could. In the meantime, Chris moved in with me in Retford. On Monday morning I received news from Rod at the estate agents in town that there was another interested viewer for my house. Coincidentally, Rod had a friend who already owned property in Bulgaria and was sure he could offer us any advice if we wanted it about the buying process there. I can't compliment Rod highly enough, he and his staff at Rightmove gave us an excellent service.

We set an appointment for the same afternoon and went about the routines you are supposed to do, get some fresh filter coffee on the go, have some nice French bread in the oven and some fresh, cut flowers on the kitchen table. At 3pm my viewer showed up and had a long look round. Megan was a young supply teacher whose school was less than five minutes' walk from the front door. She seemed as pleased with what she saw as had the previous three viewers and after fifteen minutes she left us to enjoy our coffee and baguette. The next morning Rod was calling me, she wanted to come back for a second viewing, this time accompanied by her parents. We happily agreed and the viewing went as well as could be hoped for. I was leaving my nearly new washing machine behind and showed Megan how to use it; she was also pleased that the cooker was being left behind, too. After all, where Chris and I were going we'd have little use for them. Megan and her parents were curious as to where we were going and were fascinated when we explained that we were leaving the country on a great adventure. I didn't hear anything further from Rod during the next few days and when I did, he explained that my house was one of three on Megan's shortlist and it was now a waiting game to see which house would be the winner.

We arranged to see our two shaman friends, Jon and Helen over in Todmorden for a couple of nights. On the second day with our friends I got a call from Rod with the best news we could have had. Megan had put in an offer on my house! I listened to her offer which was less than I wanted, I suggested a little more and we'd have a deal. Thirty seconds later the return call came back and the deal was done! The date was 12th October 2011 and was within the three month window foretold by our crystal divination; the universe is a very wonderful place when you begin to trust it and the energies that run through it! We had more than a few celebratory drinks at the great news and we could begin proper planning for the next step of our journey!

We returned to Retford the next afternoon and began packing up stuff to put in storage at Leeds, I put my king size bed, TV and leather three piece suite on eBay and they'd all gone within two weeks. We spent the rest of the time sleeping on airbeds and sitting on fold-up camping chairs until the 23rd November, departure day, came around.

There was one difficult issue I had to deal with, what to do with my beloved cat, Butch. He was nearly twelve years old and had not been in the best of health. The previous Christmas it had seemed like he would not last much beyond New Year. His fur had been falling out and the spark in his green eyes had faded dramatically. The vet could do nothing for him and advised that there were lumps on his chest that might be cancerous.

One of the events that helped show me the evidence and power of shamanism occurred when the four of us conducted a remote healing session for Butch. We were one hundred miles from him at the time but when I got home the following day he was a different animal. His vitality was back, his eyes shone bright and within the week his coat was noticeably thicker and healthier. I know what I saw in him, the difference it made and any tiny doubt in the new experiences I was learning, totally disappeared. We were planning on leaving the UK and there was no way at all I could take him. I couldn't bear the idea of taking him back to a cat sanctuary, my ex and I had rescued him from there when he was a month old, the idea of having him put down was one I couldn't and wouldn't entertain but fortunately for me my friend Tracey from the motorbike club offered to take him. This was the last remaining stumbling block and the way was now clear to leave old 'Blighty'.

Something else on a far deeper level needed thought too, upping sticks and leaving your home country is not something you do lightly. We were both unsure as to the reaction of our parents when we discussed our future plans. Both sets of parents were actually incredibly supportive of what we were about to do, we had their blessings as we began to plan what lay beyond.

The morning of November 23rd arrived with bright sunshine and blue skies. I'd emptied the attic and the shed. I'd also sold my motorbike and just had the issue of getting a bicycle rack for the back of the Astra van and some roof bars and top box fitting at Halfords. This took longer than expected and I knew we'd be very close to the 6pm arrival of Megan for the keys. I got confirmation late in the afternoon that the money from Megan's bank had arrived in my account. This seemed to take forever in arriving but obviously it was a massive relief when it did. I took the time to pay off the personal loan for the van, paid off my credit card and all other debts and now had both a clean slate and a positive bank balance.

We'd arranged to stop at a historic hotel in Lincoln that evening and were looking forward to dinner out on the town. Chris was getting worried as the clock ticked by that everything was taking too long and she was relieved as I drove up and parked on the driveway of my little house for the last time. We loaded everything in, filled the top box and secured our bikes to the rear bike rack. I realized suddenly that I'd forgotten to inform TV licensing that I was cancelling my direct debit with them. I'd done everything else you're supposed to, sort the electric and water readings, paid what I owed or vice versa so I immediately rang the TV people. They wanted to know my new address and they were not very impressed when I told them I had absolutely no idea. I told them I was in all likelihood leaving the country in January but if I had a change of heart I'd be back in touch. Fat chance of that! That was it, done and dusted. I was just pulling the last bungee cords around the bikes when Megan arrived. I walked around the house one last time, just as I had with my former marital home four years earlier. This time it was different, I wasn't a broken man surrounded by shattered dreams, faced with a bleak future, this time Chris and I had the world at our feet. We knew where we would be for the next three nights but after that we had no idea. We only knew that it would be extraordinary!

We arrived at the 18th Century Duke William Inn and checked in. The hotel was definitely authentic, the rooms were tiny but comfortable enough. We asked a girl behind the bar for her choice of a good restaurant in the city, she was very helpful with that and as she pulled two good pints of bitter the conversation soon got round to what we had just done and where we were going. She was from Napoli and was fascinated by what we had planned. She said that we must visit Napoli if we ever got around to travelling through Italy.

We had dinner at a fabulous Italian restaurant near the cathedral; we ordered a bottle of white wine and savoured not just the meal itself but the idea of the adventure we were embarking on. We wanted to spend Christmas and New Year with our families before we left the country so we just had to fill in the time before then. The following five weeks were spent in places as diverse as Surrey, Cumbria, Scotland, Bruges and Guernsey.

Our intention was to drive to The Algarve and check out property prices there as well as France and Spain and gain an insight into the cost of living in those countries along the way. We'd visit Paris for a few nights, Chris also wanted to visit a very old town perched on a cliff that was used in the Johnny Depp movie, "Chocolat". We'd then zigzag across France covering a lot of ground on the way to the Spanish Frontier. Portugal was where we really had designs on settling down. Chris loves Albufeira and its relaxed atmosphere and we planned on staying there for at least three weeks before returning to the UK. It is a strange feeling to have nowhere to call home anymore. No mortgage, no utility bills, no council tax, no TV licence and no work for either of us to get up in the morning for. Living out of a couple of suitcases and whatever else we could pack into the van, we could have been roadies for a rock band!

Quality time was spent with family and friends, good bye and good luck parties took place with resulting sore heads all round. The most satisfying aspect of these gatherings was the genuine good wishes and hopes we were being offered (or perhaps people were glad to see the back of us). Christmas and New Year came and went, the packing was sorted and ready after another visit to the storage facility. We had everything we could think of stuffed in the van: ironing board, clothes airers, washing powder and enough clothes for six weeks. On the 7th of January we were headed to Dover. I bought the obligatory European motorist's Travel Pack and a concise AA European road map. French law now says every driver has to have two breathalyser kits in the car so we bought these as well. Christine had one more outstanding legal issue pertaining to her divorce to deal with; this meant we couldn't book a ferry until we knew it was taken care of. Similar to the situation with my house completion, we were made to wait until very late in the day which meant that when we got the all clear, we had to pay nearly three times the price of a ticket than if we'd booked online earlier. Oh well! Now we could book a hotel in Calais and our road trip was set to begin at 7pm.

At 7:40pm I drove on to the "Pride of Calais" and we made our way up the stairs to the passenger deck for a drink. I checked the hastily scribbled notes and map I'd drawn a couple of hours earlier of the location of our hotel in case my obsolete satnav didn't play ball with me. I knew it was near the main university and I had ridden near there three years earlier on a motorbike holiday across Europe, so I was confident we could get there with minimum fuss when we disembarked. We cast a glance at our fellow passengers, wondering what their plans were; most seemed content to take a nap or were playing cards and watching the Road Runner cartoon that was on TV.

We sipped our large Costa coffees and remarked excitedly that this was it! We were actually doing it. This wasn't just idle dreaming after a couple of bottles of wine; we were on our way to Southern Portugal. We had each other and a belief in what we were doing. If we couldn't find somewhere else to live, what was the worst that could happen; we'd have to come back to the UK and start again, at the point we're at now. We had nothing to lose.

This was the first key milestone, and we were more than ready!

CHAPTER 3
NO TURNING BACK

We were tired but excited when we were eventually summoned back to our vehicles. At just after 9:30 pm we drove off the ship and set out into the cold winter night to find our hotel. My satnav behaved impeccably, listing every boulevard and side street and we found our home for the night incredibly easily. It was just along from a nicely lit Ibis hotel, we'd considered booking there but were put off by the price. Our chosen venue, by comparison, looked like a young offenders' institute. Poorly lit, had no reception desk and was without an elevator. To gain access to budget hotels in France you have to put the credit card you used to make the reservation into what looked like a chocolate or drinks dispensing machine. Once the machine is happy your details tally up, your room key drops down in the draw at the bottom. We'd never seen anything like it before, but there are definite advantages to it.

I took the bikes off the rack and locked them up, then lugged everything we needed for the next week into the room so it could be more efficiently stored in the roof box for the rest of the trip. I'd forgotten a backpack so had to find my way down the poorly lit corridor to the stairs, and out into the chilly air. There were very few people out and about and little passing traffic so a quiet nights' sleep looked to be on the cards. As I made my way off the stairwell and into the long corridor towards our 'luxury suite', I heard loud sighs, ecstatic moans and a bed headboard banging against the wall from the room opposite ours. This definitely wasn't from the "HD/3D" TV in their room. I smiled and laughed inwardly, "Welcome to Europe!"

We slept pretty well that night, all things considered and the next morning reloaded the car in such a way that we wouldn't have to mess around with the bike rack again for at least a week. We got a rather insipid coffee from the dispensing machine and checked our route to Paris. The A26 toll motorway would bring us to Arras and onwards via the A1 to Paris. The drive to Paris was very enjoyable, little traffic to contend with, rolling fields, woodlands and blue skies. When we got on the A26 it was tempting to put Steppenwolf's "Born to be Wild" or AC/DC's "Highway to Hell" on but as it was, Chris put an album from Dido on the CD player and this choice was perfect. Since we'd had no breakfast we were soon in need of refreshment and stopped at the next service area. The first thing you notice when you arrive in the car park is the lack of warning signs on every lamp post announcing that you have just entered into a contract with the parking provider and agreed to pay ten quid the moment your stay goes one second beyond two hours. There are no warning signs announcing that your details have been recorded on CCTV and fines will be sent to your house for non-payment. I liked France already! If you wished, your car can stay put for up to twenty-four hours without hassle or threat.

The next thing is the great choice of food available, from salads to soups, cooked meats to vegetarian dishes and the obligatory fast food joints. You are also given the choice of beer with your meal if you so wish. The punishments for driving over the limit in France are considerable but your passengers might like one and it is refreshing to have the choice, to be treated as an adult and not bombarded with health warnings if you do fancy a cold one. We enjoyed our meal, filled up with cheaper French diesel and rejoined the A26.

Soon you are entering the Somme region and familiar names connected to the Great War appear on the exit signs. I'd already taken Chris on the motorbike to Thiepval near Albert: this is a huge memorial to 385,000 allied soldiers whose remains were never found, and Beaumont Hamel where the trenches are still in place as they were a century ago.

We continued on until we reached the toll point on joining the A1. Ouch! Twenty euros? I was sure I'd only paid five euros when I came through three years previously. I put it down to driving what might be classed as a commercial vehicle in France. The satnav was becoming less helpful than it had been in Calais. It gave us the road, its number and the direction of travel, so we knew we'd be joining the A3 just after passing Charles De Gaulle airport. Chris was navigating from the map, as we now entered the A86, then the E50 auto route de l'Est on the edge of south eastern Paris. She did brilliantly and we knew we were now only a few minutes from our exit, and then we got stuck in the Thursday afternoon rush hour.

Eventually we found our exit and arrived outside our hotel for the next three nights, the Best Western St Maurice. We'd chosen it because it was a good price, had car parking facilities, easy access back out onto our route out of the city and not too far to the nearest metro station. There didn't appear to be any car park however, just a layby outside reception so I parked behind a VW transporter and looked for my booking number for checking in. Chris asked where was the car park with more than a hint of concern in her voice! There were two shutter doors on the side of the building, one was insanely low, the other must be the access point to an underground car park. I left Chris to guard our stuff and went into reception.

I thought I remembered enough French from school to be able to announce I had a reservation for three nights but clearly I spent too much time gazing down the cleavage of our French teacher and not on what she was teaching. Fortunately the receptionist spoke perfect English. I gave him my booking number and he started keying in my details. It was half past five and I was looking forward to getting cleaned up and I knew Chris was too. "I'm sorry monsieur, but your reservation has been cancelled as your credit card company refused payment on the room." It got worse, "We are full tonight, I'm afraid". Great! What on earth were we going to do? We knew that just turning up on the door was the most expensive way to get a room and that most of the hotels in and around the city didn't have parking facilities. It was still the rush hour outside and I knew Chris would be gutted at the prospect of trying to find somewhere else to stay.

The receptionist must have picked up on this because he announced "Moment Monsieur, there may be a way I can juggle some of the other incoming guests into other rooms and still accommodate you". After a couple of minutes on the phone and some frantic typing on his keyboard he continued, "Monsieur, we can get you a room for the next three nights but I am afraid it will cost an extra six euros a night plus another six a day for the car park". I would have snapped his arm off for that instead of the alternatives, so readily agreed. It crossed my mind that I might have had some colourful language reserved for my credit card provider, particularly as I'd informed them that I would be travelling in Europe for the next few weeks, but I let it go. I was just thrilled to be able to show Chris one of my favourite cities once we'd got unpacked and cleaned up. I asked where the car park was and was told that the receptionist would open it as we approached the door. Then his assistant asked if I owned the silver VW? I replied that I didn't and she seemed happy. As I walked down towards the car I developed a sinking feeling. Chris wanted to know why I'd been so long and I recalled the problems to her. Then as I pulled towards the two doors, the shorter one began to swing open... "Oh Hell, no!" We both got out and looked at the low concrete beam above a steep descent to the lower level. The warning sign on the beam said nothing over 1.85 metres. We knew from our recent trip to Bruges that with the roof box on, the car would get under 1.9 metres but this looked a lot lower than the P+O car park at Hull docks. Chris was convinced, "You'll never get under that beam! It's too low, you'll wreck the roof box and the bikes!" I was determined to give it a try, very, very carefully.

I told Chris to get out and watch the roof as I inched the car forwards until the front wheels started down on the slope. Chris was still very unhappy about what I was trying to do, after all we'd just spent four hundred quid on the roof bars, box and bike carrier. I inched further towards the overhead beam. I couldn't hear a scraping noise or any yells from Chris. By now I must have been under the beam so I carried on down the slope with a feeling of triumph bordering on smugness. The only thing that stopped me from punching the air with relief and gratitude was the knowledge that on Sunday morning I would have to perform the same trick the other way round. Part of me thought that would be no problem, after all I'd got in hadn't I? But going the other way? Wouldn't the angles be against me and I knew also that I couldn't have a run at the steep slope in case I did wreck the roof box. That was going to be interesting but I put thoughts of it out of my mind. We had three nights to enjoy in one of the most famous, exciting cities in the world. Chris walked down the ramp to where I'd parked the car, "You only just made that! There couldn't have been more than half an inch between the top of the box and that beam!" "No problem! I told you I'd do it" We went up to our room and got spruced up.

I looked at the view out of the window at the heavy traffic on the auto route de l'Est, parallel to that was the

River Seine meandering its way through the city. I wanted to show Chris the Basilica Sacre Coeur in Montmartre. I used to have a print on the wall that I'd bought in Athena twenty years ago. It depicted the steps leading up to the cathedral in black and white from 1950. Sadly it got damaged during the moving process and I'd thrown it on one of the many fires I'd burned in the back garden. The helpful receptionist told us where the nearest metro station was and he gave us a tourist map to help us find our destination. We set off and after a mile or so we found Charenton Ecoles metro station.

For the first time in thirty-four years I was riding the metro again, it was Chris's first visit and we were both relishing the experience. After forty minutes and a change of line, we arrived at Anvers station. The tourist information signs are everywhere and so it is very easy to find your way around, unless, like some of my biker friends who'd struggled to find the historical site they most wanted to see, they'd spent two hours wandering around in ever decreasing circles until one of them asked a Parisian lady in their best French, "Pardon Madam, où est La Bastille, s'il vous plait?" She looked like she was struggling not to laugh as she informed them that the Bastille prison had been raised to the ground in one of the first acts of the Revolution in 1789 but the monument marking the site of its location was 50 metres behind them. We duly found the bottom of the steps leading to the cathedral. I'd forgotten that there was a funicular railway leading up to the top and just how far it was but we'd wanted some exercise after our day on the road, and we certainly got it.

The cathedral was obviously closed at this time in the evening but the views over the city are fantastic. There were plenty of young Parisians sitting on the steps enjoying their own wine or beer and listening to music. It was a great atmosphere but we also wanted to find the celebrated Moulin Rouge so headed back down the long flight of stairs in search of the famous red windmill. We walked past a couple of bars and restaurants before making our way along the Boulevard de Clichy. Soon the famous landmark came into view and we checked the admission prices; €163 each for dinner and the show! We abruptly decided that was way over the top for our budget and decided we fancied our first beer in the capital at more modest prices. We retraced our steps until we walked past a delicatessen we'd noticed. They had some tempting snacks in the window from only €5 so I bought a hotdog with cheese which we were going to share. It was utterly revolting and made the need for a beer all the more important. We took a side street and walked past the La Cigale music hall, up the hill past Cabaret Michou and took the next right turn. We stopped and sat down outside the bar, taking advantage of the patio heater that was keeping the cold, winter air at bay. The waitress took our order from the somewhat limited drinks menu, not everyone likes Ricard or cognac. We asked for two large Kronenbourg 1664's and savoured what we considered well deserved beers.

I texted my parents and let them know all was well with us and Chris did the same with hers. The waitress came over as we were just about finished and advised us the bar was closing soon and did we want another drink.

We decided that we'd better make tracks as we had a long day planned tomorrow so just asked for the bill. My intake of breath when it arrived almost snuffed out the overhead heater €15! We'd definitely had enough and made our way to the station and back the hotel. Even at 11pm the traffic was still busy on the auto route de l'Est but we were ready for a good night's sleep.

The next morning we were going to go up the Eiffel Tower and if we had the time, we planned to visit the Louvre gallery. We enjoyed coffee while watching the Euro news channel in our room. I had gone down to the van earlier to check everything was in order and also to bring a thermos flask up to the room to fill with more coffee. This would save us a few euros and we would buy a proper French pain au chocolat from a Boulanger near the metro station. I put this in my motorbike backpack along with Chris's handbag and we headed down the steps to get our metro tickets.

After forty-five minutes we arrived at La Tour Maubourg station and made our way up the street. The sky was a perfect blue, not a cloud in sight and the sunshine felt wonderful after our underground commute across the city. All around us was the hustle and bustle of Parisian life: fast moving traffic which is often oblivious to pedestrian crossings, cars parked so close together that the owners have to literally bump obstructing vehicles out of the way to escape, souvenir stands, the aromas of cognac, coffee and Gauloises emanating from plush looking restaurants, and well-heeled Parisians rushing from one location to the next. I overheard one businessman on his mobile explaining in perfect English that he would be in Moscow at the end of the week to conclude a lucrative deal.

We popped into another sumptuous Boulanger and bought a fresh baguette (no one makes them as beautifully as the French) and some cheese. I popped them into my backpack, checking my expensive thermos hadn't leaked over Chris's handbag and zipped it up. It seemed as though no one had the time to just take in the pleasant mid-morning sun, except for us. The unforgettable image of the iconic Eiffel Tower loomed over us, barely a kilometre away and we made our way to the Avenue de la Bourdonnais with its big 19th century apartment buildings and expensive, properly parked cars outside. We turned into the Champ de Mars gardens that led us to the base of the amazing tower itself.

As we neared the tower we were approached by two young women armed with clip boards and pens asking for a donation to a local children's home. We explained as best we could that we had no address now; we were passing through but would be happy to donate a couple of euros. We signed their petition asking for help from the government when one of them pointed to the minimum donation that they would accept. €10! In no uncertain terms were we going to stump that up and we left them in no doubt of that either. What a scam! We made sure we weren't being followed and continued to the Tower entrance a few hundred metres away. There were huge queues for the elevators with the usual sheep pen arrangements for the visitors. By contrast there were no queues at all for the stairs and the entrance price was half of that of the elevators. We were on a fitness drive anyway so what the Hell? As we got closer to the entrance I saw that we had to go through the same kind of security checks that you do at an airport nowadays. I took off my backpack and put Chris's handbag on the conveyor belt and watched it on its way through the detector, my aluminium flask was checked, we had to hand our phones to the security guard for checks before they were returned to us and then we were allowed in for our more than three hundred steps climb to the first stage.

The climb to the first stage didn't take too long, there were pictures on the walls of the construction of the tower in 1887. Incredibly, it took less than two years to build this magnificent structure, hard to imagine such a feat being replicated today. Chris did very well on this climb as she isn't best fond of heights but she wanted to prove to herself that she could do it.

Once we were at the first stage we sat down for a much needed coffee and a slice of baguette with cheese. The views were already pretty amazing. We walked past a large gift shop and restaurant then headed for the narrower staircase up to the second stage. This was also a climb of three hundred steps and we often had to take evasive action to avoid giddy school children rushing up and down. The climb didn't take that long and we needed a sit down with more coffee and food. We felt pretty pleased with ourselves for climbing this far and savoured the views of Paris while we shared our still hot hotel coffee. Next, we went into the gift shop and bought some souvenirs for ourselves and our friends back home. When we came out Chris took me by surprise and suggested we take the elevator to the very top. What a woman! No way did I expect that so I joined the queue to buy tickets. It was €10 to take the lift to the top and back again, an absolute bargain. When the lift arrived they do pack you in like sardines and the ride itself seemed to take forever to reach the third stage. By the time the doors opened, Chris had already turned a strange colour, the thought of what she had suggested had obviously played on her mind on the journey up but she had courage enough for a photo op on the top level before a quick walk around though not too close to the edge and rejoining the queue for the ride down. This was a wonderful first for us both.

When we exited the lift at the second stage we needed something a little stronger than our coffee. We made our way to one of the best located ice rinks in the world and ordered two mulled wines. The sound system was playing "Personal Jesus" by Depeche Mode, one of my favourite groups and watching people have fun on the ice, the view beyond them and what we had just experienced? It was hard to suppress a sense of near euphoria. I knew also that this feeling would be equalled or surpassed as we continued our journey.

We walked back down the stairs to the ground and set off for a stroll in the lightly setting sun along the south bank of the Seine. We crossed over the Pont Alexandre III and headed past the Grand Palais and Place de la Concorde. This ancient Egyptian obelisk marks the spot of the guillotine that was so busy during the Revolution of 1789-93. We discussed how many of the seething injustices of 18th Century France, exemplified by the "let them eat cake" remark of Queen Marie Antoinette, were still being felt today by people right across Europe and the USA. On the opposite bank of the river from the Grand Palais, about two hundred metres away is the Hotel des Invalides, a hospital built for wounded veterans of the Napoleonic wars and a few hundred metres further south is the gold domed Army museum. Directly underneath the gold dome lies the tomb of Napoleon himself. We were now walking through the Jardins des Tuileries and ahead of us was the world famous Louvre gallery and museum. It was now half past five and we half expected that it would be closed. This was our lucky day, it was late opening on Fridays so we joined the modest queue for the €12 entry fee. To the right of us was the large glass pyramid made famous by the Ron Howard movie, The Da Vinci Code. After a wait of perhaps five minutes we were inside and planning on what we could see with the time remaining before the museum closed.

Obviously we wanted to see the Mona Lisa and Venus de Milo but there was so much else to see, it was almost bewildering. There are so many awe inspiring masterpieces hanging on the walls, the galleries containing Roman, ancient Greek and Egyptian artefacts and under the museum itself, the excavated remains of the fortress/palace that used to occupy the spot. After two exhausting but immensely satisfying hours we headed back to the escalators under the ticket hall. Here is the spot where the tips of the two pyramids meet and we took photos of it for our journal. What you don't see in the movie is that just to the side of the touching pyramids is a branch of Starbucks. Chris is a fan despite their ingenuity in tax avoidance and I'm a bit partial to their cheesecakes so we enjoyed a break there. She couldn't resist buying a souvenir mug to remember the day and she pointed out quite rightly that dozens of the biggest corporations are not paying their fair share in taxes and they should all be made to comply with tax payments due.

It was now gone 8pm so we thought it best to get some dinner nearby before returning to the other side of the city. Across from the museum exit was an enticing looking restaurant, we looked at the menu outside the front doors and were tempted by the wonderful smells coming from within. Then, almost as instantly as the smells enveloped us, I could hear the sound of an old fashioned record player scratching to a stop across a vinyl disc. The prices were more than a little terrifying and nice as it would have been to have had a romantic, candle lit dinner to finish off what had been an incredible day, we ended up around the corner having a McFillet of fish, french fries and a small beer each in McDonalds. Tomorrow, our last night in Paris, we would find somewhere better for our last dinner in the city.

Saturday morning we decided to walk to Père Lachaise cemetery. We set off towards the metro station, bought another pain au chocolat and proceeded into the park that lay beyond the right of the station entrance. This was a large park with a boating lake, joggers passed by frequently, there were many families out on their bicycles and people walking their dogs in the crisp, cold morning air. The sort of scene you'd find anywhere across Europe. What we didn't expect to see as we made our way towards Boulevard Davout, was the sight of about a dozen frost covered tents scattered around some bushes. There were also two or three cars which clearly, by their sorry condition, had not seen movement in months. People were living in them and relying on soup and coffee offered by local charities. The night before we had seen these being offered to homeless people near the Louvre. We found this sight to be very sad but reflected that at least the police hadn't come along and sent them packing. I'd spoken to a homeless man reduced to begging on the streets of Dover before we'd left. He recalled very harsh treatment at the hands of police officers in Folkestone and he was also very worldly wise as to the reasons behind his horrible predicament. His situation was definitely a case of "here for the grace of God".

We carried on our journey, using the little dog-eared guide of Paris that our receptionist had given us. We were back on the Boulevard Davout, an inner ring road named after all of Napoleon's Marshals of France, who all had one thing in common, they had been utterly unable to defeat Sir Arthur Wellesley, later Duke of Wellington, anywhere in Europe. The road was closed to all traffic because of road works and it gave this part of the city the weird feeling that we were the only people in it. The streets had none of the glamour or splendour of those we'd seen in the last two days and as we approached Nation metro station with its elaborate and ornate statue on the road junction it was easy to see how two hundred and twenty years ago, the downtrodden masses from this area had joined the mob as word spread of the march on the Bastille.

We were ready for a drink by now and after another half an hour we found ourselves on the southern edge of Père Lachaise on the Rue de Bagnolet. Here, we were spoilt for choice of which café to try. We picked one next to one of many entrances into the cemetery. Inside it looked like the perfect, typical café that you see in the movies. It was wonderful. Behind us were two English girls in their early twenties having an excited conversation which was cut short by one of their mobile phones going off. She answered and spoke in perfectly fluent French. We couldn't help but be very impressed as we waited for our lunch and small beers. I needed the WC and went down the steep spiral staircase. I opened the door, noticed the urinal and went about my business. I remembered from my first visit in 1978 that it wasn't unusual for men to relieve themselves up against a tree, or that there were some old open toilets hidden by circular, metal screens on the street, at least this one was more discreet. Just then a door opened to the side of me and an attractive lady came out, smiled at me, washed her hands on the other side of a small dividing screen between us and walked off towards the stairs. It's ok, I thought to myself, it's just Europe. I washed my hands and made my way back upstairs and recounted to Chris what had happened. She found it quite funny.

We finished our lunch and headed up the street towards the cemetery entrance. Père Lachaise contains upwards of a million burial plots, artists, actors, philosophers, statesmen, sports stars, military figures, prime ministers, presidents and great composers are all interred here. Bizet, Chopin, Edith Piaf, Oscar Wilde, six of Napoleon's Marshals and more recently, a memorial to the passengers on Air France flight 447 that crashed in the Atlantic in 2009. The most visited tomb is that of legendary front man of The Doors, Jim Morrison who died in the city at the age of 28 in 1971. Morrison's father, Admiral George Stephen Morrison was in command of US forces from his flagship, USS *Bon Homme Richard* in what became known as the Tonkin Gulf incident in August 1964. This was a "false flag" exercise that was used by the Johnson administration to justify full scale military action in the Vietnam War[2]. Perhaps the knowledge of this and the ten years of horrific and ultimately pointless war that killed 58,000 young American soldiers and between 1-3 million Vietnamese, affected the young, idealistic Jim and was a major influence in his poetry and song writing. The tomb is now protected from the kinds of vandalism that made it something of an eyesore within the cemetery.

Next up for us was a visit to Notre Dame cathedral. We got off the metro and made the short walk to the landmark cathedral. As luck would have it, we made it in time for evening Mass. What an amazing experience in such a historic building. We left soon afterwards and made our way to the Latin Quarter. You can find this by turning left out of the main entrance and following the Rue de la Cite over the Seine. You will soon find yourself in a wonderfully vibrant, energetic and historic part of Paris. We had a beer in a bar called La Guillotine. There are three price lists for the same drink, how much you pay depends on what time you visit and our beer worked out at €4 each, much more reasonable than Montmartre. We had a wander round the Latin Quarter and window shopped the huge choice of restaurants, souvenir and clothes shops. Each restaurant had a tout outside trying to tempt customers inside. We listened to one of them. He came out with at least eight reasons why we should patronise his restaurant and as we were thinking about it, the tout from the restaurant next door chipped in with "Our place has just the same, but better!" It turned out that they also had a special menu, a 3 course meal for two with a half carafe of house white wine for under thirty euros. Result! So ended our last night in Paris, we had our romantic meal, enjoyed the music and atmosphere in the restaurant and made our way back to our hotel. We were excited by the prospect of heading for Flavigny sur Ozerain the next morning, and beyond that, the open road to the Algarve.

We loaded the car and checked out. Chris positioned herself at the top of the ramp to make sure disaster was averted. It took a few shunts to get into position at the bottom of the ramp and it looked even steeper than it did three days earlier. Since I couldn't take the chance on damaging the roof box I had to really ride the clutch as I inched under the concrete girder. Chris was gently beckoning me forwards, no sound of scraping yet and after what seemed to take forever, I emerged out on to the street. Chris climbed in, "You hit my bike, not badly but it definitely got hit!" After checking everything was secure at the back I noticed foul smelling smoke coming out from under the bonnet, clutch damage! I have never lost a clutch in over twenty-eight years and more than two million miles of motoring experience. Images of breaking down in the middle of nowhere crossed my mind but I ignored them, selected first gear and set off into the post rush hour traffic. The gearbox felt fine and the smell subsided quickly.

The satnav still gave plenty of information but obviously wouldn't give route planning options; Chris was navigating a toll avoidance route toward Fontainebleau and Dijon. We only came unstuck once on this journey when I took the wrong turn at a roundabout on the D607 in Fontainebleau itself. This was a blessing in disguise as the only place I could perform a U-turn was opposite the former country residence of Napoleon Bonaparte. Just to have seen the splendour of this glorious château was enough, we were on a schedule after all and resumed our journey south east. We arrived in Flavigny at 3pm after a very enjoyable drive through the gently undulating hills of rural France.

The medieval town is an unspoilt time capsule and sits perched atop of one of the highest hills in the area. We had been told that hotels in the town were not too expensive, around €50 for a night and that the food in the local restaurants was very good. We parked on the edge of town, no pay and display machines here and walked into the old place. To me it felt like the town Clint Eastwood rode into in '*A Fistful of Dollars*', there seemed to be no one around whatsoever but we still got the impression we were being watched. We made our way to the first of three hotels that we knew were in town. It was closed, as were the other two so we now needed a place to stay for the night. We wandered up a narrow street to where the chocolate shop had been in the Johnny Depp movie[3]. It is pretty much derelict inside but was nice to see it nonetheless. We walked past the church that was also a big part of the movie, it appeared to be closed too. It was getting cold now and the sun was setting quickly on the horizon. We got back to the car after having spent a good forty-five minutes stretching our legs.

The temperature had dropped to 0 degrees Celsius as we descended the narrow, twisting road back to the D905. We turned west at the equally impressive medieval town of Vitteaux and followed the D70, hoping to find a hotel before long. It was another sixty kilometres before we found anywhere to stay. This was on the edge of the town of Avallon. Two hotels and a restaurant appeared on the right hand side of the road. One hotel was charging €65 for the night; the other was a Premiere Classe (cheap and cheerful) and was €32. Chris was less than enthused at the idea of stopping in this hotel, after all she'd been looking forward to stopping somewhere very special tonight. She thought she might be able to get the other hotel cheaper online.

We parked close to the Premiere Classe and, somewhat cheekily, tried to get online through their router and book one of their rival's rooms. The internet worked, if a little slowly but the plan to get the room at a better rate fell flat on its face. It was the same price so cheap and cheerful won the day. The room had a double bed and a single bunk running over and across the bed. There was a shower room that resembled one you'd find on the Hull to Zeebrugge ferry, it probably made you seasick when you used it. A tiny TV was in the corner and there were no coffee making facilities in the room. There was a coffee machine in the reception area instead. Chris wasn't impressed but I didn't mind it to be honest. Twenty years of sleeping in the back of a lorry cab has made me almost immune to conditions which some might call disgusting (note to my legal team, I'm not saying this hotel was disgusting, only that it isn't everyone's choice). The restaurant opposite was charging stupid money for their food and as it was getting late we just bought a sandwich and some snacks each and turned in.

In the morning I was confronted with an angry woman coming out of the shower. Chris was feeling seasick and not only that, she'd banged her head on the bottom of the overhanging bunk twice during the night and again first thing in the morning. This was my fault for being a cheapskate! To make up for it, I went and got her a coffee from the machine. This didn't go down well either as it was pretty insipid but I made her see the funny side eventually.

We checked out and headed off towards the nearby town of Clamecy. We had a relatively easy day planned, we wanted to stop in Poitiers that night and check out the surrounding villages and towns as possible future home locations. Clamecy is a typically quaint and picturesque town. On the outskirts we'd found a Lidl supermarket and bought some good beer and wine at very low prices. The cost of food was very similar to prices at home. Next stop was a traditional coffee shop and we enjoyed a proper café au lait with a delicious éclair each. We walked to an estate agent's that we'd seen after we'd left Lidl but the prices were too high to make our plan viable. We felt another quick coffee was in order so stopped at a nice looking bar. The walls were covered with rugby shirts, scarves and other memorabilia to do with the local team. I'd forgotten just how passionate the French are about the game.

We made our way back to the free car park and set off on what became one of the nicest drives I've been on in Europe. Little or no traffic, blue skies, rolling countryside and wide open spaces. It felt just wonderful. Chris was determined not to spend the night in another cheap and cheerful hotel; she came up with the idea of stopping at the next McDonalds if we saw one and could go online there and book something better. We found one after three hours in the town of Châteauroux. We ordered a meal and Chris set to work on her laptop. She booked an Ibis in Poitiers which was another ninety minutes away. We wrote down directions to it and set off after we'd finished our food. There were no signs in the car park threatening motorists with fines for overstaying their welcome, what is it with the UK that motorists are always being entered into contracts at car parks with totally disproportionate fines for infractions? There were no signs of discarded rubbish from the drive-thru window either, another pleasant change.

The hotel wasn't far from the airport and we planned on having a quiet night in with a filled baguette and some of the beer we'd bought in Clamecy. We watched

Euro news on TV, reflected on what we'd seen and learnt during the day, and turned in for the night.

CHAPTER 4
FINDING FREEDOM

The following morning there was a thick frost covering the car, it would be the last one we would see for the rest of winter as we headed further south.

We planned on stopping in Cognac for the night after another short but equally enjoyable drive from Poitiers. During the journey towards Angouleme we saw signs for a megalithic site, not far off our route. We found it but it was sadly closed during the winter but the walk through ancient woodland in the frosty air was a nice experience. We rejoined the N10 and headed south. Chris found a quiet route to Cognac using the D950 and the D731 which led us through the vineyards used for making the best cognacs in the world. The temperature was in the mid-teens now and the skies above were cloudless. This was the perfect time to pull down a side road, unlock the bikes and go for a ride through a perfectly serene setting. We rode for around an hour, relishing the exercise and fresh air and then returned to the van. It dawned on me that I'd forgotten to lock it before we set off but no one had seen fit to ransack it. I secured our bikes and we arrived in the town a short while later. It had been another hugely enjoyable journey and we now had time to find a hotel and wander round the centre of town.

We found another Ibis, there were two other hotels but one was full and the other too pricey. We enjoyed a good meal that evening, probably the first proper meal in two days. We mulled over what we had seen and enjoyed during our journey from Paris and apart from the better driving standards, the glorious countryside, beautiful château and cheaper diesel we'd noticed that many villages and smaller towns seemed to be eerily quiet. It was if the locals had all been abducted by aliens. The Christmas lights and other decorations were still up long after twelfth night but we'd seen virtually no one out on the streets. Even the fields seemed devoid of agricultural equipment or animals. It was a mystery we had plenty of time to speculate on during our travels.

Our hotel was of the usual standard we'd enjoyed before and was the same price, €62 plus another ten for secure parking. We knew the next day was going to be a long one and Chris booked a hotel for that night at a more than reasonable €28. I couldn't wait for the morning alarm call but still slept very well. A complete contrast with tremendously poor sleeps on hundreds of Sunday nights knowing what would befall me at work the next day.

Half past six in the morning and we left the hotel behind us. We stopped at a Boulanger and bought our now obligatory baguette and cheese with two cafés au lait and in the cold, misty light of dawn we set off on our way towards Bordeaux, Bayonne and Biarritz, beyond them was the Spanish frontier and more adventure.

We had a journey of six hundred kilometres ahead of us and most of it was toll free. I knew the section around the border would be tolled and I planned to come off the A63 at Castets and drive through Biarritz, stop there to stretch our legs, then continue over the frontier and rejoin the main E5 at Irun. The N10 towards Bordeaux was the main route for trucks heading for Spain and Portugal yet is free running for light traffic because trucks are not allowed in the outside lane (this is the case across much of Europe) so you don't get the huge queues caused by one forty-four ton truck overtaking the other when both are restricted to 56mph but one does .3 mph more than the other! Frustration leads to accidents and road rage incidents yet the legislators seem to have overlooked this trifling matter that impacts on millions of motorists in the UK every day. Minor rant over. Actually, it isn't. Our route took us through Bordeaux, quite a large city and it was near the end of the rush hour yet we encountered no traffic delays whatsoever. Well engineered junctions, easy access to other major roads, the lack of traffic lights and roundabouts often both at the same time, keeps traffic flowing smoothly. Ok, moderate rant over.

We stopped for fuel and a snack within the city, where we bought some local red and white wine from the shop for later and resumed our trip. I enjoyed driving through Biarritz, yes it was obviously busier than anything I'd encountered since leaving Paris but it was well signposted and I was able to keep going without getting lost. The moment we saw the beach to our right and the Pyrenees stretching out across our path in front of us was breathtaking and removed any notion of doubt about leaving the motorway. We stopped for a walk on the beach and gazed north across the Bay of Biscay. It was a special moment, one of dozens we would encounter, and still do today.

Half an hour after we set off again we were approaching the Spanish border. The architecture changed from regular French to Mediterranean as we came within 3 kilometres of the border. The border crossing itself is of course very simple and easy, thanks to the Schengen Agreement and the days of queues, passport checks and searches are ancient history. Another milestone had passed; we were now in Spain and heading for a quick coffee before rejoining the AP-8 through the mountains. It cost us the princely sum of two euros for our coffees, we had a wander round the hypermarket we'd stopped at, made use of the scrupulously clean WC's and returned to the van. The prices in the hypermarket were less than in France but the quality of food and drink seemed just as good. My satnav was by now struggling to give me proper mapping. It occasionally showed me the road we were travelling on but usually showed me driving parallel to the road I was actually on. It was still helpful and if nothing else, the compass direction was enough to keep us on track besides Chris' flawless navigation with the map.

The AP-8 passes through staggeringly beautiful mountain scenery. Beneath some of the bridges winding tortuously through the valley floor was the old road and only toll avoidance route. It would add hours to your journey yet some heavy trucks were still using it. We turned south on the outskirts of Burgos, a huge sprawl of a city that I was glad to not have to tackle after a long day on the road. By the time we left the A1 into Lerma we'd been on the road for 9 hours and the tolls from Irun to our destination had cost us €21. I reckoned we'd probably saved as much by coming off the A63 at Castets; this would pay for dinner and a couple of beers I was thinking as I consulted my hastily scribbled notes on directions to the Hotel Alicia. My notes went out the window when our intended route was blocked by a funeral cortege. It took another twenty minutes to find the hotel but at least we got our bearings on the town itself. It looked well worth having a wander round in the morning. Our room was huge and well equipped, fantastic value for the €28 and we both slept soundly.

We checked out and planned to get breakfast in the town. We needed the walk and we had plenty of time as we only had a four hour drive to get to the Portuguese city of Braganca. Lerma is indicative of much that has gone wrong within Europe since the crash of 2007/8. Outwardly it looks very impressive, especially the magnificent Ducal Palace that takes up one whole side of the city's main plaza but signs of decay are easy to see elsewhere. The place seemed deserted and there was a sense of abandonment to it. We'd seen swathes of the French countryside in a similar condition. We wandered around some souvenir shops, and checked out a couple of supermarkets and estate agent shop windows - the property prices were still above what we could afford.

Through a foliage covered archway we spotted a small café and made our way inside. Luckily for us the menu had pictures and we could point to the breakfasts we wanted. Very nice, similar to the cooked breakfasts you'd find in Tenerife or the Costa Del Sol. Time to move on, we walked back alongside the river which gently flows through the town and back to the van.

We planned on heading west towards Palencia, keeping north of Valladolid and dropping down to Zamora and on to the Portuguese frontier with a short distance to Braganca. This looked the most scenic and quiet route. I filled the van with diesel at the garage on the edge of the city as it was only €1.32 a litre. The journey towards Palencia was just as I'd hoped; devoid of traffic, beautiful scenery, amazing bird life, and a pleasure to drive.

Not long after we'd skirted the edge of the town we were stopped by police for the first time. We were out in the middle of nowhere when the officers stepped out in the road and flagged us down. I wasn't worried as I hadn't been speeding and hadn't had any booze the night before. The officer spoke good English, "Your licence please, Señor". He didn't ask for any of the other documentation that we had nor did he ask to see that we were carrying the Euro travel kit that we'd bought at Dover. He was satisfied with what he saw and handed my photo card licence back and waved us on our way. We got lost a little while later, owing to some poor road signs, but after some zig-zagging across the high ground we found our way again.

During our unexpected detour we saw more of what we'd noticed since the south of France. In most villages there were groups of old men playing chess and drinking coffee in the centre. Their wives were doing all the household chores as probably had been the case for hundreds of years. The houses around here were in a very poor state of repair, donkeys were tied up outside houses, for some people these were the only form of transport they could afford and you could have been forgiven for thinking that this was Eastern Europe, yet, on the perimeter of the village, there was a faded billboard with a poster offering large sums of cash for regeneration projects and other opportunities funded by the EU. Oh the irony of it! To the inhabitants dressed mainly in black with their decayed buildings and crumbling roads that billboard must seem like a sick joke. We'd seen on Euro news that a 28 year old lady had thrown herself to her death from her high rise apartment near Madrid as bailiffs were kicking down her front door. She'd lost her job, was behind with the mortgage, and because of the crash in Spanish property prices she couldn't sell her home either. Truly a tragic situation.

The road past Zamora began to descend through mountainous terrain to the Portuguese border and not long after we arrived in the northern city of Braganca. We'd not booked a hotel so we parked up and went for a walk around the town. This town is in decay as well, from the outside it looks normal, though not glitzy or glamorous it looks fine. You don't have to look far to see signs of systematic decline, it is here too. We ordered two café brancos from a café and consulted the Ibis hotel leaflet we'd taken in Cognac. Somewhere here was another hotel but we didn't have any idea how to ask anyone for directions. We went back into the street and wandered past some smart fashion shops when Chris saw a road sign pointing towards the Ibis hotel. Bingo! We made our way back to the car and retraced the route back to the café. The signs were useless after that and we diced with the peak hour traffic before stumbling accidentally onto the hotel. This was a very impressive looking, ten storey building with an underground car park. What was even more impressive was that the receptionist spoke perfect English and a nice room on the 7th floor was only €39. We unpacked and made our way down for a well deserved meal accompanied by one of Portugal's favourite beers, a large 'Super Bock'.

Friday morning we set off into thick fog and headed southwest through yet more stunning scenery headed for Vila Real. The Portuguese government are throwing hundreds of millions of euros on a new motorway link to Braganca. We passed at least 100km of new viaducts and bridges through the toughest terrain. The flaw in that plan is this: the project will cost a staggering amount of money at a time when the country is struggling under incredibly harsh austerity measures and these sums will have to be repaid by tolls along the length of the highway. This is money that the Portuguese people do not have.

On our last visit to the Algarve, we were delayed significantly on the charter bus out of Faro Airport because of protesters complaining about their local motorway, the IC-4 (which was built thirteen years previously to relieve the most dangerous road in Southern Europe), being re-designated to a toll road. There was no consultation, nothing. You have to have and pay for an electronic spy reader that debits your bank account each time you pass under a gantry. If you're driving a foreign registered car and were unaware of these changes you could be liable to a substantial fine. Why on earth the authorities didn't use the good old fashioned method of toll collection is a mystery. You get your ticket, you pay at the next collection point or on exiting the road and you create some desperately needed jobs, but no, too easy! You have a horribly complex system in place which the majority of people are boycotting. The toll roads are predominantly empty as the locals have gone back to using the N125 and accident rates on this road are up 15%. Be careful if you hire a car to see the sights as not only will it cost you a small fortune, you may end up being billed for journeys made by many previous customers who haven't paid their tolls. The car hire companies owe hundreds of thousands of euros to the government and many are at risk of going out of business altogether. Doubtless, the charges for the in-car equipment will rise above inflation year on year. What a dogs' breakfast of a scheme. People are furious about it and believe their lives are regarded as secondary to revenue generating. Even the hotel receptionist sympathised with our prolonged journey from the airport, but added succinctly, "The banks should pay!" It was hard to disagree with him. Another minor rant over.

We'd noticed on our journey towards the Spanish border a truck with a picture perfect representation of an ancient town fording a river on the back of it. This was the town of Amarente and we mentioned how it'd be nice to find it. Luckily it was half way between Vila Real and Porto. We left the motorway and made our way into the medieval town. We left the van and took a walk around and soon found the old bridge over the river that we'd seen advertised two and a half days ago. We found a café with stunning views of the river gorge which we enjoyed with coffee and cake. We also wandered around a beautiful church nearby. Away from the main street we found more areas looking quite sorry for themselves. A glimpse at a couple of estate agents windows confirmed that prices were still out of our reach.

We resumed our journey south west. After another 100 kilometres we stopped at a motorway service area for a light snack. Again, no signs that we'd entered a contract by simply parking at the facility. It was immaculately clean as we'd come to expect. We ordered a light meal and were watching the TV. The country's president was announcing yet more austerity measures to the angst of fellow travellers in the café. Here too, you can buy a beer from the restaurant. You are treated as an adult and not a simpleton. Very refreshing.

We rejoined the motorway and after a short while we tried a toll avoidance route. This was a bad idea, the roads were terrible and we rejoined the toll road again. It seemed that the next 150 kilometres towards and beyond Porto was just one giant urban sprawl. We planned to stop the night in Coimbra and zigzag our way the next morning towards Castelo Branco enjoying what would certainly be a beautiful drive through more forests and mountains.

We came off the IP-1 and entered the city limits. Chris was really pushed to thread our way through the intense traffic. It was peak time and the city's roads were the most congested we'd seen since Paris. As Chris found our route onto the N17 we realized very quickly that we didn't fancy stopping there at all. Prostitutes seemed to be lining the road for miles and miles. We decided to push on to Castelo Branco. Whilst we missed out on seeing the beautiful scenery, driving down the N112 through its twists and turns, steep climbs and descents almost made you feel like you were piloting a spaceship, driving through and over the mountains under a million stars, just like 'Disney's Space Mountain!'

After a two and a half hour final leg of the journey we approached our destination. It was along this small stretch of the IP-2 that we got flashed by a toll collection gantry camera. There might be a fine making its way back to the UK but I wasn't unduly worried.

Chris spotted a sign for a Best Western hotel in the town. The signs were little better than they had been in Braganca but we found it pretty soon. A very nice hotel, two large 'Super Bocks' for €3 and €60 for the night.

We enjoyed a good breakfast in the hotel then set off for a walk up the hill towards the ruined castle which the town is named after. There was no charge to wander around the medieval structure. It had fantastic views towards our intended route southwest. You could also walk along the old battlements with a sheer drop of some

30 metres without being obstructed by health and safety restrictions. Surrounding the castle were narrow streets with whitewashed houses and orange roof tiles. Their gardens were a wonderful clash of colour and fragrance, even at this time of year and we felt chilled out as we walked back down the street to the van. Now it was time to start the final leg of the journey that had started in Calais that cold winter evening. It seemed like months ago. We left the hotel and made our way out of town without touching the toll road.

CHAPTER 5
SEASONS OF CHANGE

Like so many other days that we spent in deep discussion, we commented on what we were learning on our journey. Today, it felt more significant, just as though we had driven out of winter into spring! The temperatures were much warmer the sun was shining, we could even see a heat haze on the road, daylight hours seemed longer, nature was waking up and our mood was extremely positive. We were both convinced we were doing the right thing.

Soon we were heading down the glorious N18 and again, we felt like we were the only motorists using this stretch of road. Like France and Spain had been, it was a pleasure driving these wonderful roads through rural Portugal. Again like France and Spain we saw much decay and depravation, more women dressed all in black, more old fellas drinking coffee and playing chess or cards. I saw at one point what appeared to be a strange tree at the side of the road, it wasn't, it was an old lady with half a ton of brushwood on her back! There were yet more faded billboards from the EU offering more investment and regeneration projects. We hadn't seen many signs of them apart from white elephant projects like the motorway extension at Braganca.

Fifty kilometres further on we saw a magnificent fortress atop the highest ground in the area. It was right in our path and we decided to stop for a visit. This was the five-hundred year old Castelo de Evoramonte. Inside the intact walls was a time capsule of a village. For the princely sum of €3 each we could go inside the castle. It was very impressive and probably did a good job of keeping the French out during the Peninsular War. It is still used for all manner of functions today and is a truly magical location. You cannot help but feel king or queen of the world with panoramic views in all directions. Shimmering in the sunshine was the toll road IP-2, devoid of any traffic. I kept an eye on it while I enjoyed an ice cream and saw only two vehicles heading west.

After a hugely enjoyable stop we set off again with the sun shining and Bruno Mars' '*Lazy Song*' playing loud on the stereo, this time heading for the Roman city of Evora and the main junction south toward the Algarve. On the outskirts of the city we stopped for fuel and visited a supermarket for supplies for our first night in Albufeira. First there were two, then four armed police officers wandering the aisles and I was sure they were looking at us, then I saw two more moving near to the Astra. Then I thought, hang on a minute, I know I'm probably on an FBI watch list after being informed by email that I had been reported to the Feds by an irate American over a mild comment on YouTube and to enjoy the knock at my door! Really, six armed cops on my account? Then I thought it was pretty unlikely that the FBI had shared their concerns with the Portuguese police. Or was it for the toll camera violation?! That really is zero tolerance policing! Again pretty unlikely but two of them were definitely checking the Astra out. We paid for our beer and snacks and made our way back to the car park. We had to jam in the beer as best we could into the roof box, my every move being carefully observed. I climbed in behind the wheel and started the engine. Chris was a little worried and I did my best to not un-nerve her. "It's probably nothing, just don't act suspiciously", which was of course the worst thing to say because from that moment you can't help looking dodgy.

Chris put Adele's hit album '21' in the player to create a calm atmosphere. We left the car park and headed for the road to Evora. I checked my mirrors and sure enough a police car was following us at a discreet distance. Fortunately, they left us at the next major junction and we saw our first road sign for The Algarve, it's great how they were so kind to put some signs up in English for us. We both beamed as we turned south and knew that in a little over two and a half hours we would be in familiar surroundings, on the coast of the Atlantic Ocean, in a fabulous hotel and three weeks of rest and recreation!

We reflected on what had been a fantastic journey in every way possible. Something we hadn't expected was the sight of storks, they were everywhere south of Castelo Branco. On part of our journey there had been a stretch of road about seven kilometres long with a stork's nest atop every telegraph pole on both sides of the road. What an amazing sight.

At half past seven in the evening, with Coldplay's '*Paradise*' accompanying us, we arrived at our hotel, the Areias Village. We checked in and were blown away by the size and quality of our apartment and balcony. Chris's extensive research had more than paid off! Time to unload the whole van and roof box. It must have taken me ten trips with a trolley up and down from the third floor. The receptionist, bless her, looked more bemused with each trip particularly when I came past her with an ironing board and clothes airer. She must have thought we were moving in permanently.

At the first opportunity we had a night out in the Old Town, our favourite bars were not all open at this time of year, but on the weekends our musician friend Martin had just started playing at 'Steps Bar' so we put on our glad rags and went down to see him. As we walked in the door, he spotted us and began playing one of Chris's favourite tracks '*High and Dry*' by Radiohead. This was very special and felt fantastic! Like being welcomed home, our second home. All the familiar bar staff were there and welcomed us back with big smiles. It's amazing how they remember everyone from season to season, but they do! We went on to have a brilliant time that night, as with so many others in Albufeira.

The hotel was brilliant in every way, the swimming pool was large and immaculately clean, the food in the restaurant was excellent and the laundry area in the basement meant we were able to get all our stuff clean with a minimum of hassle. The next morning I noticed in the car park that we weren't the furthest travelled customers staying in the hotel. A gold Peugeot estate from Denmark was already here and the owners from Copenhagen were still there as we left to continue our trip.

Three weeks became five and we spent our time getting exercise on our bikes, chilling out on the beach under more warm blue skies, catching up with old friends and exploring the area away from just the usual tourist venues. It became a base for us and was the most stability that we'd had in three months as we made it into our temporary home. For us it was the longest holiday we'd known, and was a necessary rest and review point for our journey.

One of my abiding memories of the five week stay, was returning to the hotel on my bicycle and noticing Chris high up on our apartment balcony, paintbrush in hand, focused intensely on a new painting. It really warmed my heart to see her so relaxed and happy to be able to paint a picture without distraction. I wanted that painting to hang on the wall of our new home wherever that turned out to be.

It was 18 degrees Celsius here while Sky News reported temperatures back home and across much of Northern Europe as low as minus eighteen. It was hard not to suppress a smile at the situation we had chosen for ourselves. Any semblance of doubt as to the wisdom of our decision had long since vanished and we felt convinced that we would find not only a new place to live but a new way of living altogether as we continued our journey.

I took the van to the local BP filling station and gave it a jet wash and vacuumed out the interior. For the five weeks we stayed there we got more and more exercise, our bikes got plenty of use and we saved a small fortune on what the rental charges would have been. The very worst that the weather threw at us during our stay was a mild breeze under warm blue skies. We explored the mountainous area of Monchique that one of our barman friends had told us about. Vasco (pronounced Vashco or just Vash as he preferred) and his friends used it as their favourite road circuit on their high powered sports bikes. It wasn't hard to see why, stunning scenery, sweeping, fast bends, tighter hairpin bends and perfect sticky tarmac. A real biker's nirvana with a great bar overlooking the valley floor at its highest point. This road also brought you out through the town of Silves, we had never seen so many camper vans parked in one place before. They'd come from all across Europe to enjoy the weather and also the hospitality of the town. They didn't have to pay any parking charges whatsoever. Good business really as the town bars, restaurants and shops made a good living from these happy customers.

We'd noticed from our balcony that a campervan was parked a little distance beyond the hotel for the duration of our stay. They weren't liable for parking charges or restrictions either. What an enlightened attitude, shame local authorities in the UK can't see the wood for the trees and be a little less draconian in their attitude to motorists. We also found a Neolithic settlement an hour north of Albufeira just off the IC-1. This amazing settlement is the same age as Stonehenge and was free to walk around and enjoy. The only noise to be heard was storks clacking loudly and quickly. The views from here had changed little in eight thousand years and it was awe inspiring.

Next we headed west across more mountains on minor roads until we found the coast. Here we headed south until we found a place called Aljezur, about fifty kilometres north of Cabo de Sao Vicente or Cape St. Vincent. Cape St. Vincent is significant because it is the furthest point west in Portugal and the next landfall is the US eastern seaboard but also because a major sea battle between the Royal Navy and the Spanish fleet took place on Valentine's Day, 1797. Despite being outnumbered two to one, the British, commanded by Admiral Jervis from his flagship *HMS Victory* (yes, the one in Portsmouth dockyard) decisively defeated their opponents, thanks in no small part to a certain Horatio Nelson. Nelson ignored his orders from the fleet commander and had he failed in his improvised plan, he would have certainly been court-martialled, dismissed from the Navy and disgraced. Fortunately for British history and in an act of swashbuckling bravery that Captain Jack Sparrow would have been proud of, Nelson and a boarding party from his ship, *HMS Captain* captured two Spanish ships simultaneously. Two other Spanish vessels were captured and their flagship, *Santisima Trinidad,* was badly damaged and got away by the skin of her teeth. For this act of courage in which he was again injured, Nelson was knighted and soon made Rear Admiral. Today there is an all too small memorial marker near the lighthouse which gives precious little information on the actual events of that day.

Aljezur is a very small town, very clean with a few cozy restaurants and shops. It also has an utterly beautiful set of beaches which are reached by a narrow winding track through the bracken and sand dunes. At the end of the track is a large car park that is also home to the campervan community, though the day we were there were no more than a dozen vehicles parked up. Again they had come from every corner of Europe and during the off season they can remain there unbothered by parking charges. We walked down to the beach and took a walk. The beach seemed to stretch off to the left of us for half a mile and to the right, the beach snaked around and out of sight, hidden by cliffs and a wooden pier connecting some of the peaks together. We watched fisherman casting their rods from a tiny outcrop of rock about two hundred metres from the shore. They had swum out there to get the best spot for some good sea fishing and apart from them, we seemed to be the only people enjoying this idyllic location. By now the sun was starting to set and we stood enraptured by the most startling array of colours imaginable. And we had a perfectly unrestricted view that many pay an absolute fortune to see at locations like Santorini.

The sun mesmerised us with its performance, every minute brought new shades of inspiring colours until it began to disappear over the horizon as a pure red ball. We then watched the fishermen swimming back to shore, taking part in a race that they probably did night after night. Another treat now made itself apparent. We could stay and watch the stars come out in what would be a doubtlessly dazzling performance. We collected some coffee and crisps from the van and walked quickly up to the wooden pier overlooking the previously unseen beach. From our vantage point we could see a dirt track meandering its way down to the beach through some quite sharp twists and turns. I then noticed the previous model Astra van to mine, parked down by the shoreline. It had coupled behind it what looked to be a boat trailer of some kind though there appeared to be no one sat in the van. This track led back to the car park some five hundred metres away and passed by a couple of small bungalows which were set back from the track. Chris had also brought her binoculars with her and we nestled down to wait for the second part of nature's performance to begin.

The night sky was breathtaking, no light pollution and no noise. We didn't see any shooting stars but high overhead we observed transatlantic flights silently chasing after the sun and we saw several satellites rushing across the night sky. Soon the tranquillity was interrupted by the low, monotonous droning noise of an approaching outboard engine. Chris scanned the seas off the beach and she soon spotted a large dinghy slowly approaching from the north. It was piloted by one person she said and she was puzzled as to why it displayed no lights. As we were wondering what might be going on, down on the shoreline the Astra van flashed its main beam lights briefly. Then the previously unseen occupant got out and stood near the calmly lapping waters. The dinghy stopped its engine and seemed to wait forever, holding its position. Chris turned towards me and silently gestured to me to shush and stop munching on the crisps we'd brought with us. The dinghy was still a hundred metres or so offshore. "Ok", we whispered to each other, "What are these two guys up to? It must be something dodgy otherwise the dinghy would have come straight in. What have they got in that boat? Is it drugs, guns or both? Maybe it's worse? What if the bloke down there heard you rustling that crisp packet?! What if he saw your binocular lenses reflecting back at him? Oh shit! What do we do now? We need to both keep calm, breathe slowly and, very, very carefully keep low and make our way back to the van. But it's miles away! I know, but if they did spot us they know where we are and if we don't move, they've got us! Okay, let's move!"

We did our best to move back from the wooden pier but at that moment the dinghy restarted its engine and was coming in and this time it was moving faster! "Right, time to go, now!" we backed away and when we were sure we were out of sight, we ran as best we could. This wasn't easy because I'd had a minor case of gout again and my big toe was probably no more than sixty percent healed. We knew it wouldn't take long to get the boat onto its trailer and even less for them to drive up towards us. Chris saw what might be a good hiding place but I thought that, though it might work, if we showed up in their headlights we were doomed. We kept running, after all I said "What's the worst that can happen? We both get shot in the head and thrown off the cliffs?" This didn't help but it did instill the urgency to keep going. Two hundred metres later and still no sign of them, we could now see the glow of lights coming from the campervans another two hundred metres away. We kept running/hobbling until we got to within fifty metres. "Okay, enough, let's just act like two lovebirds on a walk from the campsite, my toe's killing me anyway and even if they drive up now they won't know us from Adam." We walked along, arms round each other's waists, gesticulating up at the stars and trying to act calm and normal. We decided to get in the van and get out of 'Dodge' pretty damn quick. I got in behind the wheel and started the engine and we pulled off in a normal manner, not legging it like robbers in a getaway car. By now I was desperate for a leak and couldn't wait any longer. I pulled off the track into a clearing and leapt out onto the sand and relaxed with the biggest exhale of relief imaginable.

Just as I was coming back to my door I saw lights coming towards us. I climbed back in and just as I closed the door the Astra van with its potentially illicit cargo passed us by. They never slowed down as they passed but I'm sure the man in the passenger seat gave us a good stare. "I think we should wait a few minutes, then we'll go." Chris agreed and we sat there silently, both thinking about what had just happened. "We've waited long enough and I need the bathroom now" Chris advised me firmly. We set off, it was nearly a kilometre back to the main road and I negotiated the twists and turns when a horrible thought crossed my mind. What if they're parked across the way out, blocking our exit? Forget that thought, if they are we'll just blag our way as tourists. I told Chris to hide the binoculars under her seat! Two minutes later we saw that the track junction with the main road was clear and even if they did start following us I was confident of outrunning them. I wanted to put some distance between us and Aljezur but Chris's needs were more important. Within ten kilometres we stopped at a service station and bought some supplies and sorted ourselves out after our dice with near disaster. We set off again, this time heading for Portimao and on to Albufeira.

After doing so well on the journey my satnav gave up the ghost and lost the plot in Portimao. We seemed to be going round in circles and the local road signs weren't helping. Finally after ten minutes the satnav gave a tantalising glimpse of where the infamous N125 should be and we were able to get back home without further ado. We could have done without that bit of stress after our experience but after we got back to Albufeira we had a good laugh about it in one of our favourite bars, 'Sir Harry's' in the old town.

During our stay of five weeks, Chris needed her hair doing and we found a salon at the base of a nice hotel in Monte Choro. She had a good chat with the hairdresser who told her just how much the locals were struggling with the austerity measures that never seemed to end. There is no minimum wage in Portugal and many people were earning little more than €5 an hour. Many were told that they were going to have to work six days a week including bank holidays with no time off in lieu and the unemployment level among the under 25's was a terrifying forty-five percent! No wonder there are so many unfinished apartment blocks on the edge of town. Whole complexes remain uninhabited two years or more after they were completed. Another difficulty faced by hotel and restaurant owners is that although tourist numbers remain high the amount they are spending has fallen by a fifth[4]. Waiters report that customers are sharing coffees and soups, the first time they have ever encountered such a sight and combined with the extra cost and hassle of hiring a car it is really tough for people and businesses to make a decent living.

Another manifestation not used to by the locals is the stag or hen party. Albufeira is known for its relaxing atmosphere and friendliness and this is getting somewhat eroded by hordes of drunken and very loud British weekend "visitors". The numbers of these are increasing as other resorts and cities across Europe have started clamping down on them and the associated anti-social issues. Albufeira is stuck between a rock and a hard place here. How on earth is the rest of the country coping if even the Algarve is struggling? Little surprise then, at the number of protesters on the streets of Lisbon and other towns and cities. Despite these issues, the cost of property remains high and the cheapest places we found were former hotel rooms going for around €50,000. Not what we had in mind but you can rent a modest apartment in Albufeira for €300 a month plus bills. We put the idea of living here on the back burner for now.

One night after dinner in our apartment we looked at our options. So far we'd enjoyed an incredible road trip and everything connected to it. We'd learnt a lot but we still needed another alternative to try before going back home. We scanned Rightmove's web site and clicked on the overseas link. Sure enough the adverts for new, secure, gated complexes with swimming pools in Bulgaria were still there, we hadn't imagined them! We also saw an estate of new two, three, and four bedroom villas starting from €17 thousand in a place further down the Black Sea coast called Pomorie. Chris opened a new tab and checked flight details on sky scanner. We could get return flights to Burgas from Luton for little more than £200 and hotels were equally good value. We booked seven nights at the Aparthotel Dawn Park for the princely sum of £120. We now had stage two of our plan in place, all that was left to do was plan a route back to the UK. We still wanted to research and explore other places on our return home, so in order to achieve this we planned an alternative route covering more of Spain and different regions of France. This was going to take us another week to reach the English Channel.

The town was starting to come alive with more restaurants and bars opening, others were rushing to complete their refurbishment programs before the Easter holidays arrived. We'd had a brilliant five week stay, shopping locally, eating healthy meals, getting lots of exercise and soaking up the sunshine, it had left us feeling healthy and refreshed. As an extra bonus Chris' son Jamie managed to get out for a short holiday to see us and we had some positive insightful discussions with him. We enjoyed the company of Martin Jonathan and his wife between gigs and got to show Jamie the highlights of Albufeira. During our visit, we'd amassed much information on the pros and cons of living in Portugal. We could consider it mission accomplished but weren't quite ready to leave Portugal just yet.

CHAPTER 6
CONSIDERING OPTIONS

Saturday morning we checked out of Areias Village (after a slog reloading the van with another ten trolley loads including four cases of Portuguese beer), filled the van with cheap diesel and headed east for the short journey to Vilamoura and Tavira.

Vilamoura has a very smart marina and new apartment complexes surrounding it. It has excellent golf courses nearby that help the local economy keep ticking over out of season. We checked property prices here but again they were over our budget. We'd booked a nice hotel in Tavira for two nights and made our way along the infamous N125 very carefully through its many twists and turns until we arrived at our hotel. Tavira was the port where the Romans first arrived two thousand years ago. The town has quite a different feel to it than Albufeira but is nonetheless welcoming to tourists. A medieval bridge still straddles the inlet but is now open to pedestrians and cyclists only. The town also has some good Indian restaurants and a proper Irish pub on the quay side. There is also a fair sized ex-pat community here and one of the chief reasons we'd booked two nights was because we'd seen a holiday home park advertised online that looked very promising. According to the link it was less than twenty minutes' walk from our hotel and we were excited at the prospect of somewhere we could afford. Unfortunately despite having accurate directions we could find no trace of this phantom development. We used the time instead to plot a route back to England which we hoped would be as enjoyable as the journey down.

Sitting outside the Irish Pub in the sunshine, listening to the water lapping against the quayside, we discussed our options. We could live in Albufeira if one or both of us found a job there. Thanks to the hairdresser's information, we knew that would be very difficult if not impossible, not least because of the language barrier. We considered buying a camper van and just roaming the continent as we pleased. We thought about 'house sitting' as an option, or doing voluntary work overseas. We had seen a project in Belize that involved working on ancient Mayan ruins which looked very appealing. There were plenty of 'off the grid' communities in the UK and Europe that we could potentially join. Having no ties meant that we were free to pursue any of them. This was the freedom we really wanted. Suddenly all these options became apparent which a few months ago were not even visible to us! Isn't it funny that when you change one dynamic of your life, that everything else is affected and seems to open up with endless possibilities.

Someone once said there are two ways to control a population, through conquest or debt. To be free of debt opens so many doors, removes the obstacles and barriers that entrap the soul. This scenario is normally reserved only for the very wealthy among us, perhaps the greatest measure of wealth is time itself.

Collectively, we spend much time reminiscing the past and planning for the future, but what about now? 'Now' is all that any of us really have, the past is done and the future will take care of itself anyway. If you do have plenty of time, but can't contemplate spending it with your other half, what does this tell you? Conversely, if you have plenty of wealth but no time to enjoy it, what is the objective here?

Is the following scenario an isolated example or one that millions of us experience daily: when the alarm goes off, you'd give anything to just stay in bed. You go to work on heavily congested roads, in a car you're still paying for, to a job you don't like, to pay for a house that stays vacant most of the day, while you wait for a pension that gets put further out of reach.

If the human race just stepped off a giant spaceship onto a new world, who in their right mind would vote for such a system, particularly when half the proceeds of the new world were to be given to less than one percent of the population?! I can't imagine there would be many turkeys voting for Christmas, can you? With all this in mind we agreed that our main objectives were to find a life where we could spend our time together. Chris had worked thirty years at her job, I'd put in the equivalent of thirty-five, and we both discovered when we left our positions, that in todays' world loyalty is a one way street. Neither of us received a single wish of good luck and all the best from our former employers. We figured we had more than done our time in the conventional workplace and suffered as a result, so we wanted a life without full time work and the associated pressures.

We planned on skirting the border with Spain for 120 km through a large national park before crossing the border, then heading north again towards the city of Badajoz by the scenic route. We weren't disappointed. The journey was fabulous and we were by now wonderfully accustomed to enjoying new surroundings and experiences, rather than fighting congested traffic and contrived deadlines. The storks are very imaginative on the road south of Badajoz. They'd made nests on each of the three levels on the electricity pylons by the roadside. These went on for thirty kilometres or more and we wondered who got to have the top nest on each pylon. When we reached the city after a four and a half hour journey we were ready for our hotel and a good meal. Again, the directions we'd taken from the website weren't exactly brilliant, the satnav had lost the plot and we spent a good half hour in the heavy traffic in the city centre going round and round in circles. Eventually Chris spotted a sign for the Hotel Escarza on a lamp post and we quickly found it and parked the van in the underground car park. We checked in and both wanted a walk after our journey.

We made our way back into the city centre through a less than appealing industrial zone but soon found the old footbridge over the River Rio Guadiana. This led us to the old city walls that almost two centuries ago to the day, had been stormed by soldiers of Wellington's Peninsular Army. The events of that siege were highly controversial though ultimately successful as the capture of the fortress secured the border with Portugal enabling Wellington to begin marching north west towards Marshal Marmont's position at Salamanca. When the walls were breached, the damage is still visible today, the French defenders were ready for the approaching British and Portuguese troops and had 'booby-trapped' the area around the breach. In less than two hours more than two thousand of Wellington's men lay dead or dying, piled up on themselves in bloody heaps that their comrades had to trample over to get at the French. They were mown down by volley after volley of musket fire, bombs, grenades and even burning hay rained down on them. The carnage was so bad that Wellington for the first time in his military career, was about to signal the order to retreat, when men from the 3rd and 5th divisions got inside and waved their redcoats over their heads to rally their comrades outside. The French withdrew at this moment and beat a hasty retreat while their commander, General Phillipon surrendered later.

After four hours of horrific close quarter combat the enraged victors broke into local homes and bars, seized and consumed vast quantities of alcohol and went on a rampage of unspeakable violence against the Spanish inhabitants. It was estimated that some four thousand civilians were killed by the mob, their property stolen and women raped in the streets. Even some of the officers sent into stop the looting and pillaging were shot dead by their own men. It took three days for order to be restored and is regarded as one of the blackest days in the history of the British Army.

As we walked along the walls to the citadel and ventured inside where these terrible events took place, we were surprised to find not a single memorial anywhere outlining what took place. It is as if the whole experience has been airbrushed out of history and never happened. As trained Shamans, we felt that a discreet healing ceremony was required to acknowledge and send healing energy to those involved.

The city itself is now a colourful and modern metropolis. We walked further to the main plaza with its mosaic floors and walls until we found a very atmospheric tavern on the edges of the square. During our walk from the hotel we had been desperately looking for an ATM machine as we only had €10 between us. In more than an hour of walking we failed utterly to find a bank so at the tavern we could only afford a large beer each. As it turned out you got some free tapas with any large beer or wine so this was a lifesaver! We enjoyed the atmosphere in this tavern very much, and the young man who runs it deserves to be successful but on this Monday night it was only about twenty percent full. We savoured our impromptu meal and made our way back to the hotel.

The next day we were to be following Wellington's route to Salamanca but without the raping and pillaging, then on to Vitoria/Geistez and a journey of 650 km. Again this was a highly enjoyable journey and only the industrial sprawl around Valladolid slightly spoiled what had been a terrific day. We had found an ATM and pulled off the main drag near a huge image of a Spanish bull. There are many of these colossal structures around the Spanish road network and with the vast open spaces crowned by towering mountain ranges leaves an indelible memory of a beautiful but struggling country.

We found a good café next to a filling station. I took the chance to get another tankful of cheap Spanish diesel before enjoying a good meal and coffee. The journey to Vitoria from Badajoz was toll free and an absolutely stress-free drive. Chris had booked a room at the Holiday Inn Express on the outskirts of the city. This meant it was cheaper and gave us easier access to the main road towards Bilbao the next morning. The downside was that we couldn't find a restaurant or café anywhere within walking distance so instead we got some basic sandwiches from the hotel and watched a glorious sunset over the mountains we'd be driving through the next day. After a long day, and with a very comfortable bed, we slept for eight hours straight.

Next morning we checked out and prepared to rejoin the road to the French border and another run through the beautiful Pyrenees. This time we'd stay on the toll road and not combat Biarritz again. The tolls through that section only set us back €5 after all. A handy lesson learned for future road trips, though we were glad of our experience the first time around. Our destination today was the ancient port of La Rochelle on the Bay of Biscay. We were now travelling through familiar scenery and the extra volume of traffic in both directions. Another reminder of our progress north was the gradual fall in temperature. It had reached a high of 18 degrees centigrade when we crossed into Spain but was now down to 11 as we approached the exit for La Rochelle itself. Once again our directions were off the mark, but after fifteen minutes we found the Altica Hotel which was near the University campus and only a short walk to the old town. This hotel definitely fell into the cheap and cheerful category, but was more than adequate for one night.

The port is guarded by two medieval fortifications which are in magnificent condition. The marina is vast with all manner of craft moored up and we watched one vessel heading out across the bay into the setting sun on the horizon. Different coloured homes lined the quayside and the old town itself was lined with timber-framed buildings dating back several hundred years, the cobbled side streets were lined with expensive fashion and jewellery shops, bars, and restaurants, as well as far more luxurious looking hotels overlooking the bobbing boats in the harbour. It was beautiful, simply beautiful but with this came the price tag. The bar we picked out wanted €5 for a large Leffe. We didn't mind one bit, sitting here in the setting sun with such a view was bliss. Chris commented that it had the look and feel of York, but by the sea. We made our way back to the hotel as the temperature began to plummet and found a pizza restaurant popular with the university students. We'd only clocked up 530 km that day but were still looking forward to a good night's sleep.

We checked out on Thursday morning and were looking forward very much to our next location. Bayeux, the home of the legendary tapestry and a British owned hotel, the Hotel le Bayeux. The town itself, and I know I'm beginning to sound like a broken record here, is just beautiful, incredible, and a pleasure to visit. There are fabulous old buildings, a wonderful cathedral, excellent museums detailing the events of D Day, and wonderful shops and restaurants. We had to push the boat out and figured we deserved a proper meal with a proper bottle of wine for our last night in France. There are occasions when the cost of the meal is irrelevant compared to the enjoyment and occasion. This was definitely the case this particular evening and we relished every minute of it.

It was Friday morning and time to check out. The receptionist came out and unlocked the gate so we could leave the car park and he couldn't stop looking at the Astra van. I asked him if anything was wrong and he replied that he had never seen one before, not this model. It is unique to the UK and Ireland and explained why we got a lot of looks on our mammoth trip particularly from the police officers near Evora. I've found out subsequently that rear mounted bicycle carriers for cars are illegal in Portugal. No wonder they were so interested and at a loss as to what to do? I am driving the perfect loop hole, they couldn't ticket me and had to let us go. Not only had we escaped from the rat race but the Astra van had gotten in on the act as well. We had time to visit the world famous 'Tapestry' and enjoyed spotting the pro French propaganda, not only in the museum but also the 'Tapestry' itself. Nothing changes, history is always written by the winners!

Seeing the 'Tapestry' was the perfect ending for what had been the most remarkable road trip of our lives. It was with some sadness that we now drove towards Le

Havre and onto Dieppe for our crossing to Newhaven. This was a nice drive along the Normandy coast, again we'd selected the scenic route after all, and we had plenty of time to get to the port. Everything went fine until we got to the western edge of Dieppe. The signed route for the car ferry seemed to take us out of our route by what must have been twenty kilometres or more. Now we might be in trouble for not getting to the ferry check-in on time.

For the first time in over 2,500 km I lost my temper as the road seemed to go on and on until it finally brought us around a cliff to the port itself. We needn't have worried, there was a large queue waiting at the only check-in lane and passport control point that was open out of season. We drove onto the *Seven Sisters* ferry, and I had a fight on my hands to get the headlamp deflectors off my headlights, then made our way up to the passenger deck. When we'd visited Chris' parents up in Sutherland just before Christmas, we took the opportunity to drive the eighty-three miles to John O'Groats as we thought it was appropriate to drive from here all the way to the Algarve. Now we'd actually done it, we'd clocked up 6230 kilometres or just under 4,000 miles. The Astra van hadn't put a wheel wrong and we were going back to England to see family and friends, repack and prepare for our flight to Bulgaria in a few days' time. We couldn't wait!

CHAPTER 7
WHY RUN AWAY?

On returning to the UK, we found ourselves questioning the reasons for leaving the country in the first place. Partly, because we were being asking these questions by our friends.

It appears to us that the system we have been brought up in, is no longer working for the people. Values and beliefs must be questioned in order to achieve and progress our lives with satisfaction and fulfillment. The key doesn't fit the lock anymore! We either change the key or the lock, meaning that we have to alter our values and beliefs, or our expectations of the outcome and quality of life. I could no longer see hard work paying off and the impacts were on my quality of life, not a compromise I wanted to accept. There must be more, there must something better, is this as good as it gets?!

I guess it's all about whether you feel you deserve better, more, for your dreams to come true. I think we all deserve that and should aspire to dream big. There were concerns, we felt apprehensive, but we maintained a positive outlook and believed we could find our solution.

I like this quote by Roy Batty from the cult movie *'Blade Runner'*; "Quite an experience to live in fear, isn't it? That's what it is to be a slave." It seems we are all in fear of something; of losing our job, house, partner, possessions, status, reputation. To turn this around we need to focus our thoughts and energy on what we want, with motivation and passion, not what we don't want. This is what we we're trying to do.

Taking a step back and looking at the bigger picture of what was going on in the UK and around the world, the pieces of the puzzle started taking shape and we could see much more clearly what was going on, much of which we didn't like or want to be a part of. The three key areas we saw were as follows:

Overworked and Underpaid

People rush around like 'headless chickens' in their daily lives, stressed out with no time to spare. Many have to take several jobs and still struggle to pay their bills, which seem to only rise and never fall in spite of static or declining wages. The number of families having to take advantage of 'food banks' is rising to record levels, many of these would have once been described as 'lower middle class' earners. The other growing trend is the older generation seeking part time jobs, in competition with school leavers, to boost their income to manageable levels – thereby causing huge problems for our younger generation and the availability of jobs they can apply for.

'Big Brother'

Who wants to be watched 24/7 by cameras and recorded when on your telephone, mobile or PC? We've already heard that our kitchen appliances, TV's etc. are being manufactured to include devices which can monitor our activities in our own houses. Where does it end? Possibly 'chipped' like our pets so they can scan us at airports and hospitals and who knows what else![5]

Control through Programming

There are millions of sincere people who believe that their governments only have their best interests at heart, and that the status quo is the only viable option open and anything else is dangerously unacceptable. This is exactly what they want us to believe! The mindless reality TV shows we are bombarded with ensure that we are suitably disengaging our brains from thinking about the big issues and what is really going on behind the scenes in our country. The adverts are programming us in their own way, ensuring we buy certain products and giving us guilt trips regarding charities needing donations (issues which governments should be preventing and allocating central funds effectively). The TV shows are using programming in their titles, for example, we noticed an emphasis on 'war' e.g. *'Road Wars', 'Storage Wars', 'Parking Wars',* subconsciously telling us that we're constantly at war, with other programmes similarly named adding to our feelings of anger and fear. In a nutshell being spoon fed information on how to think, what to feel, is too much like 'bread and circuses' for me!

Having No Regrets

Key for me in making my decision to leave and change my life are the following points. I don't want to be in that position echoing these regrets. I'd rather have a life of "Oh well's", than "What if's"!

If we're not living a life true to ourselves and our core belief structures, we harbor regrets and resentments which in turn can make us ill with dis-ease. So it is not surprising that the results of a survey carried out in 2012 by staff at care homes across the UK, revealed that people on their death beds had the following regrets as it dawned on them too late, that they knew all along how they could and should have done things differently in their lives[6]. In order to start a new life the availability of real and helpful information is key, which is my main motivation for writing this book, to help as many people as possible find their freedom.

The list is as follows:

The five greatest deathbed regrets:

1. I wish I'd had the courage to live a life true to myself, not the life others expected of me.
2. I wish I hadn't worked so hard. (Missing children growing up and the damage done to relationships)
3. I wish I'd had the courage to express my feelings.

4. I wish I'd stayed in touch with my friends, what matters most in life is love and relationships.
5. I wish I'd let myself be happy. (Pretending to yourself and others that you were content when deep within, you longed to laugh properly and have silliness in your life again. It would be wonderful to let go and smile again, long before you die).

The Chinese philosopher Lao Tzu summed up the five regrets beautifully over two thousand years ago: "Worry what others think of you and you will always be their prisoner".

By allowing yourself to be part of the system that works on the mantra of "better the devil you know" and "keep calm and carry on" you may very well, in all probability find yourself uttering the same regrets or...? You can listen to your own inner voice, not the one that belongs to a newspaper headline, a parent or manager, but the one that already knows that life begins at the end of your comfort zone. That the leap into the dark will not result in a fall into a bottomless chasm but in all probability land on a feather mattress! The treasure that you seek will be found in the cave you fear to enter. (Kick that fear into the long grass, it is the ONLY factor in keeping you somewhere you know you don't want to be).

I'm a human being, God Dammit! My life has value! Emancipate yourself from mental slavery, none but ourselves can free our minds.

Ok, I've used the two quotes above already but they're so significant I thought they deserved to be used again! It is up to you, to decide for yourself if you want to be free, if you want the chance to follow your passions and fulfil your dreams and ambitions.

If you love football or motor sport, why not travel across Europe under your own power to watch your favourite team play, or F1 driver, or Moto GP rider, giving their all and staying in some of the most exciting cities in the world. If you like shopping, you have the best shops on the continent to lose yourself in. If you always fancied doing a "*Max and Paddy*" trip across Europe, calling in on the best beaches from Greece to Portugal or skiing at one exciting resort after another, these possibilities and countless others can be there for you, not years away when your strength is beginning to fail but NOW!

"We are not retreating, but advancing in another direction."
General MacArthur.

CHAPTER 8
IN SEARCH OF A NEW WORLD

*"God gave us the gift of life: it is up to us to give
ourselves the gift of living well."*
Voltaire

We spent nine days catching up with family and friends,
retelling our adventures and completing appointments
with dentists and GP's etc. Saturday 10th March we
arrived at the Days Inn hotel in Luton. The car park for
the hotel was on the top floor of a multi storey car park
and unfortunately for us the lift was out of action. We
had to walk down the ramps all the way to the street
level then up the street to the reception entrance. Not the
best start but the hotel room was comfortable enough.
Whether it was because we knew we had to be up at four
in the morning, the incessant sound of wailing police
sirens through the night, or perhaps what seemed to be
the endless procession of drunken revellers staggering
down the hotel corridor, we hardly slept a wink.

The next morning we made our way to the airport on
the courtesy bus leaving the Astra safe and sound at the
Days Inn. Checking in at the Wizz Air desk was quick
and easy and we made our way through to the security

area. I made damn sure I had nothing on me that would trigger the metal detector as I really despise being groped in a manner that would be classed as sexual assault anywhere else. I looked around at the couple of hundred other passengers penned into lanes leading to the front of the queue. This is a scene repeated at airports across the UK and the rest of the world every day. There is nothing to stop a determined jihadist from checking in for a flight, walking in to the security area and opening fire with a couple of pistols before detonating a bomb vest. Such an easy target, there would be so many casualties and blanket headlines in the media. Why all the hysteria about taking a water bottle through or what size toothpaste tube you can take, when the whole security area is a perfect turkey shoot, like shooting fish in a barrel!

According to repeated statements from the security services going back to 2005, there are thousands of potentially radicalised Islamic militants in the UK, this was before the latest dire warnings about Britons heading to Syria to fight with Isis and their potential return. Why the inability to prevent them from flying out in the first place? Known football hooligans are banned from travelling to away fixtures in Europe, why the reluctance with individuals who are potentially far more dangerous?

Is it because of the lack of resources given to the security services? Are cuts in public spending putting us at unnecessary risk? If it is either, then surely this demands a complete end to tax avoidance schemes that cost the exchequer tens of billions of pounds every parliamentary term.

Corporate profits should never override the safety and security of the public. Perhaps hubristic politicians should be made fully accountable for their policy decisions, particularly when they discount the warnings given by the most senior members of the intelligence community as to the very likely scenario of terrorist attacks against the UK if Iraq was invaded. Indeed, the 7/7 bombers directly linked their attack on London to the bombing of Iraq and Afghanistan in video messages made before their dreadful attack, and threatened more would follow after them.

I find it crazy that we expect the same people who effectively painted a large bullseye on the country when they voted for the 2003 war, to now find the solutions for the fiasco they helped create. I suppose it is concordant with bailing out the banks after they brought the economy to its knees and hoping they get it right next time. We ought to be asking questions of the media for their assiduousness in banging the drums of war while pouring scorn on those who accurately predicted the consequences of the invasion.

An honest look at the history of the West's involvement in the Middle East since the end of World War One would go a long way to finding a long term settlement in the region, one that would not be dependent on the protection of the US petrodollar, nor the armaments industry. I think it's fair to say if the region's primary economic commodity was rhubarb instead of oil, we'd never have set foot there in the first place.

We mustn't forget the odds of dying in a terrorist attack are 25 million to one[7]. The odds in winning the lotto jackpot are a mere 45 million to one yet most of us who buy a ticket know it is almost impossible to win the big prize. We're far more likely to be killed crossing the street, in a car accident or from heart disease or alcoholism, than ever from terrorism yet we are happy to be regarded as guilty until proven innocent in the eyes of the authorities. Last part of this mini rant is that I remember living through what was euphemistically called "the troubles" when for thirty years there were killings, bombings and shootings almost every week. Over three thousand people were killed, thousands more maimed in what was a very real campaign of sectarian violence from all sides in Northern Ireland and mainland Britain. The public were warned to stay vigilant, to look out for suspicious, unaccompanied baggage or packages, but over and above these warnings was the message that we must not change the way we lived our lives, for to do so was to hand victory to the terrorists.

Today we have people spooked and stampeding off aircraft at the gate because someone was taking photos inside! A flight arriving at New York's JFK was met by the FBI and all the passengers interrogated because a passenger had a bag with the logo '*Kare 11*' on it and a fellow passenger misread it as Isis[8]! A coach was stopped on the M6 motorway in Staffordshire and the passengers marched off at gunpoint and isolated while police looked for a terrorist bomber[9]. It turned out it was a passenger smoking an e-cigarette under his coat and a panicked fellow passenger phoned 999 seeing smoke come from their seat! The motorway was closed for 6 hours leading to gridlocked roads, mayhem on the surrounding routes and a lot of very scared people sitting on the hard shoulder with guns pointed at their heads.

Every other week there are similar incidents occurring and the levels of hysteria have ramped up to ridiculous levels.

It seems to me that we HAVE handed over victory on a plate to the likes of Al Qaeda and Isis. Where is the Blitz spirit that we are famed for? How on earth would today's generation have coped with high explosives and incendiary bombs raining down from the skies night after night? Would Health and Safety rules prevent first responders from pulling people out of bombed out buildings because they might get hurt? Would the children who were evacuated from the cities have had counselling and would the families looking after them have been subjected to Criminal Records checks before having children placed with them etc., etc.?

How the members of Al Qaeda must have laughed at TV images of thousands of passengers waiting to be screened at airports across the western world and even more so at the billions spent on such security measures. Yet, many of us are incredibly unobservant. A year after the 7/7 attacks in London I was delivering a package to a company near the London Dungeon attraction. This was a Friday and I did not fancy the idea of driving into the city centre and trying to get back out again in the rush hour, instead I drove to Epping underground station and got the tube into town. I avoided the congestion charge and would have a lot easier return route north to Nottinghamshire. A passenger boarded my carriage at Mile End station. He was in his early twenties, of Indian origin and was carrying a backpack. He was wearing a Hi-Viz tabard that appeared to be issued by 'Transport for London'. He put his backpack on the seat next to mine then he sat down and started assembling a mobile phone. I remembered reading how many previous attacks had attempted to be carried out using a mobile phone as a detonator. I looked at my fellow passengers at this point. A mother with her small baby opposite seemed oblivious, several Japanese tourists were more bothered with taking photos of themselves with their latest iPhones and others stared into their newspapers, all equally unaware that a few yards from them there may have been a suicide bomber priming a device.

What should I do, jump on him and possibly save everyone's lives, or end up being arrested for assault and causing a panic? Typical, I thought, I'm trying to save paying out on the congestion charge and an easier journey and I might get blown to pieces. Do I slowly move down to the other end of the carriage and jump out at the next stop or stay put and hope I'm only being mildly paranoid? What's the worst that could happen? I get off the train and am late delivering the package possibly resulting in suspension from work or stay where I am and get blown to bits which would undoubtedly still result in a few issues regarding work!

I made my choice and slowly got to my feet and as casually as possible, made my way to the end of the carriage and as the train pulled into 'Bethnal Green' station and the doors opened I almost ran for the exit. At that moment I had never been so scared, I was trembling while waiting for the next train to arrive listening out for the inevitable roar of an explosion and smoke and debris filling the platform. Obviously such an event never happened and I made my delivery on time and returned home in one piece, but this experience did show me how easily we can be controlled by fear.

The other incident that springs to mind was more recent. An unattended suitcase had been left near the check-in desk at Burgas Airport. We noticed it while we were in line queuing. No one was remotely interested in it. No one came from the WC to rejoin the queue with it. At the other end of the terminal were two armed police officers, though they seemed uninterested in it. When we finally got to the desk we mentioned the suitcase to the operator. He shrugged his shoulders and said "I don't know, maybe terrorist!" and handed back our passports and boarding cards, smiling before calling the next passengers up! We moved as far away from there as possible. I guess ignorance really is bliss but it must be better to have an escape plan if you do notice anything that looks more than a bit iffy!

Back to Luton airport. We went through security without a hitch and brought a breakfast sandwich and coffee. Our tickets had no seat allocation on them and we wondered if there was likely to be a stampede for the seats when boarding was announced. By the time we'd finished our meals and drinks it was already time to go to the departure gate. After the priority passengers had been allowed through, it was our turn and the boarding process was actually very quick and easy. We settled in our seats and watched our fellow passengers placing their bags in the overhead lockers and taking their places. In just a few minutes from boarding, the purple coloured Airbus was being pushed back from the gate, the engines were spooling up and our plane made its way to the end of the runway. Takeoff is my favourite part, the action of selecting full power, the brakes coming off and the acceleration down the runway- I just love it! Landing is a close second, the bit in between can be a bit boring unless you've got good weather and can make out a lot of places on the ground. My poor mother is petrified of flying, I've tried to reassure her with words of reason like "It's not the flying you want to worry about, it's the crashing that's the problem," it didn't seem to help!

When the captain came on the PA and asked the cabin crew to prepare for landing, we knew we were now flying over Bulgaria and we keenly gazed out of the window. The terrain looked similar to rural Spain and to our left we could make out the Black Sea beyond.

Something happened next that I've only observed in disaster movies or recreations of crashes on the Discovery Channel. Once the plane had touched down and the reverse thrusters deployed, there was a round of applause from most of the passengers onboard which I can only assume was because they were happy to be back on 'terra firma'! Despite requests to "remain seated with your seat belts fastened until the light in the overhead panels goes out", there's always one who ignores it and leaps out of their seat, attempting to open the locker and get their bags while the aircraft is still taxiing. "Hey, you! Yes you, Mister! Sit down please!" Why do people do this? Do they really think they're going to get out of the terminal any faster than the rest of us?! Is it a symptom of the hectic nature of modern day life?

Minutes later we were descending the steps to the waiting terminal bus and we were shocked. We'd left a cold and miserable England behind and were expecting the same weather here. Wrong. It was twenty-one degrees centigrade with blue skies and very little breeze, which was a pity as we'd packed primarily for winter. The thick jumper I was wearing was already becoming very uncomfortable. No queues at passport control, and less than ten minutes later we were carrying our cases towards the exit. Chris had booked a transfer for the thirty minute drive to Sunny Beach and sure enough a driver was waiting for us with a card with Chris' name on it. Sheltered life that I live, this was the first time that I had experienced this.

We set off and the driver spoke a bit of English and noticed our out of place winter clothing, "We had snow last week, it melted and now it is nice". We drove along the shore of the Black Sea past some fabulous hotels and other unfinished projects; the road was quiet and single carriageway. Occasionally some drivers came roaring past us in an almost crazy fashion but the driver seemed unfazed. We drove through a small town that had some fruit and veg stands by the side of the road, some shops and a couple of bars. Some houses looked quite ramshackle while others looked pretty modern. It reminded me of rural Portugal and Spain. The road became dual carriageway and on the right was a new Lidl store, a little further on was a home furnishing store and on the other side of the road was a large garden centre. A few minutes later there was a very impressive water park with some spectacular slides and not long after we approached Sunny Beach itself.

The beginning of the three mile long strip is marked by the presence of another large water park, to the right the road leads to the ancient port of Nessebar, a World Heritage Site. The main strip through the centre of Sunny Beach is filled with hotels, casinos, restaurants, supermarkets, car hire firms, fast food joints and the odd lap dancing club. Some of these hotels looked incredibly modern, the sort you'd expect to see in the Canaries or the Costa Blanca and others looked to have been around when the country was part of the Soviet Union. The other highly visible sight was the number of apartments for sale in new complexes just off the main strip or set a little further back. Dozens of them, perhaps a hundred were all available to buy or rent with prices starting from €23,000.

This Sunday afternoon though the place was virtually deserted. Hardly another car to be seen, hardly a soul about and the only thing missing was tumbleweed blowing across the road. The driver turned left onto an unsurfaced track. There were more complexes in various states of construction and a little further on was a block of complete hotels. One of these was our home for the next seven nights. We walked into reception and glanced around. The receptionist was sitting among friends having a cigarette (at the time there was no ban on smoking indoors though since June 2012 it is now prohibited) and she quickly came over to attend to us. She checked our paperwork and passports then asked us to follow her to our room. We walked out the opposite doors and past a swimming pool that, strangely, had lots of plastic bottles bobbing up and down along all the edges, and the colour of the water left a lot to be desired. At the far right hand corner was a door leading to the elevator and stairs. We made our way up to the 2nd floor and stepped out into a pitch dark corridor. The receptionist pressed a switch on the wall illuminating the corridor and revealing just how long it was. She gave us our key, pointed to the door at the far end and re-entered the lift. We looked at each other and started walking towards the door. Each step echoed very loudly and gave us the impression we were the only people staying in the entire hotel. The room was actually very good, it had a kitchen with dining table, good sized lounge, bedroom, and a decent shower room. We quickly unpacked and needed something to eat. That breakfast sandwich at Luton seemed a very long time ago and another planet away.

We showered and changed and set off for a walk towards the beach. This was a stroll of no more than ten minutes which took us past plenty of empty hotels and closed premises. The beach was empty. It stretched miles in each direction and was perfectly clean; a gentle lapping of the sea upon the sands was the only noise we could hear. We reckoned there must be a bar open along the sea front, but after half an hour we'd found nothing open anywhere. We now tried looking for a supermarket but had no luck there either. Having covered the best part of two miles without success we turned back and returned via the main road. Still nothing open and after half an hour two dogs approached us. They seemed friendly enough and decided they would be our guides. They got their entertainment from taking turns running and barking at any passing car. This was hard to watch, as time and again they were nearly splattered across the tarmac!

From first impressions there was an equal mix of poverty and overt wealth, both in property and cars. There were plenty of luxurious hotels and apartments plus some far more modest places, modern 'Mercedes Benz's' and 'BMW's' as well as ancient 'Lada's' and original 'Skoda's.' We walked past many estate agents shop windows and gazed at the amazing prices.

Finally, after another mile, we spotted an open supermarket and, better still, an open restaurant! We walked across to the '*Kamikadze*' restaurant and sat down at a table outside under a canopy. The waitress came over and spoke perfect English. She gave us a menu each, and the choices were a combination of Bulgarian dishes and some tourist favourites, with prices that were less than half that we'd paid a few weeks earlier! We ordered a spaghetti carbonara and stir fried chicken with two large beers. The beers came first and we tried our first Bulgarian beer, 'Kamenitza'. It was ice cold and just what we needed. It tasted as good as any we'd had since January and if I'm honest it was better than many lagers available at home. The food was excellent and the bill when it came, was less than seventeen levs, around seven pounds fifty! We looked into each other's eyes and thought that yes, we could make this work!

We bought some basics from the supermarket. including some bottles of 'Kamenitza', then found our way back to the hotel and its long echoing corridors. We put the TV on to see what the choice of TV programmes was like. We found plenty of music channels including MTV and VH1, as well as the local hip hop which is a wonderful blend of western European and Middle Eastern styles. Many channels offer this type of music and also there are four or five channels that show nothing but traditional folk music 24/7. Apart from some of it being very pleasant on the ears and many of the singers being very pleasant on the eyes, the scenic backdrops reveal the Bulgarian countryside in its magnificent splendour. Also available was the National Geographic channel, the History channel, Discovery channel, Animal Planet, Eurosport, CNN, and others. Many of these were shown in English. The Bulgarians love watching English Premier League football and live matches are regularly screened. The same goes for Italian, German, and Spanish football as well as the Champions League and Europa League. There are many movie channels, with some being screened in English with Bulgarian subtitles. We were very impressed and decided to have a quiet night in with our Bulgarian beer. The next day we planned to have a lie-in then explore more of the resort after breakfast.

Before we had left England we had looked at Bulgarian property websites and one stood out for us. It was called Brits2Bulgaria and was run by an ex-forces Englishman called Nick Gittings. His service included taking clients to properties, offering advice and local knowledge, and help with every step of the process involved in buying a house in Bulgaria. He emailed me back asking that we select a few places we liked the look of and he'd encompass them into a day's viewing. He arranged to pick us up from our hotel at 9am on Tuesday morning. In the meantime we checked out Sunny Beach on foot.

We found what must have been the main area of activity during the season. All the mainstream fast food joints were there and plenty of modern bars and night clubs were close by and the promenade led straight to the beach. We had another gaze across the Black Sea and just spent some time watching the world go by. This was interrupted only by the sounds of our rumbling bellies and we made our way back to the 'Kamikadze' restaurant again. We ordered another tasty meal and drinks and while we were waiting for it we heard another English voice from the table next to us. It was a Yorkshire man in his early sixties talking to a young Bulgarian man who it soon became apparent worked for him. When the younger man, called Dimotar, left I got talking to him. It turned out that Terry had lived here for six years and was doing very nicely as a property broker. He couldn't speak a word of Bulgarian but that hadn't stopped him from thriving in this environment.

He was buzzing with ideas and schemes and his mind rarely rested with the opportunities around him. He offered to show us around a few apartments in town both for sale and to rent. I was interested by the one he mentioned that had a sea view and was available for €40 a week. He also offered me a job as a driver taking divers up the coast five days a week during the summer season! Already on day one potential doors were opening for us and the sense of something good coming our way was very, very palpable. We arranged to see Terry and Dimo on Wednesday afternoon; we also arranged to look at some apartments with local Bulgarian agents on Thursday morning.

Tuesday morning couldn't come around fast enough for us. Nick was bang on time and after the introductions we climbed into his 4x4 and set off. The journey to the first property was 90 minutes and the time was spent finding out each other's stories and what life was like in Bulgaria. Nick was up front about it when he said if money was no object we'd all be living in the Bahamas, and the primary reason ex-pats chose to live in Bulgaria was the incredibly low cost of living by UK standards. He had lived here for eight years with his wife Jo and their four year old son Ollie was born here. They had fully embraced the lifestyle and self-sufficiency of his Bulgarian neighbours and were revelling in it.

He drove us past the airport and into the city centre of Burgas itself. The first thing I noticed was the number of tower blocks on the side of the road. They looked like they had long since seen better days though some frontages were nicely coloured. At the bottom of each was a large faded black number and the only thing missing was the red hammer and sickle flag that used to fly from each one before 1990. On the other side of the road were the sea gardens which are set back from the beach. This is a very nice area to take the kids to, ride a bike around, enjoy the well kept gardens, or find a nice restaurant and enjoy a freshly caught fish dish.

We drove on towards the railway station and noticed the tree lined street filled with nice shops, bars, and restaurants that would not have been out of place anywhere we'd been since January 8th. We drove past the railway station and eventually out of the city past some modern looking supermarkets. Nick pulled over to the other side of the road to buy a bag of chicken feed and was promptly beeped at by other traffic. Bulgarian drivers are as keen to use their horns as they are in Paris and don't have much patience. They also like to overtake in the most dangerous manner whenever it suits. Nick shrugged, saying you just get used to it. We set off again and were soon travelling into the rural areas, he drove us through the town nearest his village and where he and Jo did their shopping. This was Sredets and to be honest it looked pretty rough. If you watched *"The Long Way Round"* when Ewan McGregor and Charley Boorman rode through Ukraine, it looked a lot like that to me!

We were soon back on the country road heading towards our first property, which was in the village of Fakia. We pulled off the road and soon found ourselves looking at a very nice view of forests on both sides, sloping steeply down towards the village itself, and beyond them on the skyline were the mountains of Turkey. Coincidentally, Nick lived in this village and after we'd looked at the house we were going around to meet Jo and have a nice cuppa at their place. As we descended into the village Nick pointed out one of his local bars that already had plenty of customers, mainly men, some enjoying an espresso but mainly beer. One of them called out to Nick and he pulled over, the entire conversation was all in Bulgarian and we couldn't help but be impressed. A matter of minutes later he pulled up at our first viewing. It looked derelict but had had a new roof fitted not long ago and was structurally sound. It had its own well, a huge garden of two thousand square meters and was on the market for £5,000. We were both impressed with the potential it represented.

Nick commented that his home was almost identical to this one when he bought it and by going around to have tea there we'd be able to get a good idea of what this house could be transformed into. Nick and Jo's home oozed warmth and rustic charm. The kitchen/dining room was a good size, there was a wood burning stove in the corner which supplied heat throughout the house in winter. The lounge also was a decent size and the bedrooms upstairs were both spacious and cozy. The garden was vast and well stocked with all kinds of fruit and vegetables, they also had chickens and rabbits, Nick showed us a few baby rabbits and mentioned, to Chris' horror, that they'd need a few more kilos before ending up in the freezer. Behind the house was another cluster of wooded hills which he loved to ride his quad bike through. There are miles of off road tracks which the locals often use to get between villages and as long as no one rides or drives across the farmers' fields these tracks are open to all to enjoy.

Nick and Jo's home reminded me of the Weasley's house in the Harry Potter films and we sipped our tea, already excited at what we'd seen. Nick told us that if we were interested in it he could assemble a team of local builders and for around ten thousand pounds we could have it looking like his home. He planned to show us some homes that other ex-pats had already bought and others that were part way through being renovated on the way to our next viewing. We thanked Jo for the tea as we set off again and travelled through some rugged countryside.

The road ran in parallel with a winding river lined with forests. The wildlife consisted of wild boar, wild horses, and from March till August storks are everywhere. There are seventeen types of eagle in Bulgaria and they are a regular sight in the countryside and mountainous regions. Within half an hour we had met three English couples, one whose terrific house he had renovated himself, another family were mid-way through fixing their place up, and another man who was selling up to go back to England. Chris commented afterwards how this was like a *Blue Peter* moment demonstrating how many ways of making the transition are available.

We carried on towards our next viewing and Nick continued to tantalize us with the amazingly low cost of running a home and the level of local taxes we'd have to pay, council tax and the like. We came on the trip armed with lots of questions and a notebook so that we could assess the properties we were going to view. The day with Nick was a huge part of allaying any fears or worries we had about the reality of making a move here. This was largely due to the fact that he was English so we could ask and understand everything, but also due to his helpful, relaxed attitude and customer focused approach. This, I would highly recommend to anyone doing the same, whether in Bulgaria or elsewhere.

We made our way to the next largest town called Elhovo and here we met one of Nick's business partners who ran an estate agents in the main street. This was Elvira, both a solicitor and a highly experienced property agent who spoke both English and Russian fluently. She explained the legalities involved and how all the help needed to complete a purchase would be included in the price. One of her employees, Mitko, was going to come along with us for the next few viewings. He too spoke perfect English and explained that the language was a very popular subject in schools here.

The next house we looked at was the polar opposite from the previous one. It had been fully renovated to a very high standard and was a blank canvas, fully ready to move into and was going for €25,000. It ticked every box but we still had another five houses to look at. We were confronted with another fully renovated detached house. It was only a few kilometres from the Turkish border but still less than 25 minutes away from Elhovo and its supermarkets. It was on the edge of a wood, close to a stream and had a large garden which, like the house, was a blank canvas. It wasn't as large as the previous house but was more than adequate, especially for €21,000. The next three houses didn't float our boat, they had some minor work needed on them, nothing dramatic but the locations didn't appeal as much as the others. The next house was owned by a late middle aged couple who were selling up and going home to England for health reasons. They had been living here for eight years and loved every minute of it, they were sad to be going and were selling everything lock, stock and barrel including their car. The house was nice enough but not our cup of tea.

The next house was another renovated three bedroom detached property. It had more character to it than the other renovated homes that we liked and the only negative thing about it was the crumbling factory opposite that looked like it might have been used as a backdrop for '*The Professionals*' or '*The Sweeney*'. This could be ignored particularly at €24,000. Nick then offered us a two for one offer; on the edge of the village was a renovated house that had been empty for some time and the sale included the partially derelict house on the neighbouring plot.

We dropped Mitko back at his car, as Nick had one final property he thought we might be interested in. It was not far off the route back from Elhovo and although we'd had a long day already we thought "Why not?" Nick put his foot down as he wanted to get there before it got completely dark. Half an hour later we arrived at the house. Nick had called the builder doing this renovation, Ivan, who was a friend, and arranged to meet him there. He had renovated the house and was the seller. Ivan was already there when we pulled up outside and had put the lights on as Nick had lost his battle with the setting sun. It was a large and solidly built detached property with very good quality double glazed windows all round. It had a large animal shed 30 metres away and a vineyard beyond that. Inside was scrupulously clean with whitewashed walls and new laminate flooring in the rooms and corridors. It had a large extension added to it that we could use as a kitchen though at the moment it needed the laminate putting down and was just a bare room. The other benefit we could see was the terrace roof above the future kitchen. When we went upstairs to see it you could comfortably sit twenty people up there and it had great views to the mountains fifty kilometres away. What struck me most was the contrast between this wide open spacious landscape and the feeling of freedom it generated, and the hemmed in properties back in the UK, which leave most of us feeling compressed and suffocated.

There were three very large bedrooms, one of which looked out over the terrace and which Chris could already see being used as her art studio and Reiki room. We could use one of the downstairs rooms as a substitute 3rd bedroom. There was a good sized upstairs wet room fitted with brand new tiles, shower, sink and toilet. There was also the potential for a massive downstairs wet room, like the kitchen it was a bare room at the moment but we could imagine it being fitted out very easily. There was also an outside toilet, barbecue area and sink. We couldn't help but be massively impressed. This place was huge, the garden was equally large, and there was probably enough space to park thirty cars on it. All this and it was on the market for thirty grand! We thanked them for showing us around and we made our way back to Nick's Honda, we looked into each other's eyes as we opened our doors and both mouthed "Wow!" at the same time. Nick and Ivan shook hands and we were soon on the road again heading the hour and a half drive back to Sunny Beach.

The journey exposed one of the worst problems faced by Bulgarian motorists apart from other Bulgarian motorists - the condition of most of the roads. The UK, even with the levels of dissatisfaction with the state of repairs on the road at record levels, really doesn't know it's born. Nick had to take regular evasive action to avoid what were more like craters than mere pot holes. Fortunately many motorists avoid driving at night so he wasn't playing chicken with oncoming traffic. Paying out for new track rod ends and wheel balancing was a regular scenario he explained.

We stopped at a Lidl store to get some shopping in as we wanted an early night when we got back to the hotel. They are as well stocked and fitted out there as they are in the rest of Europe, we bought some basics and set off again. By the time we arrived back at the hotel it had been a twelve hour day and our heads were spinning with all the amazing potential! Nick still had another hour to drive home to Fakia, we wished him goodnight and paid him the equivalent of £80 for his fuel and his time. We told him we'd be back in touch after looking at some places in Sunny Beach.

We opened a bottle of 'Chateau Karnobat' chardonnay (very nice at under seven levs) and mulled over what we'd seen. We were both very tired and needed a lie-in the next day, so that we'd be ready for our afternoon with Terry and Dimo.

We made our way to 'Kamikadze' and had lunch with a 'Kamenitza' each. Terry and Dimo were prompt and arrived at 2pm. We paid up and set off for the apartment with the sea view. This was on the northern end of the resort and was a good size especially for €40 a week plus the annual maintenance charge of €400. We looked at other one or two bedroom apartments in complexes set further back from the beach. They were well fitted out and quite spacious and had access to several swimming pools, some also had shops, restaurants, and wellness centres. The pools also had plastic bottles bobbing up and down around the edges and Dimo explained that it was protection against the winter weather which, though not as harsh as it is inland, can still get very cold. As we'd already discussed work options, Terry suggested that one of these complexes would be ideal for Chris to do her Complementary Therapies from, as guests tended to spend lots of time on these all-inclusive resorts. Another plus point, we thought.

Terry then took us to a more exclusive block on higher ground giving excellent views from the sea to the mountains behind. These looked really very impressive and carried a higher price tag of over €50,000. Terry suggested we get him dinner as payment for his time during the afternoon and wouldn't accept any other offer. He dropped us off near our hotel and explained that with Dimo's help he was going to ask one of the young ladies at his bank in Nessebar out for dinner that night. He seemed very confident of success and waved goodbye as he set off into the light traffic. The thing about Terry is that he is so full of energy, he buzzes with enthusiasm with new ideas, new ventures which help keep him a young sixty-something. A situation which would have been unlikely in recession-hit South Yorkshire.

That evening we were going to take Nick up on his recommendation of a good restaurant in town. It was ten minutes' walk from our hotel and was called 'Djanny's'. We were very impressed! There were more staff than customers, they were immaculately turned out, and the food was a revelation, absolutely delicious and hardly more expensive than 'Kamikadze.' We reflected on what we'd seen, many apartments priced from €26,000 to €50,000 and the resort was obviously quiet now but what would it be like living here during the height of the summer? Then we considered what we'd seen with Nick and it was a no brainer as to what made financial sense. We both had been thinking a lot about the final house Nick showed us and wanted to see it again but in daylight. I called Nick and we arranged to meet him in Burgas on Friday at the bus station. He'd collect us from there after we'd negotiated taking the bus from Sunny Beach. We spent Thursday looking at other apartments with some Bulgarian agents who I'd also emailed before leaving the UK. They were very professional, not at all pushy and fluent in English and Russian. The Russians were very big investors in the resort, closely followed by the British and Irish. In fact, Terry had mentioned how many of his clients were from Ireland, and how in the next resort up from Sveti Vlas (Saint Vlas) there was a dental practice he'd helped get started and many Irish tourists came over for their treatment because of the huge difference in treatment costs.

Sveti Vlas is a more upmarket resort and has a fabulous marina with some very flashy vessels moored up. Few of them would have been out of place at the marina in Vilamoura. Some of the Irish contingent had come to Bulgaria from other European countries to escape the slump as the economy was taking a nose dive and investments had stalled. We must have looked at a dozen apartments in total, some ready to move into, others nearing completion, and all were around the price or higher than the houses in the rural areas we'd looked at with Nick. The difference though was for the price of three rooms and no garden we could have a whole house and spacious garden. No contest. We had lunch with Terry and mentioned to him we were going back to the rural properties tomorrow and that if anyone we knew wanted help with getting a place in Sunny Beach we'd put them in touch with him. Terry finished his meal and rushed off to another appointment and I'd forgotten to ask him if he'd got that date! Being the cheeky character he was, I was optimistic for him.

Friday morning and we made our way to the bus station. You pay on the bus not at a kiosk and we settled in our seats. The journey to Burgas took an hour as the bus stopped at several villages on the way. This gave us another opportunity to look at the sort of houses there are in Bulgaria. Some really are very basic and the construction methods would probably be outlawed by UK standards. This is the poorest country in the EU and you have to keep that in mind and not be judgemental. It works for them and we had seen some places that would not be out of place in more wealthy parts of Europe.

What you wouldn't get in these wealthier parts of Europe however is the sight of people using horses and carts and this was quite common in the rural areas the bus drove us through. We remembered we'd also seen some in Tavira three weeks earlier. The bus took us through the town of Pomorie, which looked to have a vibrant pedestrian precinct with smart looking bars and restaurants. It also took us past a very plush looking hotel that could have come from the strip at Las Vegas.

The fare to Burgas was only three levs each and Nick was already waiting for us at the bus station when our bus pulled in. We exchanged pleasantries and set off. On the way out of the city we spotted a modern shopping mall and as I needed the toilet Nick pulled in to the car park. This mall had excellent clothes shops, a huge 'Carrefour' hypermarket, sports shops, 'Marks and Spencer's', 'Costa Coffee', 'Subway', 'KFC', 'McDonalds', and what really pleased Chris, a big 'Starbucks.' We all bought one to have on the road and it was Nick's first time in the place. He enjoyed it quite a bit, commenting that most Bulgarians drank Espressos like their Greek neighbours, and that we would never find a coffee like we're used to in the UK, "cappuccino is the closest you'll find", he added. That was more than a reasonable compromise for us with all the benefits of living here becoming apparent (these will be listed later), getting upset about coffee would be a bit daft.

We were travelling along the A1 from Burgas to Sofia, one of the most important connecting roads in the country and construction on it had started in 1974. It still wasn't finished! The alternative route was further out of

Nick's way than he wanted, so with the aid of a decent map he zigzagged across country and the pot holes towards the rural location. The route crossed over construction of the final stretch of the new road and Nick reckoned it would be fully open in a couple of years. Money from the EU was helping to give the project the final push to completion. We noticed up on the high ground a very large tower like structure, it was a memorial to the country's war dead, both from WW2 and the war of Liberation against the Turks in 1878. This could be seen from a hundred kilometres away or more, and if we were to go up there we should be able to see the village not far in the distance.

Soon enough we arrived at the house, where we had a small reception committee waiting for us. Ivan was there with the elderly couple who lived opposite. The old gentleman was wearing a Bulmers Cider fleece and he shook my hand firmly. His wife was quite frail but her eyes shone very brightly and she exclaimed through Nick that they always kept an eye on the house and that no harm would come to it. We went inside the house in daylight hours and were left to wander around on our own while Nick and Ivan were chatting by the vineyard.

We went from room to room imagining what use we could make of them but we also wanted to check out the roof terrace again. It was a bright, clear day and we could now properly enjoy the views to the mountains. We both could see ourselves sitting up here on a warm summer evening with a cold beer or wine or coffee on a Monday morning. We were under the flight path from Istanbul and there was a regular stream of aircraft passing high overhead but there was no noise to be concerned with at all. We also realised that the sky at night here would be incredible. We had 360 degrees of vision and no overhanging buildings anywhere near us to dent the view. Many Bulgarian homes are quite modest in size, but they do have vast gardens for growing vegetables for both their own use and to sell as supplemental income. The feeling of space and privacy was awesome. To have a house of this size and the accompanying land would cost at least ten times as much back home, more in some parts of the UK and we'd need a lotto win to have it.

There were a few niggles we weren't happy with; the kitchen area didn't have the laminate flooring down and, despite them describing the interior as open plan, it would be nice to have some doors to the rooms! Nick suggested we go to the nearby town of Yambol and get a coffee and have a chat about maybe putting an offer in if we were interested in the house. He had a look on his face that meant he already knew we were more than interested. Yambol was only twenty minutes away and we drove the main route into town. Like in Burgas and Elhovo, the standard Soviet ten storey tower blocks were everywhere. So too were some nice looking bars and shops. We pulled in to an Austrian owned filling station. Ivan pulled in behind us in his car. He was off to a meeting later on in the opposite direction. The garage had a good coffee and snack bar and the toilets were immaculately clean. He bought us a coffee and light meal each and we sat outside in the spring air. We soon got around to discussing the house and the possibility of putting down a deposit on it once we'd negotiated a price. We could have the place as it was for €25,000 or we could have the additional jobs done that we wanted, specifically the doors, floors, and choosing what tiles, fixtures and fittings we wanted in the downstairs wet room. He would also finish off the terrace roof with either tiles or astro turf according to our choice. Ivan also explained that he knew a very good kitchen fitting company that he had worked with before on jobs for his hotel and that he would put five hundred levs towards the purchase of units and worktops. Chris also wanted a fence fitting on the edge of the terrace, she didn't want anyone falling off the roof! He would do all these extras and the house would be ours for €30,000, around £25,000!

We wanted time to think it over obviously and we would be in touch from England with a decision as soon as we'd made it. This was agreeable to all parties and Nick confirmed that he would be with us every step of the way in the legal process of buying it, all included in the price. There would be no nasty surprises or hidden extras, the process would be above board and secure. We thanked Ivan for his time and the meal but before he left he suggested if we wanted the house we could stay there as long as we wanted to without charge up to the moment we went to the Notaries office to sign on the dotted line. The house would remain on the market until we made up our mind and if we did want it, a transferred deposit of €2,000 would secure it. Very fair we thought, a fine day's work and one worthy of a few beers later that evening. Nick dropped us off at the bus station at

Burgas and we retraced our journey back to Sunny Beach. Excitedly, we got showered, changed and headed off to 'Djanny's' again. We ordered our meals and tried a different beer called 'Shumensko.' This was only a few pennies more but had a more malty twang to it.

We toasted our day's success and each other's health. We went over what the risks were, what other options we might still consider and most importantly, the benefits of living in Bulgaria. No mortgage, minimal outgoings, early retirement, long, hot summers, making our own wine, Greece and Turkey on our doorstep, new experiences to enjoy, new friends yet to be made, and new skills to be learned, not least the language.

CHAPTER 9
'WE MUST BE THE CHANGE WE WISH TO SEE IN THE WORLD' -GHANDI

The thought process that we went through was weighing up the pro's and con's (bearing in mind we didn't have all the information contained in this book, just our first impressions).

We needed a house, stability, a base somewhere for all our belongings, and we were considering what was right for 'now', not necessarily long term. Weighing it all up, this seemed our best option for now. We could explore most of Europe from Bulgaria as a base, driving trips which I couldn't wait to plan out, plus we could provide a holiday location for family and friends to come out to relatively cheaply.

We validated our thoughts and concerns with each other and then with our families back in the UK. Our parents were brilliant; they backed us one hundred percent and were equally impressed by the property we had found for that price. Chris' parents had done a similar bold move in middle age, from Leeds to a remote village in Scotland. A decision that changed their lives and created excitement and adventure they never otherwise would have experienced, so no regrets. There were in fact many parallels with what we were planning, which we only fully realised over the following months.

These were some of the considerations going through our minds on our return flight to England, we decided we were going to ring Ivan within 48 hours of landing, to transfer a deposit to him and take the house off the market. He generously suggested that we could come back and live in the house as long as we wanted until the day we signed on the dotted line at the Notary's office in Yambol for no charge. This was brilliant news and would save us a few quid in hotels and other expenses. We decided to spend a few weeks in the UK catching up again with family and friends and planning to return in the Astra van during the second week in May. We'd fill it to the gunnels with everything we needed until we decided on just how we'd get the rest of our belongings out of the safe store lock up in Leeds and over to our new home.

When we returned to Luton airport, a couple of situations occurred that reinforced our wish to leave the country. The lift at the hotel had still not been repaired. The wall by the doors was festooned with *Post-it* notes from irate drivers. You're only given a few minutes to get to your car and leave the car park before you get charged. By the time you've walked up five floors and driven down, you've run out of time and have to park in not only the exact bay nominated, but go back to reception and get another exit disk. My patience was running on empty by now but it failed completely when we got stuck in a sixty minute traffic jam within moments of joining the M1. Once we began moving again, we saw no evidence of what had caused the delay, it made me wonder just how many days of my life I'd lost being stuck in traffic jams!

We made several visits to our storage locker deciding what we needed out and where it was located. The process of extracting the relevant items and fitting them onto the van was nothing short of a work of art! Every square inch was filled, we couldn't insert a cigarette paper into any remaining gap. We just hoped we wouldn't be asked to unpack at border points along the way!

Dover, May 8th, 2012. We left England once more, this time with no trepidation about what to expect when we rolled off the ship in Calais. We were going to take a leisurely route to Bulgaria and take the opportunity to visit Chris's younger brother Kevin and his family in Detmold, Germany as our first stopping point. We had also borrowed Chris' eldest son's satnav, a state of the art 'TomTom' with most of Europe mapped in so we expected few navigational issues. Sean had changed the voice of the satnav to that of Yoda from '*Star Wars*' and, as I'm not too bad at impersonating the Jedi master myself, the journey could get entertaining if I ignored his route instructions along the way. The journey time to Detmold was five and a half hours across Northern France, Belgium and Holland. This is one of the busiest roads in Europe and it pays to take your time and not get flustered.

The day after we arrived in Detmold, Kevin and his wife took us and two of their sons into town for a bite to eat and to see the sights (the eldest was at school). As you'd expect of Germany the streets are immaculately clean, the architecture is wonderful, the pull of a German beer and home cooked meal is hard to resist, the streets are thronged with shoppers, and the beautifully kept flowers lining a bubbling brook through the town centre presented a tranquil scene.

On this particular Wednesday afternoon there was an under 12's five a side football tournament taking place right in the middle of town. The pitch was enclosed by a series of nets, with the result that passing shoppers wouldn't be knocked over by flying footballs but that spectators could watch the fun with a coffee and hot dog or hamburger bought from a nearby stall. It was as perfect an image of the dynamic and successful country the media would have everyone believe it is, and then, all of a sudden, there was a sight I didn't expect. A well dressed, middle aged man on his knees in the middle of the street, cap in hand and utterly shamefaced, begging for a couple of euros. Even the idea that begging was taking place in Germany was a real eye opener. This wasn't Berlin, Cologne or Munich, it was a modest, normal town that could have been anywhere else we'd seen on our travels. It's certainly true that travel broadens the mind and one's horizons. It's also incredibly liberating too, to no longer have to be informed by those who believe it is their place in this world to have dominion on your opinion. The mainstream media will not inform you of things like this, it is something you can only know by seeing it for yourself.

A journey south towards Passau and the Austrian border beckoned after we'd said our farewells the next morning. The journey was pretty much stress free, the satnav performed faultlessly and we enjoyed the scenery as we headed through Bavaria. The radio tuned itself into the American Forces channel (AFN Eagle) and I enjoyed listening to it while Chris caught a nap. I thought it might be like listening to Adrian Kronauer in 'Good Morning Vietnam' but the DJ was not as remotely funny as the late Robin Williams. I listened to the news bulletins and commercials and one in particular stood out. It was supposedly a couple of GI's talking about where to go for a vacation and one mentioned going to Havana, Cuba. The other one instantly cut him off, warning him that to go to Cuba would result in a $10,000 fine and up to five years in prison. Bloody Hell, I thought, this nonsense has been going on for over fifty years and they still haven't found the ability to reach a mature agreement? No wonder there is no sign of peace between the Israelis and the Palestinians. Then I passed another US military convoy and I wondered just what the hell are the Americans still doing in Germany nearly twenty-five years after the end of communism? There are over a hundred thousand American troops stationed in the country, but there have been no opposing Warsaw Pact divisions to counter in all that time, the cost to the tax payer has to be immense but what do they have to show for it? Since it is pretty unlikely that there will be a new Adolf Hitler rising to power to trouble this occupying force, it seems utterly preposterous that they are still in Germany 67 years after the end of the Second World War.

Soon, we approached the border and signs appeared about road vignettes for Austria. I pulled in at the next service area and filled the van with diesel and bought a ten day vignette. Four years previously I'd not known about them and had been on the receiving end of an 85 euro fine imposed at a spot check near the border. Ten times the cost of a vignette, I wasn't going to repeat that mistake again! German motorists bitterly resent having to pay these taxes when their Austrian counterparts can roam the autobahns to their heart's content, free, gratis and for nothing. I remember the then Chancellor of the Exchequer, Gordon Brown announcing during the fuel strikes of 2000 that he would introduce vignettes for foreign vehicles using the UK road network, but when push came to shove he bottled out of it. What an incredibly stupid and short sighted thing to do?! It would be so easy to enact at all the cross channel ports and raise a small fortune every year for the hard pressed British tax payer.

We'd booked a hotel on the outskirts of the charming Austrian city of Linz which included breakfast for €65 (I knew Linz was historically significant but for the life of me I couldn't remember what for). We went for an early evening stroll and watched the sun go down over a beautiful vista of meadows, forests and mountain peaks beyond. Our hosts were very good and spoke perfect English, as do most of the population here. They were fascinated by our plans and had heard similar ideas from other nationals passing through. The next day was going to be special. We'd booked a hotel in Budapest for under twenty quid and the city was only four and a half hours away but better still, the half way point was the beautiful capital city of Vienna. This was too good an opportunity to miss and we planned on using the park and ride scheme to get into the city centre.

We left Linz after the rush hour and rejoined the main E60 eastbound. It then hit me why Linz was significant, it was the birth place of Adolf Hitler but I guess a big sign on the approach to the city proclaiming "Welcome to Linz! Birthplace of...." was probably not a good idea! Just as the inhabitants of Badajoz had done, the information has been kicked into the long grass.

The views from the E60 are stunning, the majestic, snow covered Alps are seldom out of view on the right hand side of the road. It seemed that many Austrian and German motorists were bored of the view as they sped past us at warp factor 3, often driving within inches of each other's front and rear bumpers, a nice reminder of not having to be in such a stressful situation anymore. We followed the road into the outskirts of Vienna and singularly failed to find the park and ride station that our guide book mentioned. I had to drive further into the city than I'd have preferred but soon enough found an alternative site to use the subway into the city centre. It was less than ten euros for the both of us to the centre and back, plus another €4 for the car park but it was money well spent. The city centre is breathtakingly beautiful. We wandered around in the warm spring sunshine in awe of our surroundings. We bought some obligatory souvenirs and had an equally obligatory caramel latte with half syrup when Chris spotted a large Starbucks not far from the Opera House where Mozart had conducted his finest works in the 18th century. This was a city we wanted to come back to in the future and enjoy properly. We made our way back to the car and set off east again, careful not to take the road to Bratislava by mistake.

We had to buy another ten day vignette near the Hungarian border and this is why you need your original V5 log book, photocopies aren't acceptable and you'd be completely in the foul smelling stuff if you wanted to get into Hungary legally. Unlike other European countries, original documentation is mandatory here. It's less than two and a half hours to drive to Budapest but we'd spent more time than we'd planned in Vienna and it was now the evening rush hour as we approached the outskirts of the Hungarian capital. The traffic was heavy but flowing well enough. The outskirts of the city are pretty bleak to be honest; we spotted a very large Tesco amongst other familiar shopping brands as the speed of the traffic flow decreased. Our hotel was on the eastern side of the Danube and had free and secure parking. We soon spotted the hotel and went in to ask about the car park, which was around the back. It was brilliant value for money and we were looking forward to going out for a beer and a bite to eat after showering.

The city reminded me of the old Michael Caine spy movies; there was more than a hint of exotic tobacco coming from some of the bars lining the main street. We watched the bustling crowds of commuters boarding their trams home, taxis jostled their way through the traffic and as we got our bearings and spotted which bars we'd check out. There were large numbers of homeless folk claiming the best spots they could find for somewhere to sleep later. The city had quite a Parisian feel to it, there is an exuberance about it that is almost as intoxicating as the vapours coming out from some of the bars we'd passed by. Though it was nine thirty in the evening it was still warm enough to not need a coat, this just added to the enjoyment we felt after a great day's exploration and we also knew we'd barely scratched the surface of what the two cities had to offer.

Saturday morning and time to leave town and country. "Yoda" navigated us perfectly through the well-worn streets and out onto the M5 motorway, south towards the border with Serbia. Much of the heavy goods traffic veered off for the signs for Ukraine, most of the rest were Turkish, Hungarian, or Serbian trucks although we did see one or two from Iran. It had been more than 800 miles since the last sighting of an Eddy Stobart motor heading back to the UK from Germany. It was dawning on us just how far we had travelled from "home" but the experience gained from January was invaluable. This part of central Europe was pretty uninspiring scenery wise, very flat, monotonous and largely agricultural. We saw some decent houses along the way but more dilapidated ones were becoming the norm. Despite the lack of scenery, we were enjoying our experience immensely. It reminded us of '*The Long Way Round*' (Ewan McGregor & Charlie Boorman) where they rode into unchartered territory and encountered many different landscapes and cultures. This was our

'*Long Way Round*' and with this in mind Chris put on a Stereophonics CD and we let our imaginations take over.

Very soon the van needed fuelling and we needed a break so I pulled in to the next service area and filled up for the second time since leaving Calais. After a hot pastry and coffee we set off south again. Soon enough we approached a large intersection with the choice of non EU member state, Serbia, or left towards Romania. Since I had no Green Card for this trip, Serbia was out of the question and I wasn't sure if it was that good an idea to travel across a country we'd been bombing only a decade or so ago, especially in a UK registered vehicle, perhaps painting a bullseye on the roof might really hammer home the message. On this occasion it was prudent to be better safe than sorry.

Not long after the intersection the road reduced from motorway to dual carriageway and then the road stopped, it was waiting for authorisation from Bucharest before any more construction work would be carried out. The quality of the road declined rapidly, reducing to a single carriageway and it didn't take long for the alternative route to become a near demolition derby with insanely suicidal overtaking manoeuvres every few minutes, it got worse when we neared the actual border. Here, at least three kilometres from the crossing point of Varnanadlac, a line of trucks waited to cross the border, this was the last thing we needed and we looked like being stuck here for hours. There is no Schengen agreement here, no easy transit across the borders like there is between most EU member states. Then a few cars passed us on the wrong side of the road, then some more and a helpful trucker gestured at me to follow them. This seemed crazy! Where are you supposed to go if a line of wagons is coming straight at you from the opposite direction?! I checked my nearside mirror and waited for a chance to fall in behind the next group of cars that passed us. I pulled out and kept up with them but left enough of a gap to take evasive action if I needed to. Sure enough the inevitable happened and up ahead I could see cars veering out the way in all directions as three trucks came the other way. Fortunately the truckers queuing on the Hungarian side had left big enough gaps at regular intervals to allow for this borderline mayhem to work and we all managed to avoid any collision before repeating the process again and again until the road widened at the border itself. It was total relief to follow the Audi in front of me to passport control undamaged, we showed our documents and repeated the process at the Romanian barrier.

We needed another vignette here so I pulled over to buy a 7 day permit for the equivalent of four euros. Before leaving the UK we'd bought all the currencies we'd need from the Post Office and taken out some appropriate travel insurance, just in case. No sooner had I got back in the car with my paperwork, three Roma women were almost fighting with each other to clean my windscreen, before they'd decided who was going to actually do it we'd driven off. We were heading east towards the large city of Arad where we'd turn south towards Timisoara and south east towards the Carpathian Mountains, the banks of the mighty river Danube and our stopping point for the night, Drobeta-Turnu Severin.

Within fifteen minutes of arriving in what was now officially Eastern Europe, the clocks go forward an hour once you leave Hungary, it looked like we'd solved the mystery we'd encountered in France four months earlier. As we passed through village after village we saw dozens of French registered cars parked outside houses, shops and restaurants. There was also a smattering of UK and Irish registered vehicles as well. It was a mini version of the United Nations, however, these people were united in finding a more affordable way to live just like us.

We stopped at a large roadside café and parked the car where we could keep an eye on it while we enjoyed a break. It was dusty and humid and, without air con in the van, all we fancied was a fresh orange juice even though the menu looked very tempting. The building itself was really charming, and it was easy to imagine the place heaving with families enjoying a good meal. It took what seemed like forever for the drinks to turn up and this would probably cause friction in the UK but here there is no rush, no problem and no worries. When they did finally appear they were well worth the wait, utterly delicious and enough to keep me energised for the rest of the journey. We paid up and set off towards Arad. The amount of traffic began to subside as did the number of suicidal drivers, a relief for us both.

On the edge of Arad we saw signs for Bucharest and saw the beginning of a new dual carriageway. "Yoda" didn't recognise the road at all and he insisted "At the roundabout, the third exit you must take". "Wrong you are, the first exit I will take!" I replied and the wise satnav went into melt down. I turned off the route planning section and got some peace while I enjoyed the empty and pristine highway. The country felt vast, wheat fields stretched off for miles into the distance on each side of the highway. It looked like Kansas or Nebraska from the movies and we made better time than we had expected. After thirty kilometres the road came to an abrupt halt and we had to once again follow the alternative route which didn't even bother with destination signs, "Yoda" wasn't much help either so I trusted to my inner sense of direction or just hoped that the car in front was also headed our way. Sure enough, we picked up signs once more for Bucharest and relaxed, on the horizon we could make out the western edge of the Carpathians and so we knew that we were heading in the right direction.

Romania is the second poorest nation in the EU and many of the villages we passed through reflected this. People had placed produce from their gardens onto stalls by the side of the road to hopefully sell to passing traffic; children were often helping their parents do this. It reminded me of my honeymoon in Crete. We'd hired a trail bike and gone exploring the middle of the island away from the tourist areas and up in the mountains we'd found a beautiful cantina where we stopped for lunch. The owner looked like Uncle Albert from '*Only Fools and Horses*' and he had quite a story to tell. He was English and had been a sailor in the Merchant Navy but in 1973 he jumped ship in Heraklion harbour and made his escape to the mountains. There he'd met and fallen in love with a young local girl, got married and had four children and twenty-one years later he was still running this cantina with her. Opposite his place there was a small table filled with bags of nuts, jars of honey and several different fresh fruits, four children aged between 6 and 12 were sitting there playing cards waiting for customers to arrive. We were there a good or hour or so and not once did any of them kick off about being bored or start messing around. It was quite an eye opener and now in Romania it appeared to be common place as well.

I'm sure it always has been and it occurred to me, just how cosseted and overprotected we have made our children in the West. Maybe we try to be our children's friends more than parents and boundaries become blurred as a result? We buy them everything they ask for (even when we can't afford it) and give them high expectations for material possessions; this is a key difference we see across Eastern Europe. The outlook and expectations of these children are not for material belongings, but for satisfying their daily needs and looking after family. Anything else is a bonus, this teaches us a lesson in what's really important in life and being grateful for what we have.

As we drove closer to the mountains we saw people in the fields working them by hand with ancient looking tools. There were structures that looked like wigwams but they were comprised of hay gathered up by hand, these were everywhere. We saw small groups of people walking by the side of the road in the middle of nowhere. They weren't thumbing for a lift, they were in between different plots of land and they were picked up at the end of their working day in a clapped out car and taken home. It really is a hard way to live but one thing we noticed was that, to the traveller passing through their village, it looked like the land that time forgot and the small houses looked one stage above being derelict. What they DO have is self-worth, they have community, they have enough to live on and they don't have boarded up pubs and shops blighting their main streets.

Later we stopped at a roadside filling station that had an unfortunate resemblance to one in the Rutger Hauer movie, "*The Hitcher*", but I needed the rest room after the orange juice and we both needed some snacks for the last part of the journey. We bought some crisps and a can of ice cold beer, the temperature was in the 70's after all and I thought Chris could do with a drink after our escapades on the highway. We set off again and this was the moment I needed Steppenwolf's "*Born to be Wild*" on the CD player. There were some stunning views to enjoy as we crossed the Carpathians, some maniacs to avoid, in buses not just cars and we reached the Danube in one piece. Well, the scenery along this stretch of road was amazing, on the other side of the river was Serbia, and in between was a large number of huge barges carrying all manner of goods bound for either the Black Sea or the Rhine. Much as I was enjoying the view I had to keep my wits about me as I took part in a real life version of '*Grand Theft Auto*' through the twists, turns and tunnels along the route.

Some of these drivers are totally and utterly mad! There were plenty of reminders of the country's past along the river. Huge, sprawling and crumbling ship yards, vast rusting rail heads and long since disused watch towers overlooking them all. Shortly, we arrived on the edge of Dobreta itself and began the now common scenario of pot hole avoidance, not so much pot holes but more like craters. I also had to swerve around a tortoise that was lumbering across the road. "Yoda" refused to help find the hotel Traian that we'd booked online, but I knew it was one of the tallest buildings in the town so it shouldn't have been too difficult to track it down. We'd paid the princely sum of £18 including breakfast so we weren't expecting The Ritz but what we got was more like Colditz. The place was clean enough but the décor hadn't changed much since the days of Reagan and Gorbachev. The lift car dropped half a foot when we got inside and creaked and banged every foot of the way to the 5th floor. The room was very spacious with a good view but the walls and ceiling were well stained with nicotine, the bath and shower had long since seen better days, and the TV? Oh dear but at least the bed was comfortable-ish. We wondered if this building had been the HQ of the secret police during the bad old days and decided to go out for a walk and grab a bite to eat.

The city centre was vibrant enough, high powered motorbikes tore up and down the main street, and there were plenty of smart looking bars and restaurants to choose from. We enjoyed our Saturday night here but were glad to be heading out of the hotel in the morning. "Yoda" again lost the plot minutes after we set off and wanted to select a route to the river crossing at Calafat that was twice as far as the AA map suggested. "Silent you must be" I advised him and again shut him off. It was little more than an hour to the port of Calafat and we followed the signs to the ferry port. We had to pay for the ferry just outside the barrier and a local tax, but what we didn't know was that there was no timetable. We had just missed one boat and were first in the queue for the next one but it wouldn't leave until there were enough motors there to make it worth their while. It was ninety minutes until enough vehicles were waiting and the crew finished their coffee and cigarettes and began waving us all aboard.

The river crossing was quite choppy and the waves often splashed over the front ramp and onto the car deck. It took twenty minutes to arrive at Vidin on the Bulgarian side and we immediately bought our month-long vignette. The road from Vidin to Sofia isn't long as the crow flies but has plenty of twists and turns and the condition of the road, even through some of the big towns along the way was very, very poor. "Yoda" was behaving himself now with accurate information and we felt very relieved to be on Bulgarian soil after an exciting but tiring journey. The journey was all dual carriageway beyond Sofia but once we neared Stara Zagora the satnav was stumped. A new stretch of the A1 was now open so we followed it until, like in Romania, it ground to a halt. Our destination was Ivan's hotel on the outskirts of Elhovo but for whatever reason "Yoda" was completely unable to find it. We'd phoned Nick for directions, Ivan said he'd come and find us if we were still having problems and "Yoda" seemed to be finally making sense.

He took us to what he believed was the centre of Kynazhevo where Ivan would be but in fact had taken us twenty kilometres in the wrong direction on some of the worst roads I'd ever seen. To say I was rather annoyed at this point, eight hours after leaving Vidin, would be a serious understatement. I was as close to joining the Dark Side of the Force as I'd ever been in my life, I was ready to take "Yoda" outside and jump up and down on him! The only thing that stopped me was Chris reminding me it was Sean's satnav. His little trick had added an extra hour onto our journey and I was spitting feathers but Chris helped calm me down and out of the darkness came Ivan in his little white Fiat Uno. We were saved! We gratefully followed Ivan to his hotel, where we dumped the car, unloaded our stuff as quickly as possible and headed for the bar. The restaurant staff were waiting to make us a meal which we gratefully accepted. Ivan had reserved us the VIP suite and both it and the hotel felt like an oasis of luxury after such a long and challenging journey. We certainly needed it to be, and the beer tasted extra special this particular night. We'd made it!

The next few weeks were spent looking at furniture shops, designing our own kitchen for the first time in our lives (in Bulgarian), and all the other things you need to do when you buy a house. At the same time we were coping in what felt like glorified camping conditions, with a kitchen missing and no furniture except a loaned bed. Ivan and Nick were incredibly helpful and generous with their time and with addressing any issues we had with any minor jobs that needed doing on the house.

Ivan had also arranged both satellite TV and broadband internet to be set up at the house before we arrived. He also knew a company that could measure up and install some good quality blinds, and he arranged for a couple of air conditioning units to be fitted at the same time that our downstairs wet room was being fitted out. He took us 60 miles to the Bulgarian equivalent of B&Q to choose the tiles, shower, bath tub, and WC that we wanted and would be included in the price as promised. All jobs would be completed and the new kitchen would be installed by the time we came back on our second roadtrip with the rest of our belongings.

At that time Bulgarian law required overseas buyers of property to register themselves as a company, which Ivan helped us do at the local Notaries office in Elhovo and thus Blue C International came into being. This was a brief and simple process. The purchasing experience is a good deal easier and less traumatic than it is in the UK. The Foreign Office advice on buying property in Bulgaria was very specific about the need to hire an independent lawyer during the purchasing process. I now called Rod's friend (friend of my Retford estate agent living in Varna) and asked him his opinion. He'd bought four properties and all without the need of a lawyer. He was convinced of the safety and legality of the Notary service and had every confidence in it. This was good enough for us. We'd asked for and been given a structural report on the house to our satisfaction and all that remained was for the money to be paid, the Notary to be satisfied that proof of payment had been made and that all parties were in agreement. By the way, for transactions such as this a cash handover has to take place in front of the Notary, so we had to withdraw our 28,000 euros in cash from the receiving bank. Then we had to drive in convoy with Nick and Ivan to Yambol (30 miles) where our Notary was waiting for us. This was a very strange experience, making us both a little nervous until the handover was complete. We also had the services of Dilyana, she acted as an independent translator for us during the process in Yambol. Once signatures and stamps had been applied the Title Deed was ours and the next step in our lives was underway. Job done!

CHAPTER 10
THREE WHEELS ON MY WAGON

Within a week of moving in our first van load of belongings we'd met our new neighbours' son and his family. George is the son of the elderly couple we met in March and he speaks good English. He works for the water company in Yambol and also does many farming jobs in and around the village. His wife Yordanka speaks better English than he does and their daughter Desislava, who's nine, is nearly fluent in the language. Utterly amazing and within a few days she and her younger brother Gogo had introduced us to almost the entire village! We've all become firm friends and in such a short time; I now knew more people than I'd known in seven years back in Retford. The hospitality we were shown was incredibly heart-warming and made us feel both welcome and accepted. George and Yordanka, or Danshi as she likes to be called, took us out to dinner with the kids to the smartest restaurant in Yambol. It is called Borovets and sits on the highest point of the town. The food is to die for, the décor is immaculate and wouldn't be out of place in any of the cities we'd travelled through, and the views of the sun going down over the Stara Planina Mountains were incredible. We felt both very lucky and incredibly happy at the same time.

We also soon found out that our neighbours down the road are a British couple from Somerset. We learned from George that they only come out for the summer months, and that they have owned the house for 6 years. We've become good friends with them, too. Each year, around May time, they drive over with their two dogs and spend three to four months in their 'summer house' here in Bulgaria. An ideal opportunity to get family over in the holiday season and do some exploring themselves.

Another local, a former T-72 tank commander in the Red Army and best bee keeper in the village, told me that his neighbour was Peter from Manchester though he hadn't been seen for years. Our village no longer has a bar but the next village has two and a new hotel with a swimming pool is being built on the outskirts of the village. There is only a small shop in our village selling a wide range of essentials for those who have no transport to get out to the big supermarkets in Yambol. The shop also takes responsibility for the village post, and the lady who works there delivers letters once a week. We met six ex-pats in the local bar who live in the village and two of their friends who were over on holiday and we have become good friends with them too. This was just getting better and better.

All we needed to do now was find the best way to get the rest of our stuff over here. We could either pay a professional removals firm in the UK to collect and transport our stuff and have to wait several weeks for it to arrive or we could follow Nick's suggestion of buying a second hand large van, deliver our stuff ourselves, and then sell it once we were finished with it. We researched the costs of removal companies, hiring a van ourselves, and the cost we could do it for if buying a vehicle, this decided it for us. I didn't mind driving an old van over to Bulgaria, in fact I saw it as an exciting challenge. This sounded like the most cost effective method and convenient to us, so we settled for this idea. The storage space we were renting was eighty square meters and it wasn't full all the way through and I was convinced it would all fit in a Luton box van. They're ten a penny on eBay and other web sites like Autotrader.

Before we flew back to the UK I had the Astra re-registered with Bulgarian license plates, tax and insurance. It was a simple yet drawn out process but with Dilyana's help we had the whole exercise completed in one morning. Next, we needed a lift to get close to Burgas Airport and George kindly offered to drop us off after he'd dropped some gear off at a friend's garage in the city. This worked well as we paid towards his fuel costs making it a win:win situation. He took us out the scenic route from the village, literally through the fields surrounding it. We were stuffed into his wife's VW Polo and I wondered how on Earth he could see where the tracks were for the three feet high weeds. Going this way knocked eight kilometres off the journey, he explained. He dropped us off at the hotel we were staying at, close to the airport in the town of Sarafavo. This is close to the beach, and after we dropped our stuff in the room we went down to the sea to get some food and a beer before turning in.

The temperature was around 35 degrees centigrade as we sipped our ice cold beers watching the waves caressing the shore and we wondered how warm it would be in Leeds the next evening. We couldn't get direct flights from Burgas, the best we could get was a seven hour stopover in Prague before our connecting flight to the UK. We didn't mind as we saw this as a good opportunity, we'd get five hours exploring the beautiful Czech capital, a place neither of us had been to before.

We'd planned on spending two weeks in the UK catching up once more with family and friends.

We flew into Leeds Bradford airport and collected Chris's car from its current base in Leeds, this gave us the freedom to get round everyone, attend appointments and collect what we needed ready for the move. We also took the opportunity to travel down to Avebury for the mid-summer solstice with our shaman friends, though they wouldn't be able to get to the camp site till after the festivities had finished. We loaded Chris's car with some of the camping gear from the lock up and headed south. The Hill View campsite south of Marlborough is brilliant value for money at £11 per night, a large saving on what we usually had to pay at hotels. We realised on our drive down how much we'd missed beautiful old English villages with thatched roof buildings, churches, and traditional pubs that had so far escaped being converted into Indian restaurants. We walked down to the local pub on the banks of a canal and ordered two pints of proper real ale and two bags of crisps. I hardly got any change from ten quid! I sat back down and looked like I'd seen a ghost according to Chris. "Take your time with this pint, twenty-five levs for this! You can get a huge juicy steak and a glass of wine for this at home" I complained and we hadn't even bought one of those yet as it seemed a tad extravagant. We hadn't missed being charged these prices for a drink! We made two pints last the whole evening; we spent most of it chatting to the landlord and regulars about Bulgaria before walking back to the tent. We could not believe how bloody cold it was either, it was the longest day tomorrow but we could see our breath in the night sky like it was mid-December.

We spent an uncomfortably cold night in the tent, got up and headed off for the Red Lion pub at Avebury. We'd packed another smaller dome tent in case we could camp near the stone circle itself. When we arrived we were in luck, there was camping at the site free of charge and on a first come first served basis. We had a great time listening to other folk talking outside in the beer garden about 2012 and the end of the Mayan Calendar. The festivities in and around the portal stones were very impressive, powerful and hypnotic. Perhaps they were similar to the kinds of rituals performed there over five thousand years ago before the new age religion of Christianity showed up. Within an hour of the ceremony finishing the heavens opened with a torrential downpour. Fortunately our tent wasn't flooded out like some other poor souls a short distance from us. The next morning we had our alarms set for ten to four in the morning, but truth be told we were already awake. We set off towards the altar stone back in the stone circle and joined the crowd already there. Three druid priests were facing where the sun was supposed to be and conducted a simple ceremony. The senior figure explained that he'd been watching the sun come up yesterday so he knew where it should be. Some lad with a guitar started strumming the Beatles track "*Here Comes the Sun*" to much merriment. The lead druid asked those gathered as to how many would be coming back for the mid-winter solstice and he relayed his belief that the end of the Mayan Calendar didn't mean the end of the world, just a new shift in consciousness globally. This sounded good to me and we made our farewells, packed up our tent and went back to the current reality for the rest of the day.

We still had a van to buy and I'd spotted one that looked perfect. A Luton Ford Transit with 12 months MOT, 3 months road tax and under my budget ceiling of £2,000. The eBay auction finished at midnight and the toilet block was the only part of the camp site that we could get a good enough Wi-Fi signal from. We holed up in the washing up room and waited for our chance. Having had little sleep in the last 48 hours this was a big ask. With ten minutes left mine was the leading bid at £1600, we were struggling to keep our eyes open with two minutes left, another bid upped mine by £50, Chris gave me a gentle nudge and my finger hovered over the increase bid option. I was going to wait until the very last second to go for it; the red countdown clock was becoming tortuous. As the seconds clicked down from 5 to 2 I hit the increase bid option and punched the air in triumph. Then the reality hit me hard, we hadn't won, somehow someone else had beaten me to it. Damn it! It was back to the drawing board for me. I found out later that there is an app that allows a bidder to always get the item they want on eBay so I gave up on the idea and decided to buy one from a dealer when we got back to Wetherby.

Our friends arrived at the camp site around teatime the next day. We spent some great catch-up time with them, much animated conversation took place, lots to talk about and stories to tell under the starry night sky. With the aid of a dozen cans of beer from the local supermarket in Marlborough we all caught up on some much needed sleep.

The next day after our friends left, we made our way north after buying some paint for the house. Now the planning for the return route home could begin in earnest. From our hotel room I scanned the internet for the right van and it was unexpectedly bleak. Not one affordable vehicle anywhere. The only other option would be to hire a suitable van, drive it all the way to Bulgaria, unload it and drive all the way back again as quickly as possible then fly back, not an enticing prospect. The next day however my luck changed. A Mercedes sprinter box van was available with one month's tax for £1400 or £1600 with a new MOT. I called the seller up and told him I'd have it with a new MOT and he agreed, stating that it would be ready for collection in two days. That would do nicely.

I made my way over to Rochdale by bus and train and walked the last couple of miles as I was early. I saw the van parked outside the garage and walked around it, checking it out. It was a 1996 N registered motor and I knew it could comfortably take all our gear, I just needed it to be a good runner. I went into the office and announced myself, the dealer looked very apologetic and explained it hadn't gone for its test yet, it was about to go and that I'd have to wait for an hour or so. That didn't bother me, I needed to sort out the insurance on it anyway. I watched one of the mechanics get into it and I wanted to see how much, if any smoke came from the exhaust when he started it up. It seemed clean as a whistle, a good sign and he drove off up the street. The engine sounded just fine, another good sign and the decals that were still on the sides suggested that it had spent its life transporting mattresses and beds about, so it was likely that the engine had not been overly stretched.

I hadn't cancelled the insurance on the Astra van so it was a simple process to call up my insurers and transfer the policy to the Merc. It would cost me an extra £150 in monthly instalments which was fine as I planned on selling it once we arrived home. I'd also arranged with my good friend Andy from Gainsborough to register the van at his address so I could get the V5 logbook changed with the DVLA. I needed a temporary document to allow me to leave the UK because it would be well after we'd left the country before the new document arrived in the post. The van returned and I now completed the formalities after having a look under the bonnet and in the cab. Under the bonnet seemed ok, no signs of oil or coolant leaks. The interior was a mess and the stereo didn't work, the directional air cooler on the passenger side was missing, Chris wasn't going to like that. The dealer gave me the keys and the new MOT certificate. Now it was time to head back to the hotel in Wetherby.

I climbed in started the engine. Again it started on the button and I put the indicator on in readiness to pull away but it didn't work. I put all the lights on and rested my backpack on the brake pedal so that I could check the brake lights too. One of the brake lights wasn't working, nor was the side light or indicator. Hadn't this just gone through a very strict inspection by a Vosa inspector? I went back into the office and spoke to the dealer about it. He sent over another mechanic to sort the problem and as the rain started coming down he was soon pretty soaked. He fiddled around with the wiring and after fifteen minutes or so it was fixed. Then the nearside dipped headlamp stopped working. He gave the light lens a thump and it came back on again. He gave me the thumbs up and I selected first gear, the biting point was really high, this would take a little getting used to but wouldn't be a problem. As I approached the end of the road I applied the brakes.....eventually they stopped me. Hmm, there were no advisory's on the Test certificate about the brakes. There was no reading from the odometer either. I had no idea what the mileage was on this motor. The engine braking was pretty good on this van and should help with slowing down. On the motorway it pulled very well but it had a lot of play in the steering. Normally I would have kicked off about this, threatened the dealer with suggestions of reporting his firm to Vosa, as there was no way on earth this motor had passed a real Test, and demanded my money back, but there was more to consider here. Our storage space rental was up for renewal in 36 hours, we'd booked a ferry from Dover and we were set for going 'home'. The engine was the most important component and it seemed to be pretty good to me. Did I think it would get us the 2,300 miles back to Bulgaria? Yes I did, I had experience enough to cope with the van's shortcomings and would just explain to Chris that it had some "quirks" but nothing serious.

It took us three and a half hours to load the van, it was about 80% full. Ivan had asked us if we could bring back some stuff he'd bought on eBay and we'd left enough space inside the back for his gear. Oh, the other thing I noticed was that there was no spare wheel anywhere. The tyres looked ok though one of them wasn't far from being illegal. It should manage to last the trip and I made sure it and the other tyres were inflated to the correct pressure.

We stopped at Andy's house that night after our failed attempt to reach the DVLA office in nearby Lincoln for a temporary certificate, we had been beaten back by flooded roads. The only other office near to our route was Maidstone in Kent where hopefully we'd pick up our certificate the day before we sailed from Dover, failing this we'd be snookered!

We bought some shopping at Asda in Leicester and filled up with the cheapest diesel we'd seen on our journey south. The indicator began playing up on the journey but I learned to get it to work by some wiggling of the switch. On the way to my aunt's house in Berkshire the temperature gauge started to rise (at least it worked!) so I stopped at the next services and topped up the radiator. It behaved itself the rest of the journey and we reached the house after dark. Reversing into the drive was a neat trick as the reversing lights didn't work either. The next morning we bade farewell again and headed over to my parents house to load Ivan's stuff and have a good bye and good luck meal before heading to Maidstone and Dover. I'm not sure if my aunt or my mum and dad believed the van would make it to the end of the street let alone the rest of the journey but I was convinced we'd make it, it would be the our own '*Top Gear*' challenge!

Suffice to say we did make it to Dover with our certificate and the next morning we left the ship and headed back to Detmold again. We enjoyed another night with Kevin, Leanne and the boys and they too had doubts whether we'd make it back the 20 kilometres to the autobahn, never mind to the border with the Czech Republic and beyond. Having watched a certain motoring program on the BBC for years I've watched a procession of bog standard cars and vans perform above and beyond the call of duty and I believed our German built van would not let us down either, especially on the way to Berlin as our intended route suggested. I wanted to avoid any unnecessary stress to the engine by taking it over the many long climbs through Bavaria towards Passau and the Austrian border. We'd head for Berlin, crossing the old West/East German border, hotbed of potential intrigue and the likely front line of World War 3 for forty years, then pivoting south at Magdeburg toward Leipzig, Dresden and the border with Czech Republic.

We got stuck in horrendous traffic jams on the autobahn after an hour's driving because of a minor accident. This added an extra ninety minutes onto what we knew already would be an extraordinarily long journey to Budapest. The old Mercedes continued to do its job well, I had to top up the radiator every morning and suspected that the cylinder head gasket was on its way out but would not fail until after we got home (I hoped) and again I attempted to reassure Chris that it was just another quirk of an older van. The trick that I'd been using to get the right hand indicator to work had now given up altogether but, thanks to the efficiency of European roads, I could get away without using it too much and the left side worked perfectly. I drove at a fuel efficient and steady 60 mph which kept me out of conflict with the other more frenzied traffic, allowing me to relax a little more. We stopped at a signed layby to buy a vignette for the Czech Republic and were soon having headlamps flashed at us by oncoming motorists. I wondered if they'd spotted something else wrong with the van, like flames and smoke coming from behind or something but soon realised that all motorists are required by Czech law to have dipped lights on day and night. A nice earner for the bulb manufacturers I thought as we pushed on towards Prague and although we'd been travelling for over six hours Prague was only the halfway point to Budapest! We unfortunately had to travel across Prague during the rush hour thanks to the delay near Hannover. We lost more time here but "Yoda" at least was performing well and successfully put us on the way to Brno and the Slovakian border beyond. This road surface was shocking for at least fifty kilometres and we were in need of fuel and a pit stop as we passed Brno. As I pulled in to the Shell filling station I noticed that the headlamp had gone out again. Another quick thump sorted it. I finished filling the third tankful of the journey since Leicester and headed towards the forecourt shop. I walked past a German registered car and while the driver was refuelling it one of his passengers stumbled out and threw up on the forecourt floor. Nice, I thought but the way some people drove here it wasn't that surprising.

We set off into the dark once more and within an hour we needed yet another vignette, this time for Slovakia. This took the last eight euros that I had to my name, I was just glad that I didn't have to wake Chris up for any more change. She'd had a long day and needed the nap. The volume of traffic had reduced substantially and the van was still behaving itself as I approached the Hungarian border, and it grieved me a little that I needed another vignette barely an hour after buying my last one.

Two hours later and "Yoda" guided me perfectly to the front entrance of the Ibis hotel on the south eastern edge of the vast city. We'd arrived at last after a thirteen hour and 1175 kilometre journey. Chris checked us in and we made our way up to the third floor. The interior of this hotel was absolutely identical to one we'd stayed at in Bradford before leaving the UK in January. We'd gone to a party at one of Chris's former work colleague's house. He'd referred to Ibis uncharitably as the Abyss but on this night I didn't care. This was the

Ritz to me, and I was asleep before my head hit the pillow.

We didn't set the alarm for the morning; we needed the sleep more than an early start. I went downstairs and out to the car park and checked the van was as we'd left it. The heavy duty padlock was untouched and once more I topped up the radiator, though this time it didn't need as much as it had been using in England. A good sign with just one more push today until we crossed into Bulgaria. It was already warm and sunny, the weather had been unseasonably miserable across Germany with heavy rainfalls across the Czech Republic and Slovakia. This had probably been a blessing in disguise and made the journey a little less wearing on the van. I looked around at the now busy street opposite the hotel. Commuters were buying coffee and hot pastries and joining queues for the tram service into the city centre, car horns beeped sporadically, aimed at motorists too slow away from the lights or jaywalking commuters who'd left it too late to catch the bus or tram.

Today would be hard for Chris with no cool air from the fan to help her, in fact it was quite the opposite, she had hot air blasting through the vent from the engine, which in thirty degree heat was not going to be a pleasant experience. On the flip side it would be a change from yesterday when she had water running down her arm and leg from a gap around the window! Not to mention the worrying hole in the floor, no one could say this van didn't have character! Chris managed to fix the problem with the hot air vent by adapting a used sandwich box and diverting the hot air away from her, this kept her occupied for the start of our journey.

We headed off onto the now familiar route towards the Romanian border. I'd estimated that we had enough diesel to reach Bulgaria and pay for the final length of the journey from our stash of levs. It had been quite tricky keeping on top of the many currencies we needed to cross these countries, especially as they weren't easily available in the UK before we left.

This time at the border there was no chicken run to negotiate but a traffic police officer insisted I pull into the truck section despite our protests. I saw him getting a mini ear bashing from a colleague in the mirror which was scant consolation for trying to get through two dozen trucks all trying to get to the only open lane. We lost a good forty minutes as a result but at least they didn't want to have a look inside, hey ho, take a deep breath and forget it. There were no Roma trying to clean windscreens this time as I bought our penultimate vignette, we speculated on this, maybe they were in the back of a truck heading west to Calais, or it was their day off?

We repeated our journey from before but this time I intended to head further east to Bucharest and cross the Danube south of the capital, it should be less hard work on the van and we'd booked a hotel in the Bulgarian river port city of Ruse. I was ordered to pull over by a traffic officer on the approach to the Carpathian mountains, he politely asked me to put my lights on and explained in very good English that it was the law here to have them on day and night, he also informed me that it was the same in Bulgaria, I apologised and thanked him with more than a hint of relief.

We passed through Drobeta again but it was dusk already, a brightly lit neon sign informed us of the time and the temperature. It was 39 degrees centigrade as we pulled into an OMV filling station for a pit stop. We probably had just enough Romanian money for a sandwich and drink, we hadn't eaten since we left Budapest over seven hours ago and we were starving. We were startled at the next set of traffic lights by a young Roma girl clutching a baby standing by Chris' open window with an outstretched hand. We tried to explain that we had no money so she pointed at the mini baguette sitting on the dashboard. Normally we would have considered giving it to her but not on this occasion, I still had another four to five hours driving to do and could have eaten it four times over myself. Chris and I needed the energy to get us to Ruse. The lights changed and we set off into the traffic once again. The van continued to pull well as we crossed the plains, each hour completed was a small triumph as we nudged nearer the Romanian capital. There seemed to be no sign of life for miles on end and then suddenly we'd pass a really large, smart looking restaurant whose car park was filled with modern, expensive cars. In the warm air we could hear the loud, vibrant music coming from within and delicious aromas of great food wafted in through the windows. This was nice to experience, but tormenting for us as the mini baguette had long since worn off!

It was nearly midnight as we finally passed through the edges of Bucharest and followed the signs for

Bulgaria. Bucharest also looked like a very modern city replete with swanky bars, restaurants, and plenty of young, really smartly dressed clubbers queuing to get in to their favourite haunts. Eventually we found ourselves pulling up to the border point and now we had a problem, we had neither euros nor enough Romanian currency to pay the bridge toll. We showed our passports and had to try and explain our issue. The officer was less than impressed and eventually demanded twenty levs. This was more than double the actual toll but we couldn't do anything to change the situation so took it on the chin and put it down to experience. We pulled away from the customs point and swung left onto the pot hole strewn carriageway over the Danube. I couldn't help but yell at the top of my lungs as we came off the bridge and on to Bulgarian territory. Chris joined in and we whooped with joy, relief and excitement all at the same time. We'd made it, the van had made it and "Yoda" informed us we were less than ten minutes from our hotel. Oh but life was good, wasn't it? We were exhausted yet elated as I parked near the hotel. We checked in, got a cold Shumensko each from the mini bar in our room and toasted each other. It tasted fantastic this night/early morning and I looked out the window at our hard worked van across the street. I gave it a nod and toasted it too, if anything were to go wrong now I could ring George in our village and between us we'd be able to find a way of getting home. Needless to say, we slept very well and the next morning enjoyed a shower and a wonderful Bulgarian breakfast. At the table next to us were two English friends who'd ridden all the way here on their BMW motor bikes. One of them lived in Varna on the Black Sea coast, his friend had just wanted the chance to enjoy a "*Long Way Round*" style adventure and was riding all the way back to England after a few days chilling out. We finished our breakfast, made our farewells and wished the guy riding back home a safe journey. We checked out and walked over to the van in the hot, morning sunshine. Naturally, it started on the button; we put some fuel in to get us home and bought a couple of cold drinks to enjoy as we headed home. "Yoda" then conspired to throw a mini spanner in the works and like our previous trip, added an extra hour and a half to our journey. Instead of pulling over and flattening the annoying little git as I might have done once upon a time, I turned him off and dropped him into the door bin. I knew where we were now and decided that we'd stop for lunch at a really nice looking roadside restaurant that did fantastic BBQ's. We phoned our parents to let them know we'd safely arrived and they were overjoyed at the news as well as greatly surprised that we were here already.

At around two in the afternoon we pulled up outside our gate. The house looked great but the grass was about three feet high, cutting that could be tackled another day. We drove in and parked the van not too far from the front door. The Astra van was sitting where we'd left it and we rushed to the kitchen windows to see if the kitchen was fitted as promised. Our newly fitted blinds were open and as we peered in we could see the kitchen units, work tops and cupboards that Chris had designed and chosen weeks ago. We jumped up and down with excitement, we also saw that the air conditioning units had been installed and we couldn't wait to get in and examine everything! No sooner had we finished enjoying looking at the results than Desi and Gogo had excitedly come running over to us offering to help unload the van. We embraced each other then gave the kids a hug and thanked them for their offer of help. Within an hour we had everything that we initially needed to set up home inside the house. Everything else could stay in the back of the van until we found homes for it another time. We were home, back to a house that was paid for, we didn't have to ask what time we had to check out by, we had a new life to enjoy, we knew we had new friends to share good times with and more important than these, we had each other. We'd already explored and seen so much it was like a whirlwind but we also knew deep down that this was just the beginning of something more incredible to come.

Within a month I had sold the van for about half of what I paid for it. We calculated by adding on the fuel and vignettes that the cost of fetching our stuff amounted to less than fifteen hundred quid. Result.

Fast forward to our life now

With this section I want to paint you a picture of what life is like for us now and what you too could create for yourself:

Chris and I enjoy a fabulous lifestyle together and our relationship solidly reflects this. We have shared the experience of this adventure and faced challenges along the way, which have taken our relationship to another level. For instance, we've been able to drive 2,000 miles and talk the whole journey. To the extent where we now feel lost when we are not together. We've met people here who were single, had already lived extraordinary lives but have met someone new and realised that it's never too late to start a new life. In the example of *'The Best Exotic Marigold Hotel'* you don't have to go to Jaipur to experience the colours, smiles, and new opportunities, but it will feel the same.

In our new life we have a home and land that is paid for and obviously removes the financial pressure that otherwise would be there. Our home is larger than what had been my dream home. The kitchen is brightly coloured, light and welcoming; Chris loves to let her creativity flow. It is larger than my lounge had been in Retford, with views across miles of open fields to the mountains beyond. In the other direction, forty yards away is the vineyard where I regularly tend the vines and keep the weeds at bay. I also enjoy having cherry, plum and walnut trees in the garden. We have created a Feng Shui garden, again Chris's imagination and my physical work brought it into being. To this we added a plunge pool to enjoy during the long hot summers.

Our roof terrace is a perfect place to enjoy a filter coffee in the morning (whatever time we decide to start our day). It tastes very special as we watch storks glide over our heads on the warm thermals. In early August we are treated to the sight of hundreds of them circling high up in vast hypnotic patterns. What is taking place is flight training for the youngsters before they head back to Africa a week or two later. It really is an astonishing sight.

We relax on our sun loungers at the end of the day, to watch the amazing sunsets, often with an ice cold beer, the temperatures still high enough to be wearing shorts and t-shirts, it is very relaxing and tranquil and makes us feel very grateful for what we have here. Often these occasions are accompanied by music from the initial road trip, reminding us of how amazing it's been and how far we've come. On top of this we have a feeling that the best is yet to come.

Stargazing on a summer's evening is a revelation due to the low levels of light pollution. You can see millions of stars, pick out constellations easily and monitor satellites and shooting stars. Not to mention the regular displays put on by the fireflies. It's often hard to drag ourselves away, but we don't have to set an alarm in the morning so we have that freedom.

We've met many new friends and there's no shortage of events to attend and places to go. We are learning new skills including, Bulgarian language, growing food, winemaking, artwork and small construction projects like our walk-in wardrobe room.

As an added bonus, there is a new hotel in the neighbouring village which is a great facility that we can get to easily. It has a superb outdoor swimming pool, spa, and gym. The food is very good and rooms are less than £20 a night. One of many nice places we have to visit in the area.

Half a day's drive from here will take us to Halkidiki. A few hours further on, on similarly empty roads, will take us to Athens and Pireaus. We can leave the car in a secure underground car park for five euro's a day while we go island hopping before returning to explore Athens.

Bulgaria itself presents the most surprises, the Black Sea coast, the Pirin Mountains, the Valley of the Kings, we have found truly beautiful places and hear about yet more to explore. Budapest is a day's drive away as is Bucharest, and Istanbul is even closer. It's a great base to explore Europe from, and we have planned many road trips we'd like to do. Our next one takes us west through Serbia, Croatia, Slovenia, Italy, Switzerland, France and onto the UK.

I haven't mentioned half of the experiences we've enjoyed. It would take another book and there would be many who wouldn't believe it in any case. But suffice to say the free time I've had here is equal to forty years of average holiday entitlement which is also astonishing. If I got struck by lightning I'd go happy because I've enjoyed life so much. Consequently, my levels of fear have reduced dramatically. I know there is so much more to see and enjoy. We've barely scratched the surface but have been totally captivated by our shared experiences so far. The concept of boredom is utterly irrelevant and unknown to us.

This leads me to the very best part of all: Christine. In the depths of my pain there was just no way I could have believed that I would meet someone like her. She has been my rock, she has helped me in living a life I could not have remotely conceived of. She has shown tremendous courage, and belief in not just me, but in what we set out to do. She has shown me how to believe in love again. She has shown me another way to look at life and it has totally transformed mine. She has also helped countless others with her Reiki, crystal and colour therapies and Angel Card readings since we left England. I never would have believed I would be this happy again. This time though it is far, far better than before. She's amazing and I love her very, very much.

Believe in love, believe in yourself, believe and trust in the Universe. You <u>can</u> do these incredible things only better because they'll be your ideas and dreams you'll be turning into reality.

This is the time, this is your time and as Gandalf the Grey once said;

"All we have to decide is what to do with the time that is given to us."

Top of the Eiffel tower and what a view! With our coffee and baguette gone it was time to head back down for a calming mulled wine on stage 2.

Flavigny Sur Ozerain, we felt eyes watching us from behind every curtain as we found the location of the shop in Johnny Depp's "Chocolat"

Amarente, northern Portugal, a beautiful place to stop for a coffee in between Vila Real and Porto, and all thanks to an advert on the back of a truck.

The January frost of Poitiers was hundreds of miles behind us now. Rediscovering the joy of driving was wonderfully unavoidable on the warm, empty, rural Spanish roads.

The time capsule of Castelo de Evoramonte in central Portugal with the very expensive, empty IP7 toll road in the background.

Aljezur, Portugal. Our night of drama took place five minutes' walk from where this photo was taken.

Only a few hours away from The Algarve, it was hard not to feel on top of the world.

A perfect place to get some exercise. Albufeira enjoyed 18 degrees centigrade, while across much of northern Europe temperatures had plunged to -18.

Areias Village - Up on the third floor balcony Chris enjoys the chance to paint. I wanted her creation to hang on the wall of our new home – wherever it happened to be…

The Citadel courtyard in Badajoz and the location of our beer and tapas salvation.

The beautiful medieval port of La Rochelle in France, or 'York by the sea' as Chris described it.

March, 2012 our first view of Sunny Beach, Bulgaria. The murky gloom of Luton airport seemed a long, long way away.

The beautiful turquoise pool and waterfall at Hotnitsa, situated close to Veliko Tarnovo. A great place for a BBQ and swim.

The hotel Par Avion, near Apriltsi in Central Bulgaria. We had this great place to ourselves for less than £30 for the night.

One of the many beautiful sunsets we've been treated to since living in Bulgaria.

Stunning view of the 'City of the Tsars' Veliko Tarnovo,
former capital of Bulgaria, is one of the most popular
settlements for ex-pats.

Bulgarian Black Sea coast - Empty beach, blue skies, tent – sorted!

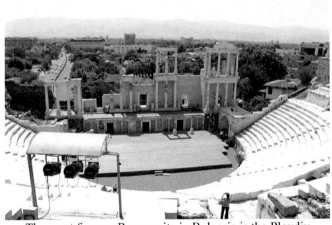

The most famous Roman site in Bulgaria is the Plovdiv Amphitheatre.

Bulgaria, what's there? Not just grey crumbling buildings as
you can see. This place is a magical forest with several
stunning waterfalls and diverse wildlife, high in the Rhodope
mountains.

My new running track, five minutes from the garden gate. This reminds me how grateful I am not be stuck in traffic on the M62.

One of our favourite beach locations on the Black Sea coast,
just south of the popular tourist towns.

A typical colourful Bulgarian street market, where you can
enjoy fresh local produce in the summer months.

The majestic Pirin mountains. The perfect location for skiing, hiking, mountain biking and golf.

In May and June we see a glorious carpet of colour in the fields around our house.

Alfresco dining at our favourite restaurant in Yambol.
Delicious food served with great local wines in a water garden
setting - and all for less than £5 each.

Autumn on the lower slopes of the Pirin National Park near Bansko.

SECTION 3
Your opportunity

I am the master of my fate; I am the captain of my soul

I hope I've covered all the bases with this book; the key element is that nothing is impossible, everything is possible. If your car is in good condition and you haven't thrashed it within an inch of its life it should serve you well on your future adventures.

There are plenty of alternative places to live a great life apart from Bulgaria. Property prices have been falling across France and there are bargains to be had. For example, if you don't need huge amounts of space you can buy a new mobile home north of Le Mans in a park with beautiful surroundings and great facilities for as little as €17,000. You can only stay there ten months a year but why should this be a problem? Eight weeks to see family and friends or perhaps head south for sunnier winters on the Riviera, Portugal or Spain.

You can buy an apartment in the Austrian Alps from €40,000 but beware, like Belgium and Greece, there is no ban on smoking indoors. Of course, if you like a cigarette with your meal and don't like being sent out into the cold to enjoy your habit, these countries could be just what you're looking for.

Wherever you decide to make a new life, you'll find all the help you need is available to you. Start with the 'Rightmove Overseas' website as we did and the world is your oyster! There are lots of handy pages of information regarding each country featured, these will help in your decision making process. It won't be like the Krypton Factor at all. The toughest part is making the decision to do it. After that it gets a lot easier.

"Don't try to eat the elephant in one go" as the saying goes. Break it into bite sized pieces, that's what you must do with big changes and projects in life. Develop a set of milestones that are achievable and celebrate reaching each one. Before you know it you'll be well on your way. If you think of the whole thing at once it appears unachievable. It's all too easy to talk yourself out of doing something like this. 'What if' is something we hear all too often in our lives, when we stop ourselves from doing something we know we can do, how do we feel later? Pretty terrible is the honest answer, isn't it? Little issues and minor snags begin to fester away at the back of our minds and become much larger than they really are. Either we snap, hit the bottle, comfort eat or develop an eating disorder, or partake in some other manifestation that temporarily hides our deep sense of discontent, frustration and powerlessness.

The more unfairly we get treated at work, the lack of reward for a hard day's work while those at the top get richer and richer, adds to the unease and simmering resentment. When you're told you'll have to work harder for less for longer you'd be inhuman if you didn't ask yourself just what the hell are you doing it for? Loyalty is supposed to be a two way street but it is a rare scenario today. Companies and corporations will not hesitate to dump you if it suits their agenda and no one is indispensable. There have been too many examples of employees being fired by text message or finding out through the media that they have lost their jobs after what may have been many years of hard work and sacrifice.

These conditions and the others already mentioned will inevitably lead to those mournful regrets when it is all too late. Another survey published in the autumn of 2014 listed the top ten regrets of the over fifty's and they mirrored those taken from the care homes with one notable exception. The biggest regret was marrying the wrong partner though it didn't reveal the percentage of those who were still married to them. This is really a terrible statistic; those people are being totally unfair and selfish not only to their poor spouse who deserves better, but also to themselves. It's never too late to let go and find real happiness.

It's true that you can feel completely stuck in a situation without any options to improve it, but once you change one dynamic of your life, everything else just begins to open up and options appear to you that you couldn't imagine possible. It has been observed that no one likes change. Growth can be painful, change can be painful. But nothing is as painful and damaging as staying stuck somewhere you no longer belong. "Ruin is the road to transformation" (Liz Gilbert – '*Eat, Pray,*

Love') Once you decide to move forward a weight will be lifted, you'll be helped and opportunities will arise which you could never foresee. You will be creating space for new positive energy to rush in. We have both personally experienced this and met many others in Bulgaria who have as well.

Imagine if you met yourself from a few years in the future and that person had two pills, a red one and a blue one. Taking the red one means you would remain as you are, living the life deep down you know isn't making you happy but you'll be ok, bordering on feeling comfortably numb OR take the blue pill and POW! You'll be out of your comfort zone for a while and have challenges, but you'll do everything you imagined and amazing things you could never have imagined, see places you always promised yourself and constantly learn and grow from the experience, revitalize your zest for life all the while. Which would you take?

We've driven from Eastern Bulgaria to Albufeira and back again. The equivalent distance of Perth to Sydney and back, and during all of that incredible journey we were held up twice on the Belgrade ring road for a grand total of ten minutes. Ten minutes delay from 5,000 miles, try finding any roads at home that offer that experience.

We also learnt from driving along the French Riviera that rents are no more expensive in Monte Carlo than they are in Britain, restaurant prices are not much different, even near the Marina, and parking your car under the world famous casino is a quarter of the price of parking in York. You can walk in off the street in

Cannes and get a hotel room from €70, little or no different from the UK. If you're just passing through the famous town and you don't mind walking along the beach for ten minutes, you can park for free. If you had your own motor home you can drive from Greece to Portugal and find somewhere to park without charge. The options are limited only by your imagination. I'd take the blue pill every time and as Terence McKenna said about being caged by our cultural programming, once you've expanded your horizons, your experiences and your consciousness, you can never go back to who you once were. This will not be a bad thing at all and will help open your eyes to the truth of the way the world really works.

The more of us who decide we've had enough of the system and it's warped machinations, the more we reject living in a state of media induced hysteria and quit, there will be a more than tangible improvement in the opportunities to make a better life for the next generation. After all, they are being helped not one jot by those who are having to work into their 70's and 80's, occupying jobs through necessity because of the exorbitant cost of living and insufficient pension provision. This is more evidence of a system that is catastrophically flawed and not going to change for the better for decades.

Another factor to consider is that we don't look after ourselves nearly enough. We try to look after everyone else and their interests ahead of our own needs and desires and are then made to feel guilty for it. This doesn't work because eventually simmering resentments and frustrations ultimately lead us down the road to addictions, ill health, broken relationships and an overwhelming sense of powerlessness. When you start loving yourself the way you deserve, you will project that outwardly to the benefit of not just yourself but your nearest and dearest. You will be content to just be the best person you can be. Everything will flow from that moment on, it's that simple. We weren't born to live in fear, we weren't born to run around like headless chickens sinking under debt, struggling to pay bills and burning ourselves out before our time. Our time here is a magnificent gift from the universe, it is here to be enjoyed, cherished and celebrated.

From Shakespeare's Hamlet:
"What a piece of work is man, how noble in reason, how infinite in faculties, in action how like an angel, in apprehension how like a God!"

It is really hard to attribute Shakespeare's writings to the state so many of us are in now.

Do you deserve it? Yes, you do, everyone does and we don't hear this enough. No need to go on......

SECTION 4
The how-to guide

DISCOVERING BULGARIA -
PROS AND CONS

"If you want to reach the castle, you got to swim the moat!"
Eat, Pray Love

This chapter is an attempt to cut out some of the leg work necessary to help you make a choice. We feel we have been on a huge learning curve since leaving the UK and my main objective for this book is to share our knowledge and information to enable you to make your transition to freedom and an amazing life.

Property

There are property agents aplenty with studio apartments available to buy from 15,000 euros and one bedroom apartments from 25,000 upwards in tourist locations. However rural house prices can be a good deal less than this.

The crux of the matter: How much do I need, to be able to successfully do a runner?

As I've mentioned, you can buy a good, renovated house for £25,000, you can rent a two bedroom apartment for twenty quid a week plus bills which aren't much. If you've a house with equity that is lost to you because of the cost of property in the UK, that is the key to living like a lotto winner in Bulgaria. If you don't want to sell your UK home you could rent it out and live very well indeed off the income here. The UK pension works out at £105 a week for a single person or £420 a month. This isn't much to live on with the cost of living and the trend is only going to get harder as time goes on. So £420 equals roughly 1000 levs and to put it into perspective the Bulgarian state pension is as little as 177 levs per month. Clearly there is a lot of spending power to be had with just the UK pension in Bulgaria. If you have the equity to be able to comfortably live off it until your private or state pension kicks in then you've cracked it!

(values valid as of 2014)

The Cost of Living

As Nick put it to us on the way to look at our first viewing; council tax bands in the UK were drawn up in 1991 and haven't been raised in price to match the current real value of property. The same is true in Bulgaria and the council tax charge for all the properties we looked at was, wait for it, drum roll please £28! Not per week, not per month, not per quarter but per YEAR!

Road tax or Vignette: For a car, motor bike or vehicle below 7.5 tons it is £28. This has been the same for years and doesn't go up as a matter of routine each budget day. There is another annual charge from the local municipality which ranges from £2.50 to £50, depending on the engine size and emissions of the vehicle concerned. Trailers are classed as another vehicle so incur all of these charges too.

Car insurance: Again this depends on the engine size and it is the car that is insured, not the driver which means a seventeen year old with a full UK license will pay the same premium as someone thirty years older. Cover is basic third party only and you are covered for every member state of the EU, Turkey, Serbia, Russia, Ukraine, in fact the only European country you're not covered for is Kosovo which is as likely a tourist venue as Iraq, Libya, or Syria. The Green Card comes as part of the basic insurance. The insurance for my Astra van would work out around £80 per year with no excess or stipulation of vehicle use. You can get fully comprehensive insurance which is called 'Casco' here and is more expensive but still less than the UK. It is also possible to get breakdown cover here at competitive rates. As the car is insured and not the driver, any additional driver for your vehicle will need to apply for a Power of Attorney to be legally able to drive the car, this is a simple process costing around 20 lev.

Diesel, petrol and LPG prices: These work out at around a pound less per gallon compared to the UK apart from LPG which is half the price of the UK. The quality of fuel is questioned in advice issued by the Foreign Office, particularly from local retailers but Shell have forecourts everywhere, Austrian owned OMV have forecourts from Salzburg to Sofia and beyond and Russian owned Lukoil sells equally good fuel at the same price as smaller retailers. You don't get ripped off either for buying fuel on the motorway type roads either. They have the same prices as those in town or rural areas.

Electric prices: Ours is a large house and the monthly charge comes to around 55 – 70 levs a month though it can be less. This equates to between £23- £28 a month. We are in the habit of reading the meter regularly to ensure our bills are correct, which they have been. You pay your bill in the middle of the month at the post office (as you do with the water charge) and getting accounts set up was part of the property sales service we got from Nick and Ivan. When you get your accounts you get a red card for the electric and a blue one for water, you present them at a counter that says handily in English, 'water and electric payments' and there's no worry if you have lost your cards, just present the previous month's receipt at the counter. You won't receive a bill in the post! The plus side is that you don't get bombarded with mail, specifically junk mail, it doesn't exist here....yet!

Water charges: These work out to around £3 – £4 a month. It is hard to complain too much when there is a failure!

Winter heating costs: Nearly every rural house is heated by wood burning stoves. Ours also pumps hot water to radiators in every room and heats up the boiler for hot water. We order twenty cubits of wood from a local yard who deliver it for a nominal charge. The cost of wood for the whole winter is around £500. Result! We had our heating system installed after our first winter here. The firm we used was very efficient and professional and we'd recommend them to anyone. We had the wood burner, radiators in every room and hallway, a new hot water boiler and a solar panel which heats up the boiler from late spring to autumn all installed for £2000.

Most Bulgarians have an annex to their home where they bunker down for the winter. The cost of wood to last the winter is a fifth of what we spend and this explains why no one dies in winter here or the rest of Eastern Europe including Siberia because they don't have to choose between heating and eating. It is both unacceptable and uncivilized that thousands die every winter in Britain because of that monstrous choice when the country is supposed to be the 6th richest in the world.

Internet options: Internet access is excellent across the country and there are several providers. Monthly charges work out from £10 per month and there are English speakers at the companies who can give quotes on initial installation costs. As I mentioned, ours had already been set up as part of the deal. English friends here have said their connection is faster than they can get back in the UK!

Weather

When we see the sun here we are learning that we don't have to rush out and make the most of it for fear of it disappearing the next day and we missed our chance! The summers are long here with temperatures in the mid to high 30's from the end of June till mid-October. In May it is in the high 20's and it isn't unknown for it to be that temperature in November either. Having sunshine more of the year is so uplifting and gives you a sense of wellbeing. It allows for the days to be fully enjoyed even into the balmy nights preceded by glorious sunsets. This is one of our favourite times of the day, especially accompanied by a cold drink and soft music.

Scenery

There are more than two hundred miles of wonderful, sandy beaches along the Black Sea Coast with water parks, water sports, great restaurants, shops and hotels with full spa facilities and historic sites offering something for everyone. In Western Bulgaria you'll find excellent ski facilities with the season running from November till April. Bansko, Pamporovo and Borovets are the most popular resorts, all easily reached within 3 hours from Sofia. The same mountains offer hiking, golf, pony trekking, mountain biking, quad bike safaris, and paintballing during the summer months and again there are fabulous hotels and restaurants to enjoy during your time there. The Rila mountain range is also home to the incredible Rila Monastery, Bulgaria's most visited tourist attraction and the Seven Lakes of Rila are a must-see location.

Scattered throughout Bulgaria are well preserved archeological sites including Roman and Thracian. Veliko Tarnovo, Plovdiv, Nessebar, Kazanlak to name but a few. One site in particular 'Perperikon' is where Alexander the Great is purported to have had his epiphany of conquering the world. The ground he stood on can be reached by a hefty climb and when you reach the top it is hard not to feel you are on top of the world! The country really is a treasure trove and once sampled, any preconceptions soon melt away.

Wildlife

With such a Mediterranean climate it is not surprising that there is an abundance of creepy crawlies in the rural areas but you hopefully won't find your house under attack by them. There are snakes, lizards and tortoises and in the woods you may see wild boar. The positive side to this is that there is so much life around from insects to birds and small mammals which keeps itself in balance naturally. It means we have seen an array of different species of birds, mammals and insects and feel very privileged to have done so. We might find one centipede or field cricket in the house every month, that isn't much to deal with. Fitting fly screens to the windows that open is a good defence against them. We never tire of watching the storks flying over our house in the summertime and eagle spotting in the mountains.

Community Life

There is a very strong sense of neighbourliness and friendship in the local community. It manifests itself not just in putting out fires, but in generally helping each other out in small but important ways. On public holidays, like the orthodox Easter Sunday, many of the locals will meet in the centre of the village. They'll bring food and drink from home or buy it from the stands available. There'll be traditional dancing which you'll be encouraged to join in with and is actually a lot of fun. Everyone from every generation takes part in the festivities and the atmosphere is really enjoyable. In our village, people exchange intricately painted hard boiled eggs instead of chocolate ones, and at the end of the occasion, the mayor will hand out free food and even a beer or glass of wine to all the adults, or soft drinks if they prefer. The music will end, the equipment will be packed up it will all move on to the next village.

In the bigger towns and cities they really pull out the stops for the festivities and the firework displays that light up the night sky on New Year's Eve are pretty spectacular too! We've found the acts of kindness and hospitality offered us since our arrival to be both many and incredibly sincere. There is a strong bond between the people themselves, the communities they live in and the land they work on. It teaches us a lot about what really matters in life. I mentioned earlier about the water supply problems. You will see everywhere across the country, natural springs in every village, they are scattered by the roadside everywhere and unless there is a warning sign attached to them by the authorities, the water is perfectly safe to drink. It is reassuring to know it is tested regularly!

The Language

There are probably a large number of ex-pats who can barely utter a word in Bulgarian, just as there are immigrants in the UK who have been there for years and can't speak English to save their lives. Travelling around gives you a new reflection on issues you may have had a different opinion on not that long ago.

There are many British people who speak fantastically fluent Bulgarian and we take our hats off to them. We are taking lessons from a very good and patient young teacher. She charges ten levs an hour and though we are far from where we would like to be, we can make ourselves understood in the village, shops and bars etc. At least we are trying and this is appreciated even when we get it wrong. It is challenging but does add to our enjoyment of life in general. We do have time on our side and we will master the language eventually.

Chris is very good at reading the road and other signs we come across. Luckily for us, many of them are in English anyway which is another bonus. Watching Bulgarian TV also helps pick up the language. Google translate is also a God send for requesting transaction statements in the bank. Fortunately for us, our local branch has more than one fluent English speaker and many younger Bulgarians are very good at speaking it. You will not be left high and dry.

There are quite a lot of similarities between Bulgarian, Russian and other eastern European languages which we have noticed. This gives us a little more confidence in making ourselves understood in surrounding countries, or at least being able to spot things we recognize on menus, road signs etc.

English TV

No problem, apart from the English language programs I mentioned earlier you can get Sky TV packages here, they are a little more expensive than in the UK but at least you can get them if you wish. There are other ways to watch most live UK programs through your laptop and your new English friends will be happy to tell you how to get them. You are unlikely to get a knock at your door from TV licensing staff two thousand miles from the UK!

Satellite TV

We have a 'Premium' package from Bulsat, the largest provider. It gives us the choice of 75 TV channels and 20 radio channels. It works out at less than £5 per month and currently if you pay 8 months up front you'll get 4 months free! This is an HD package, it contains the stations we sampled when visiting Sunny Beach. Mostly Bulgarian, with CNN, Eurosport, MTV, Discovery type channels and film channels, which are sometimes in English, so we find it great value for money.

Becoming a Resident

This is a simple process. First ring your translator for an appointment, meet them on the chosen day at the police station and fill in the forms, sign on the dotted line, get your picture taken in the same room, pay your modest fee and the translator's charge, leave the building and go and have lunch! That's it, done and dusted. The next step is to go back to the police station in a couple of weeks with the form they gave you, hand it over and you'll be walking out with your residency card that is valid for five years. You might get asked for your residency card when making purchases with your credit card, until you get it your passport is equally acceptable. You are supposed to keep your residency card on you at all times and there is a fine for not having valid ID with you (ten levs).

All paperwork processes in the country require everything being signed in triplicate, sometimes more, stamped, checked, and maybe stamped again before being completed. It's like the UK was thirty years ago, in fact some of the 'computers' used in official locations look like they fell off the back of a lorry or have been round the globe a few times before being bought at a car boot sale on the outskirts of Sofia. To be fair, there is no such thing as a throwaway society here, if it can be fixed why chuck it? There is ample evidence of this with the fleet of hand-me-down buses and trains from Germany that are used across the country. Even the bin lorry that comes round our village each week is still carrying its original decals from Greater Manchester where it started its career more than a decade ago.

Nothing happens quickly here but what's the rush? We rush enough in our lives and where does it get us? We remarked at the time, it's like going back in time about thirty years. The processes are long and drawn out, paperwork trails are still key and things we take for granted can take a number of attempts to achieve. However, most people have jobs, and computers have not replaced people, yet. We hope they learn from the issues in the west and don't adopt all of the measures and new technology, well known to us and labelled 'progress.'

Anyone who worked in an office thirty years ago as Chris did, would recognize the scene: four small workstations in a room, an in-tray on one side of each desk and out-tray on the other. Piles of paper waiting to be processed in the in-tray's; girls wearing casual dress and relaxed in processing their work. A window open, and a precession of external customers coming in and waiting at your desk to be seen. Even a communal box of chocolates was open on the spare desk. Chris said it was like deja-vu, it took her right back to her first years working at the local electricity board.

You'll need your own stamp when you buy a property here and getting it is part of the service you'll receive. It's very quick, easy and inexpensive. Just remember to manage your expectations, it can take several attempts to achieve what you set out to do. Your translator can always be of help so don't worry.

As I mentioned earlier, we had help setting up our company, bank and utility accounts and complete with your residency cards that is all you need in a nut shell. Simple!

Health Issues

There is no NHS in the country but there are English speaking doctors, dentists and vets available. Medical insurance costs around four hundred levs a year (£160) and the hospitals are scrupulously clean, there are no super bugs here and there are no waiting lists. Private hospitals have the very latest equipment and are as good as their counterparts in Western Europe. Feedback from ex-pats who have lived here six years or more, is very positive. They inform us that hospitals have specialist units and for the latest technology you need to find the right hospital for your issue. That said waiting lists are a thing of the past and the cost of surgery is more than affordable, especially if you belong to the country's health service. Vets are also abundant and very cheap compared to the UK. People travel here for high quality, affordable cosmetic surgery.

Power Supply

The main power provider is the Austrian owned EVN Company. They are doing their best to update the country's infrastructure but in the area we live in, power failures are not uncommon. Sometimes they last no more than a couple of hours, sometimes it has been three days. Most people have petrol generators as a standby measure.

Water Supply

In our area we will usually experience several failures a year. The extremes in temperature can cause cracking in sections of the pipe work; the longest time we were without mains water was five days. Each village has its own spring and so, with the aid of 11 litre containers and a wheelbarrow, it was possible to get enough water to fill the toilets and by leaving them out in the sun for a few hours we could jury rig an outside shower. Alternatively, we'd use a water shortage as a good excuse to go and stay somewhere else for a little while and do some exploring. We've cured the problem now by fitting a powerful pump to the bore hole well that the builder had installed near the vineyard. We now have water 24/7 and the cost of the pump was around £200

Drinking the water out of the taps here is probably best avoided due to the amount of limescale evident in our kettle. We haven't seen any official warnings about the quality of it but bottled water is so plentiful and cheap so it's best to stick to it instead. The country is lucky enough to have huge reserves of natural spring water and even the best, most expensive brands will not set you back more than £1.60 for eleven litres.

Working Options

Never having to work again? How many times have you been queuing at the check in at the airport to go home after a good holiday and realise you've only just started to unwind but now you've got to go back to work? A recent survey revealed that 1 in 4 of us has been in tears at the prospect of having to return to the grind of work. This book is the easiest way to prevent that situation from ever happening again. If you do have to work its only for things you want to do like travelling, socialising, gardening, home improvements, making your own wine and rakia etc. Looking at your alarm clock with fond nostalgia at half nine on a Monday morning or come to think of it, any weekday morning.

Of course I'd like this to be the reality for everyone, however if you do need supplementary income, there are several ways to achieve this. If you have a trade, you'll never be short of work. Friends of ours have opened their own shops including; UK foods, clothes & crafts, gifts, café's, bars, restaurants, beauty salons, and hairdressers. Another option is Internet working which is flexible in terms of where it can be done and will provide income in pounds, euros or dollars all of which are above the Bulgarian equivalent wage per hour. Another scenario we are aware of is where people spend a set number of months working in the UK to fund the rest of the year off in Bulgaria. There is a scenario to fit all requirements, achieving the right balance for your situation.

Work for us these days is all about managing and maintaining our assets; the gardening, house repairs, maintenance, decorating, financial investments, managing annual payments & obligations, practicing Reiki and other healing therapies, keeping on top of Bulgarian policy changes affecting us, planning and booking our trips around Europe. This leaves plenty of time for new hobbies like painting and writing!

Car maintenance

You must re-register your vehicle if you plan on remaining within the country longer than six months. If not, forget about it, but if you are going to go the whole hog, your translator can arrange the process. You can have the whole process completed, insurance arranged, taxes paid, documentation issued and shiny new number plates on your vehicle in around five hours. It will cost you approximately £400 and this process involves an inspection of the vehicle by a couple of mechanics. Your translator will doubtlessly reassure you that they won't find any issues to raise with your car. There would be no old bangers from a bygone age left on the roads if the annual inspections were as rigorous as they are at home.

In twelve months you will need to go for a new MOT which you can just turn up at a garage and ask for. You will need your documentation with you; the process takes about twenty minutes and costs between thirty to forty levs.

If you're like me and the limit of your mechanical expertise stretches to putting oil and water in the engine, checking your tyre pressures and changing a wheel (blowing my trumpet here but I have managed to take the back wheel off my motorbike, take it to have a puncture repaired and successfully replace it back on the bike) you'll want to know about keeping your vehicle looked after while you're here.

Bulgarian mechanics can fix just about anything from a lawnmower to a Tupelov airliner, the parts they use are generic to western Europe but the labour charges are a fraction of what you'll pay back home. You'll soon discover on the grape vine just which garages are popular with ex-pats, primarily because one of the mechanics speaks good English.

Buying a car is a simple enough process here, again you'll need your translator's assistance and whether it is a second hand or new one, it will be a lot less than the UK equivalent. I'm still running the Astra van as it is so cheap to tax, insure and run, it seems daft to sell it. There are already seven potential buyers for it in the village so I'll not be needing eBay for help. Which reminds me, you can buy things on eBay and they will find their way eventually to your main post office or be delivered by courier to your address if it is your passport you have sent off for, for instance. Some High Street brands do deliver to Bulgaria but it is a tad much to expect deliveries from your favourite supermarket in Croydon!

Shopping

Lidl has dozens of branches across Bulgaria as does Kaufland, a German owned store which has branches from within Germany right across to the Black Sea. There are many other smaller supermarkets around Bulgaria, however Kaufland, Billa and Lidl are the largest chains and can be found in all towns and cities. An equivalent can be found for most items on your shopping list, the things that we miss can be found at the ex-pat shops if you're willing to pay the extra money. These are items like sauces, pickles, bacon, double cream, biscuits. Once you have been here a while you start to enjoy the local foods and don't miss your old foods so much. Particular favourites are; Serene (white crumbly cheese), the cold meat selection including many varieties of salami, pickled vegetables and breads baked with fillings. The tasteless tomatoes and cucumbers are a thing of the past, here they are delicious. In the summer fresh vegetables are abundant and cheap so you can have a very healthy diet. It's fair to say we're still discovering new tastes but draw the line at things like pig's ears and sheep's head!

Some products like tuna and salmon cost the same as they do in the UK, lamb is more expensive than steak for some reason which is hard to get, and milk is quite expensive at 70p for 1 litre but for most other necessities the price is a heck of a lot less. You can fill a shopping trolley up for £60 which is good for two people for a week.

In the drinks section at Kaufland you will find a litre of Vodka, Gin, Bourbon or whisky for the equivalent of £4 a bottle. These are nationally produced with brand names that will make you smile. The familiar brands are available but obviously more expensive. Rakia is the national favourite and is very similar to brandy. The most popular derivatives of it come from either grapes or plums, though it is also made with apricots or peaches. There is a 'Still' in every town and village in the country and your new neighbours will be happy to show you how to go about making your own stuff.

The wine selection is excellent with all manner of Western European and North American vintages available in addition to the very good Bulgarian wines. Prices start from 3.50 lev a bottle. We have a couple of favourite Bulgarian wines, one is 5 lev (£2) the other 8 lev (£3.50). The more exclusive brands; Cycle, Khan Krum, and Karnobat are among the best that we've tried.

As I said when we had our first Bulgarian beer I was very impressed. We made it our mission to sample all brands, they are all very good and prices range from 80p to £1 for a two litre bottle. I especially enjoy the dark beer they bring out in the winter months, cautionary note: it is very strong! (6%) In the summer months there are lemon fresh and grapefruit fresh variants with reduced alcohol, perfect for a summers' day. The quality and price makes it very painful to purchase a pint in the UK now! Guinness is available here but relatively expensive at 3.45 lev a can, so not on our shopping list!

There are large modern shopping malls in Bulgaria's main cities which contain many of the outlets you'd find at home. They usually include a food court and cinema complex. It's nice to visit these if you're missing home. In smaller towns there are a wide variety of weird and wonderful shops! Old fashioned hardware shops are a plenty so you can find all household items you might ever need or want. Each town has a fresh fruit and vegetable market and often a meat market where quality is high but the prices are low. You will not find any GMO products in Bulgaria. High streets are very important to the community, it is very rare to see a boarded up shop, this gives the impression that everything is ticking over nicely and people are thriving. Perhaps Bulgaria has a better way of nurturing small businesses than we do in the UK?

Restaurants

Even in a small town such as Yambol, we have been surprised to discover just how many high standard restaurants there are and with unbelievable prices compared to the UK. It's not uncommon to get a good meal for two including drinks for £7. The menu choices are varied and they often feature grilled meats, liver and kidney, stews, soups, along with an impressive range of salads. There are usually a wide range of wines available that can be expensive, however if you choose half a carafe of house wine you can expect to pay around £2.50. A large 500ml beer in a restaurant will set you back about £1.

Along with traditional Bulgarian restaurants, you can find Irish, Italian, Turkish, Greek, Chinese and the odd Indian. In tourist cities you'll also find English menus offered. We discovered early on that you can get roast beef dinners and real bacon sarnies at ex-pat run restaurants and cafes which is massively reassuring! Although we have discovered that Bulgarian cuisine is actually very good and many visitors prefer it to the other choices available. What we really like, above the great choices in food and drink, is enjoying wining and dining in the outdoor sections. There are dozens of places with fantastically relaxing beer gardens, water features, overhead grape vines and sitting under large parasols, enjoying a great meal and a cold one, it really feels like you are on holiday. The restaurants and cafes that line the beaches between Burgas in the south and Varna in the north are a revelation. Sharing these experiences with our families and friends has been massively rewarding. They have all been stunned with what they have discovered and enjoyed about a country they knew (like us in the beginning) next to nothing about.

Café's

Bulgarian coffee is strong and sweet in a small measure similar to an expresso. If you like long coffee with milk as we do, you'll struggle to find anything similar. Cappuccino is the closest and in many café's Nescafe '3 in 1' or '2 in 1' sachets are the best you will get. It's a good excuse to go to the 'big city' every now and then, to find Starbucks or Costa's for a coffee fix!

Tea is served black or green and you have to ask if you want milk. Due to the language barrier, we ended up with green tea and milk one time which is not recommended!

On the plus side, no one bats an eyelid if you go and buy food and bring it to your table which is a nice change. We can also do the same at our local cinema. In fact, our local cinema is so easy going that if their own shop has run out of chocolate, crisps, popcorn or beer then they'll happily point you in the direction of the nearest shop and welcome you back in with your stash. There is none of that business of trying to stuff every pocket you have with fairly priced minstrels and m&m's, then trying to walk innocently past staff at the screen entrance without making a crunching sound!

Toilets

In this respect Bulgaria shows why it sits behind the rest of Europe when it comes to the toilet. It is not uncommon to find in many bars that the WC is just a hole in the ground with foot marks. Some are cleaner than others, some even have a flushing chain or a handy hose pipe for washing away any spills. This sounds horrendous to those of us from over the English Channel and we wonder how on earth do the locals manage with it, particularly the elderly? As a man they are not that problematic but for the ladies, well, going out for the night in your favourite outfit becomes a lot more challenging! Some bars have a communal hole in the ground and, thanks in no part to the negative comments from many British and other ex-pats, they are being phased out but this is a slow process. To be fair, across other parts of Europe it is not that unusual to discover similar 'facilities' and we have gotten used to it. I always remember the cafe in Paris with the smiling French lady and have accepted that Europeans are more uninhibited in many areas, not just the toilets and this helps to explain the more relaxed attitude to life in general.

Over time, we've discovered where to find the bars, cafes and restaurants with proper facilities. Petrol stations generally have very good facilities, they don't charge a fee like the German autobahn service areas but we'll buy a token chocolate bar if we've not bought fuel.

Like many poorer European nations, some of Bulgaria's sewage infrastructure really is a load of crap. The pipework often cannot cope with paper and there will be signs on the wall asking for the bins to be used instead. It didn't take long to get used to this however, but it is a little embarrassing asking visitors to our house to do the same. Perhaps we'll have to make up a sign instead!

Like many rural properties, we have a septic tank at the far corner of the garden and in the three years we've been here, we haven't experienced any horrendous incidents at all and when it does need emptying eventually, George across the road will send a mate with a tractor and vacuum tank trailer round to do the necessary for us, this will set us back around forty quid.

If you buy a modern apartment somewhere, you won't have to do this, and if you have the know-how, you can always sling out the old, hopeless pipework and fit modern, 21st century plumbing instead.

Crime

Being targeted by the mafia? Not as stupid as it sounds, one of my friends from England was convinced we'd fall foul of them. We'd seen part of Ross Kemp's series on gangs when we had spent some time in Edinburgh. It was about the effect of criminal gangs in the city of Plovdiv, one of Bulgaria's largest and oldest cities. I say "seen" it but that's a bit inaccurate. The hotel we'd stayed at had negative reviews on the quality of the TV reception in the rooms and promises were made by the management to fix it. Months later we turned up and nothing had been done to fix it. We could hear but not see the program. We could hear Ross Kemp talking to a gang member but we were stumped when we couldn't read the subtitles of his reply. During our stay in the Scottish capital we saw the film *"The Best Exotic Marigold Hotel"* and like millions of others we thoroughly enjoyed it. We couldn't help noticing the parallels with what we were doing and the characters that'd gone to India. I'd asked Nick about the Mafia. He replied that most people knew who they were and what they did but if you kept out of their business they would keep out of yours. People also assumed that anyone driving a big, expensive car was Mafiosi, they're probably right. It's widely suspected that number plates featuring four of the same number are Mafia owned. You won't find a thirty year old 'Lada' with that kind of number plate, so perhaps these are more than just rumours!

Plovdiv doesn't sound the most enticing of places to visit but this is the modern derivative of the city's original name Phillipousis. This being the name of the city's founder King Phillip II of Macedon, father of Alexander the Great. The city has some fantastic Roman sites to visit and the whole country is in fact the third best in Europe for Roman architectural sites and museums.

Corruption

A friend mentioned how he got pulled by the police for speeding and the officer asked him "Ticket or no ticket?" He thought about it and said no ticket; "Twenty levs" came the reply. He handed over the money and was let on his way. Of course corruption goes on in official circles, right to the very highest levels but this is not unique to Eastern Europe or Russia. It goes on everywhere and in every country. The more industrialised countries have found more sophisticated ways of describing it or hiding it but it is essentially the same thing. The EU, for instance, has not had its accounts signed off by any auditor worthy of the title since the mid 1990's because of widespread and systemic fraud, nepotism and corruption running into billions upon billions of euros. The whistle blower who uncovered this situation was not promoted, he was not praised for uncovering this misuse of public money, he was sacked and his name rubbished in the business community making him unemployable. Bulgaria need take no lessons or lectures from any outside agency.

Unstable government

The Bulgarian people are not shy in making their feelings known on any given subject, whether it is political corruption or unfair and unaffordable increases in electric bills, they will take to the streets and protest until something is done to remedy the situation. As a result, politicians know they cannot take the electorate for granted. This gives us confidence that the Bulgarian society is headed in the right direction. Italy has had more than forty governments come and go since the end of the Second World War yet they seem to have, on the whole, a good standard of living. Since the end of communism, coalition governments have become the norm in Bulgaria. As the UK has now experienced a coalition government themselves, life carries on quite normally and is not a problem.

Security in the Banking Sector

Since Bulgaria is a member of the European Union, their banks are obliged to offer the same levels of guarantees to their deposit holders that you will find in the UK or other member states.

But when you look at the amount of taxpayer money given to just one UK bank, Lloyds to the sum of twenty billion pounds amongst a dozen others, and the taking of customer money in exchange for shares in Cyprus in 2013, is any financial institution truly safe and run in accordance with the rules? Probably not, with situations like the Libor scandal and the manipulation of the precious metal and oil prices amongst many other commodities, and in any case this is even more of a reason to get out of the rat race with your money and escape.

Since we've been in Bulgaria interest rates have fallen, however they are still higher than in the UK. It is still possible here to live off the interest on your savings. There was an issue with certain banks liquidity in the summer of 2014, which had the potential to crash the Bulgarian banking system. We were reassured and impressed by the way this was handled and the savings guarantee process was upheld.

Tax Considerations

Another consideration is beating the tax man. He has been,very sneakily and stealthily, pulling more and more people into inheritance tax by not moving the tax thresholds of property values as they have soared during the last 25 years. It is called fiscal drag and means that people of modest means are now paying the amounts of tax that only applied once to the very wealthy. Don't feel too bad for the tax man, he has been letting his mates from the corporate elite avoid paying £25 billion every year by not clamping down on tax avoidance schemes. If you sell your house, pay off your debts etc., you will be able to legitimately avoid being stung for inheritance tax and you'd be able to help your children get a leg up in life rather than them having to wait for you to snuff it. It is a win-win scenario, particularly if thousands of people left for a better life and the Chancellor would have to pursue the colossal sums from the big boys after all.

For non-Bulgarian citizens, tax on savings interest is currently 10%.

Future Prosperity

Bulgaria is the poorest member state of the Union but paradoxically it is one of the few nations in the world that actually has a current account surplus. The UK owes £1.4 trillion pounds and rising, the US over $16 trillion. Sooner or later these huge economic chickens are going to come home to roost and when they do, the fallout from it will be nothing short of colossal. The only way is up for Bulgaria no matter how long it takes.

National Security and Occupation from Russia

There is a split in the population between young and old as to those who would not mind being part of a new USSR. Many believe they were better treated and better off under the old system than they are today. Many younger people feel that they haven't yet received the better life that they were promised when communism collapsed twenty-five years ago. Bulgaria is a member of NATO and the chances of an invasion from across the Black Sea are incredibly remote, probably the same as being killed by a terrorist: 25 million to one.

What happens if I need help?

Whatever situation you might be faced with, there is a very strong support network here amongst fellow ex-pats, your translator will be happy to help with issues like tax returns, residency permits, registering with GP's, and most other scenarios that life might throw at you. They charge ten levs an hour and the peace of mind that this help brings is invaluable.

You will not be alone, cut off or adrift from the rest of the world. In fact, you'll discover more of it than you may ever have dreamed possible. There are numerous Facebook community groups where you can ask about anything you are faced with, or interested about and lots of willing members will impart their knowledge and experience.

The emergency services can be reached by dialling 112. The police officers in our local town have been given English lessons in the last few years so that, in the unlikely event of you needing their help, you will be able to make yourselves understood. The Fire Service - hmm, I've seen the equipment at our local fire station. No disrespect but the majority of the fire engines appear so old the fire-fighting instructions are in Latin. They are modernising their equipment and the dedication of their crews is not in question. From what we've heard, most people in the outer villages like ours on the outbreak of a fire, depend on neighbours to rally around together to put out the flames. A bell at the mayor's office will be rung by the first person available to alert everyone else and put out the fire before the fire brigade arrives. This isn't due alone to a lack of faith in the Fire Service.

You aren't billed in your council tax for the emergency services so you will be liable for a bill if you need their services. This isn't as bad as it sounds though. How many times in your life have you needed the police or fire brigade in the last twenty years? I've needed the help of the police perhaps four times, the fire brigade came to my door in Retford during the flood, I didn't call them. If I worked out the amount of council tax I've paid in all that time in comparison to the help given, I could probably have gone on an around the world cruise, first class.

Missing family and friends

This is the hardest issue to deal with and we would be lost without Skype. By having a home here we actually spend more quality time with parents, children and friends by having them out here for holidays. The cost of dining out and buying shopping is half the price and as they stay with us, there are no hotel bills which makes it a cheap holiday for visitors. This is a stark contrast when we go back to the UK, where we find the price of food, drink and hotels is eye wateringly expensive! The tip here is to book your hotels well in advance for the offers and similarly, the flight prices are cheaper booked in advance where possible.

Lifestyle Changes

I often reflect on how I used to spend my Saturday mornings after a long week at work. The chance to have a lie in instead of my 4am alarm call was bliss, until the 0630 to Kings Cross went thundering past, 200 yards from the end of my garden. Then it'd be the 0650 to York, the 0700 to Kings Cross, the 0715 to Edinburgh, that one always rattled the doors and windows!

Now, I'll go for a walk under warm, blue skies, along a quiet lane occasionally lined with fruit trees, gazing at the mountains beyond and the storks drifting over my head. Sometimes I'll see an eagle, one flew so low near to me that I could see it scratching itself under its chin with a huge yellow talon, before it gracefully flew away over the fields and out of sight. I try to run 5 kilometres a few times a week as well. In these temperatures it has helped me lose around fifteen kilograms, the fantastic salads have helped in that process as well. I'm in the best health I've been in for probably fifteen years or more.

I can do these things on any morning, not just the weekends and that is priceless to me. I've put in twenty years of sixty-five or more hours a week driving trucks. I've driven another four-hundred-thousand miles on top of that doing my courier work. I figure I've put in a life's work of graft already and feel no guilt whatsoever for having effectively retired at the age of forty-five.

Chris has similarly powerful reasons for doing what we have since January 2012. We wanted a base that we could afford without a mortgage, without debt and the chance to explore Europe together. It has worked out better than we could ever have imagined. We've driven right across Europe and back again, we've driven down to Piraeus via Mount Olympus, left the car behind for five euros a day in a secure underground car park and gone island hopping to Santorini. We went up the Ionian coast past Kefalonia, across the mountains to Thessaloniki and back to Bulgaria. We never got stuck in a single traffic jam, yes the journey to the port cost twenty-five euros in tolls but the result was empty highways, stunning scenery and sheer driving pleasure.

We've driven along the French Riviera, the Italian Azure coast, stayed in the Austrian alpine village where the legendary movie '*Where Eagles Dare*' was filmed. We're planning future trips across Switzerland on our way to the UK, I have an urge to drive on a circular trip from Sofia to the top of Finland, then return along the edges of the fjords, Copenhagen and a ferry trip to Hamburg and eventually home again.

Before we even drove on to the ferry on that distant January evening three years ago, two certainties comforted us. What we were setting out to do would be extraordinary and the second was that we would be together 24/7, every step of the journey. What has been an incredible bonus ever since has been the number of times we have been literally stopped in our tracks by a sight, a view of such beauty and wonder it has taken our breath away. There have been too many to list, we still experience them regularly and there is no reason for this to change for the foreseeable future.

I've experienced so many special moments in the last three years, learned new things and met so many interesting people along the way that if I was struck by lightning tomorrow I'd go to the next world incredibly happy. No regrets, just a wonderful ride. That's what I want as my epitaph! I'm grateful for everything that has happened to me in my life both good and bad, they've brought me to where I am today and I wouldn't have it any other way.

Talking of epitaphs I have to mention one last consideration in our journey - death.

Passing Over & Funerals

This is the ultimate taboo in our lives. We have been conditioned to be terrified of it, to do anything but talk about it when really, it is the great leveller that awaits us all, rich or poor, prince or pauper. Our fear of dying has kept us in thrall to those who claim to keep it from our door as much as is possible. In reality, those claiming to be our saviours and benefactors have been the ones who have caused utter carnage and destruction throughout our history. The sad reality is that there is no profit to be made from peace. War makes vast amounts of money while keeping the people in an endless state of fear. The cycle continues endlessly, new enemies continue to be found whether real or imaginary and the status quo continues largely unchecked. Jimi Hendrix summed the situation up perfectly when he said "When the power of love overcomes the love of power, the world will know peace," This day will dawn when the majority of us have had enough of war. From conversations we've had with people across the continent, it will happen sooner than the powers that be actually expect.

Eventually, when one of us dies the cost involved in burying or cremating us is obscenely expensive. Many of us struggle just to live at all so it really is a kick to where it hurts that we can't afford to die either[10]. Proof if it were needed that our society has gone utterly mad!

The process seems so cold and clinical that the human element has almost been overlooked. In Bulgaria, the neighbours rally around when someone passes away. Help is provided with funeral arrangements, a coffin is made locally and the deceased person remains in their home one last night before being interred the next day.

A friend of ours lost her husband recently after a long and debilitating illness. She found the experience of having him in the house one last night to be incredibly comforting. All the signs of pain lifted from his face and he visibly looked to be at peace. His body was transported to the cemetery on a simple cart, pulled by his own horse and the Orthodox priest gave a very calming sermon. Though she couldn't understand all of his words, the kindness and sincerity were very evident and she found the entire experience to be very natural and dignified. The cost involved is but a fraction of what it is in the UK, the rallying around of friends and neighbours is massively comforting to all concerned. I will have no qualms about being laid to rest near our home when the time comes. I don't plan on it happening anytime soon, in fact I plan on living forever, or to die trying.

The body dies, the mind or soul is energy, and any good (or bad one, come to think of it) physicist will tell you that energy cannot be destroyed, only relocated or transmuted.

Whether that relocation is the Spirit World, a parallel universe or a doorway to another dimension, is immaterial. I believe we go on to another world, complete in spirit but without our physical bodies.

Many people down the ages have described near death experiences and the one constant they all articulate is the sensation of complete, unconditional love that is there. Our long lost friends and loved ones are there, even our beloved pets!

I certainly believe it is better than the vision handed down by 'official' religious institutions down the centuries. These organisations, similar to our political institutions like to say all the right things while behaving in the opposite direction. How can you be made to believe in the Ten Commandments yet made to sing 'Onward Christian soldiers, marching off to war?"

Thou shalt not covet? How does this square with building the largest empire the world has ever seen? Did we march across Africa and the sub-continent from a fine sense of altruism or did we believe from our military might that we could take what we wanted, where we wanted? Food for thought…

DRIVING IN EUROPE

Road movies are among the most favourite genres on the big screen. We love them because deep down we want to be that person, freed from the chains of responsibility and obligation and revelling in new experiences, new surroundings and the means to go where you will.

'*Top Gear*' is enjoyed by tens of millions round the world precisely because of the amazing challenges they get to enjoy. '*Long Way Round*' was another massively successful series chronicling Ewan McGregor and Charley Boorman's trip around the planet. Who wouldn't want some of that excitement?

Modern cars are far better built than their counterparts of thirty years ago. If they haven't been abused they are easily capable of giving over two hundred thousand miles service or more. In July of 2006 when I started working as a self-employed courier I bought a six-year-old Vauxhall Combo 1.4 petrol/LPG van with 50,000 miles on the clock. By the end of 2008 the mileage had increased to 240,000 and in that time, apart from replacing two alternators, tyre changes, new brake pads and a few headlight bulbs, the only maintenance performed on it were regular oil and filter changes plus replacing the cam belt at each 80,000 mile mark. No oil leaks, no water leaks, same clutch, same exhaust, same battery and suspension. I think that's pretty good going and in the end it was a water pump failure that took out the engine just after passing 240,000 miles. Nine times round the world and it could have been more if I'd thought to have replaced the water pump before it went but it gave no indication it was on its last legs.

The van I replaced it with saw me clock up another 150,000 miles with regular oil and filter changes and nothing more than brake pads and tyres. No oil leaks, water leaks, same exhaust, battery clutch etc. The Astra van I still have is now up to 134,000 miles and has been to the UK and back here twice. I haven't had to replace the turbo either, this I put down to not having a heavy right foot and though it might not be that exciting, neither is getting a repair bill of over a thousand pounds every 50,000 miles. I fully expect it to reach 200,000 miles before replacing it again. The upshot is 420,000 miles without adhering to the service guide from the main dealers. Like Captain Barbosa said in "*Pirates of the Caribbean*", "They're more mere guidelines than rules" and had I adhered to every suggested action in the service booklet the cost to me would have made my job economically unviable. I have managed to do this by keeping a good distance between myself and the vehicle in front, using engine braking as much as possible, (this has enabled me to clock up as many as 90,000 miles between brake pads) and keeping my speed at around 60 mph or 100kmh outside urban areas and on motorways. This means I don't have to worry about police speed traps and reduces wear and tear on the engine. It also has the benefit of knocking 20% off my fuel bill that could go to better causes like buying our dinner in the evening! It's called defensive driving and combines all of the above with looking as far ahead in front of you as you can and read the road conditions more effectively. This has the added advantage that you'll arrive at your destination more relaxed and will have seen more on your journey other than trying to keep up with the traffic flow. If you've decided to leave the rat race long behind you, you don't have schedules to keep or meetings to get to, it's liberating to let all that angst disappear from your life and just enjoy the journey.

If you haven't decided to quit, the above tips will still save you a small fortune in running costs and down-time. Driving on the continent is often portrayed as too scary, too many lunatic drivers, poor or unreadable road signs, corrupt police, bandits, pickpockets and other undesirables to deal with. As I've described earlier, the truth is somewhat different. Driving can be a pleasure once again and the above techniques can add to the experience by keeping your costs and stress levels to a minimum.

You'll need your Euro travel kit before you board the ferry. You can get these from Halfords, the channel ports or onboard the ferries. You'll also need your two breathalyser kits by law in France, (I've never been asked to show them on any part of my journeys across France, twice now we've never even had our passports checked at Dover or Calais!) but its best to have them anyway. I also bought a small fire extinguisher as it is compulsory to have one in Bulgaria and Greece, though again, I've never been asked to show it to a traffic cop in these countries.

You will also need both parts of your driving licence, your MOT certificate and V5 logbook, the originals not photocopies. You won't need an international driving licence unless you are going somewhere well off the beaten track like Mongolia, China or Russia. Another must is a good quality satnav. I'd recommend a Tom-Tom or Garmin, preferably with Europe mapping already supplied. I have a Garmin Nuvi 50LM as it comes with mapping for forty-five countries and has been an invaluable companion for us, though sadly this one doesn't have the 'Yoda' option. I also bought an AA map of Europe as a backup, another good investment. I've covered driving across France, Portugal and Spain and even taking the big cities into consideration, it was some of the most pleasurable driving I have ever encountered. I'd put it on a par with driving around Death Valley and Yosemite Park in California or along stretches of the old Route 66 in Arizona.

Belgium and Holland can also provide enjoyable motoring experiences, though the main route east from Calais and Dunkirk (the E40 and E34) will be very busy with freight traffic and the best time to use them is early morning or better still the weekend. The vast majority of trucks are off the road by law unless they are carrying perishables and won't be back on them till early Monday morning. There are economists who believe this is madness but at least the drivers get to spend weekends with their families which I think is more socially acceptable than making a few extra pounds in profit. Some of the road surfaces on the E411 south east of Brussels are appalling and great care is needed to avoid damage to your suspension. Clearly Belgium isn't as well off as we'd believe because this road surface would normally be completely unacceptable to motorists and businesses alike.

Germany is full of unrestricted sections of autobahn and you need to be watchful of black or silver cars (the favourite colours of 90% of Germans) coming up behind you at speeds approaching warp factor seven. The roadside services put ours to shame, the food is fantastic and very reasonably priced. You have to pay seventy cents to use the toilets but you will get a voucher to recoup this in the restaurant. You won't get charged ten quid either if you stay beyond two hours.

Austria has vignettes and tolls on some sections of motorway, mainly the alpine sections. The vignette price is €8.50 for ten days and the cost of the tolls is worth every cent for the breathtaking views through the mountains.

Driving through Slovenia or Hungary towards the rest of Central and Eastern Europe is very straightforward as well. You'll need vignettes for Slovenia (they have put them up to €15 for ten days), Hungary, and the Czech Republic. Croatia and Serbia have tolls on their motorways but these are again a pleasure to drive and well worth the small cost. There are road signs in English in all these countries and plenty of roadside adverts, too. Any concerns I initially had about driving through Serbia have since been put to rest.

The border staff speak good English, are polite, professional and courteous. Border crossings between Croatia, Slovenia, Serbia and Hungary are nothing to worry about. They usually last no more than fifteen minutes, often no more than five and you will be on your way again.

The cost of fuel is a lot less than it is in the UK. Euros are accepted in Croatia to pay for your tolls and the forecourt shops on the motorway network also exchange euros into Croatian Kuna making other purchases easier. It also works out cheaper at the toll booths to pay in the local currency.

Greece has a brilliant road network, roadside services and again, the road signs are in English as well as Greek, even the overhead gantry signs on the motorways. These have tolls but again, like Austria, they are worth it for the spectacular scenery and less congested roads. I have heard some folk say they are nervous about travelling to Greece because of the levels of public protests in the streets regarding the punishing levels of austerity inflicted on the country. Having driven from close to the border with Turkey right down to Athens, Sparta and back up along the Ionian coast past Kefalonia and Corfu and back, we have never seen any trouble or felt remotely threatened. Unless you wander around the country espousing the virtues of Goldman Sachs and the European Central Bank you will find only warm hospitality and kindness coming your way.

At the time of writing this book, we haven't yet explored Turkey which is crazy as it is only 40 minutes' drive to the border and another 3 hours on to Istanbul. It is yet another adventure waiting to be undertaken among many others…

I have to temper the good stuff with a serious word of warning. The border between Slovakia and Hungary is known to the police as a high risk crime zone. Gangs target the vehicles of foreign drivers when they are parked at service stations 15 miles either side of the border. They cut a small square shape on the inside of a tyre wall which isn't enough to puncture it but it will cause the tyre to blow out when higher speeds are reached. This will happen within minutes of the unsuspecting motorist resuming their journey and they will be helped by a seemingly good Samaritan who pulls over to warn you about a fire coming from what remains of one of your tyres. While they are showing you this, an unseen colleague will slip out of the other vehicle, unseen and unheard by the noise of passing traffic and help themselves to anything of value in the front of your car. By the time the victim has realized this, the perpetrators are long gone and over the border.

Don't leave your motor out of sight, if there is no space to park outside the forecourt shop, leave a passenger with the car, or better still, plan your fuel and rest stops at least half an hour away from the border. You will not have any problems with the rest of your journey. Don't be overly worried by this warning, common sense is all that is needed and the bad parts of driving in Europe are literally dwarfed by the enjoyable aspects!

PRACTICAL STEPS
(PROPERTY SEARCH & OPTIONS)

Whilst there is specific reference to Bulgaria in some places, these steps are generic and can be applied to a search in any country.

Research

Your adventure begins!

Find out as much as you can about your selected location/s. Things like property taxes and legal requirements for residency vary drastically across countries. Your research can be done a number of ways.

- Internet searches of overseas property agents e.g. Rightmove Overseas (Warning! If you look at these you may find your own head spinning uncontrollably with ideas, excitement, opportunities & dreams)
- Talking to ex-pats via Facebook groups and other network sites. Asking questions about lifestyle and practicalities to satisfy any concerns or issues.
- Reading books and articles written by ex-pats or about them and about the country in

question. Lots of amazing information can be found in travel books, the *'Dorling Kindersley Eyewitness Travel'* range are very good.

- Attending travel shows like *'A Place in the Sun'* roadshow which has events annually with lots of information on buying a house overseas.
- Watching the TV shows featuring people buying abroad and the house prices available such as *'A Place in the Sun'*, *'A Dream Home Abroad'*, *'Escape to the Continent'*.

Selection

This is your choice!

All the steps necessary to buy the house are included in the price with most agents, their staff speak good English and they are both thorough and professional. They also have properties on the coast to tantalize you with and the ski areas have all year round facilities to enjoy. The prices are cheaper in the ski resorts than the coast and are only a couple of hours drive from Sofia or Plovdiv airports. Decisions, decisions but it's great to be spoilt for choice!

Select your criteria:

As with any house purchase, you need to decide the purpose of your property; is it holiday only, seasonal or full time living.

Do you want to be in the country, rural village, the mountains, by the sea or in a town/city? Consider transport links and local amenities you require.

Do you want a plot of land to build your own place, a renovation project (where planning permission is already granted), a partially renovated property, a fully renovated property, a fully renovated and furnished property, a modern building i.e. apartment or complex with facilities and security? Consider the re-sale potential of a property if your plan is to sell it on, or the rental options if you will only use the property for certain weeks a year.

Choose properties you want to view, and request a viewing online or by phone call.

Contact details of the agents can be found on the websites and you can request appointments to suit you. You can ask for a translator to be on hand, but would incur their hourly rate. The agents speak a small amount of English usually. Alternatively if you like a place, arrange a second visit including a translator so that all of your questions can be answered fully.

Plan

The fun part!

Once you have selected the properties you want to view, plan your trip. Visit the country for as long as you can to get the feel of the place and see as much as possible.

Friends of ours were able to book a month over in Bulgaria to explore several regions and decide where they could see themselves living. It is possible to rent in most regions and get the local feel. The ex-pat groups will help you with contacts for rental properties in their area. If you only have a small window of time to visit, do more of the research mentioned above and fine tune your search to a particular region or a couple of regions that you can cover in your trip. Choose which time of year you want to see the country in, it may be wise to see it out of holiday season, if you plan to live there full time.

This would also be a good opportunity to meet up with some ex-pats that you've contacted online through the various groups, ask people in your chosen area if they are able to meet up and give you some local information. This may help your decision making process.

If possible, take advantage of cheap flight offers to Burgas, Varna, Sofia or Plovdiv, be astonished at the number of great value hotels available in those cities. The choice of rooms available in the ski areas or on the coast is huge and brilliant value and makes viewing apartments there a very easy process.

Determine which airport is closest to your chosen region and find flights and accommodation. We have found *Skyscanner* is a good flight comparison site and *booking.com* is usually best for hotels.

For those of you with more time, hiring a car and exploring the four corners of the country to find your dream location is also a great option.

Visit

The really fun part!

Whichever area you want to explore you'll soon discover how much better it is to see it up close and personal. All will have stunning scenery, fabulous restaurants and not be too far from the airport or big cities with their modern shopping malls and other attractions.

Try to balance the need to be focused on your objective, with the ability to relax and take in your surroundings. Enjoy searching out restaurants and bars you like the look of and sample what they have to offer.

If you have a week, arrange viewings every other day to give you time in between to digest what you've seen and analyse the possibilities. This method worked well for us, and we then had a spare day at the end of the week to arrange second viewings of our favourites.

If your budget allows, you could have an apartment in the ski areas AND one near the beach. You could rent one out and get some income while living in the other. Decisions, decisions....again!

Review Options

The serious part!

Now it's time to analyse your findings and decide which of the properties satisfy your criteria and how you want to proceed. You may want to arrange another viewing of your favourite at this stage just to confirm your decision. This is perhaps best done over dinner and unless you don't like what you have seen and can't wait to go home (unlikely, but it isn't for everyone), your heads will be spinning (again) at the choices available to you.

Consider how you would make the move work. How will you be financing your property purchase and running costs; will it be from savings and monthly pension income, rental income from the UK or a wage. Will it be an outright (cash) purchase, or will you be seeking finance and repayment terms. There will be annual maintenance costs to enter into the equation too. This analysis will help you decide how much you can commit to for the purchase price.

Friends of ours have set up businesses here in Bulgaria; hairdressing, nail manicures, holistic therapies, gift shops, cafés, building services, joinery, plumbing, electricians, to name a few. Others are working online jobs, teaching English which is a very good way of bringing some income in regardless of where you reside.

You could also buy an additional property where rental income is maximized and provides a good return.

There is a spectrum of options, these are some of the ways we have witnessed and discussed amongst the expats:

- Stay in a caravan on your plot and renovate or build your own house
- Live in your partial derelict house and renovate yourself
- Pay for local builders to renovate your property to your requirements and stay locally in a hotel, or rental house to supervise the project
- Recruit a builder to project manage and renovate your house, while you go back to the UK and wait until its ready to move into
- Bring your own team of builders (friends) over and spend the summer working on your renovation and getting it ready for occupation. This would be a great recipe for you to build each other's houses for very little cost and all move out to live.
- Buy two places one ready to live in and another as a renovation project, and supervise a building team
- Take out a long term rental in your chosen area. Get used to the place and locals and way of life before committing to a purchase
- Seasonal residency, staying for certain months (summer usually) then working and living back in the UK until full transition is possible.

- Working several months in the UK then having several months off here living on the proceeds. Flexible contract working arrangements.
- Buying a property as a 'Summer House' using it only for holidays and retreats

I'm sure there are other scenarios, but this is to demonstrate that there are lots of options and ways of implementing your dream way of life.

Once you've decided on a property your agent will be with you every step of the way in purchasing your dream home. An independent translator will accompany you to the Notary's office to ensure you are reassured and confident in the purchasing process and with this help you can easily complete the paperwork necessary. Remember, you don't have to form a company to buy property anymore. Your translator will be able to help with issues like not for profit tax returns if you are going to be happily retired. They can also help if you are going to try and run a business - you will not be left out in the cold, all the help you need will be available. A deposit is usually required to start the process of purchase to secure the property and take it off the market.

Whether you want a permanent home, holiday apartment or investment opportunity, they're all here for you. There's no rush either, the gap between the UK and Bulgaria is not going to close for many years, probably decades so you will still have the chance to try a new life in the future if you decide you can't do it now.

Another factor to consider if you like the sound of the rural life, growing your own fruit and veg, making your own wines and enjoying the sense of community it brings is the weather. Heavy snowfalls often result in power cuts and blocked roads but these aren't that insurmountable if you have stocked up before it happens. The large amounts of gardens that you'll have do require a lot of work during the summer, I enjoy this as it helps keep me fit, I enjoy a few grapes from the vines or plums or cherries in between work before joining Chris up on the terrace for a couple of hours sunbathing. This beats being stuck in heavy traffic or crowded commuter trains any day but if this isn't your scene, having an apartment near the sea or up in the mountains removes the idea of grafting in the garden altogether.

The very worst thing that will have happened is that you've had a cheap holiday in the sun; the very best thing is you may have just found the life of your dreams!

Initiate Move

A Feeling of Liberation!

If you are moving house completely as we did, the transport of your belongings is the next consideration. There are a few options to choose from:

- Buy your own van, drive your belongings over, sell the van in due course - if you like the challenge and have cash to buy the vehicle.
- Rent a van, empty the contents, then take it back to the UK - very time consuming, tiring and costly since you hire it for a number of days, which can be difficult to keep to given recent border delays.
- Hire space with a removal company for them to transport your belongings (insured option) - most costly, but least hassle.

I described in chapter ten how we brought our belongings over from England. It was an adventure that we both enjoyed and at least we were able to keep an eye on our belongings by day and park them somewhere safe at night. This isn't everyone's cup of tea and there are the alternatives I described.

If you want to move small amounts at a time, you have the option of driving them across in your car or having one of the many transport companies bring your goods to Bulgaria. You can order items in the UK and bring them over this way too, for things you can't find out here. These deliveries are usually charged by weight.

The important thing is, by this point your transition has begun, you are 'leaping into the unknown' but that's the zone where we really live, and the amazing stuff happens!!

EPILOGUE
January 2016

Events have changed dramatically since I began writing this book and I feel obliged to talk about them with complete honesty.

Interest rates here have dropped sharply and now offer the same miserable returns as those in the UK. The explanation for this from the government stems from the collapse of the Credit and Commercial Bank and the deliberate undermining of one of the country's largest banks, the First Investment Bank. False rumours of the impending collapse of this bank on social media sites caused the kinds of scenes we saw in Britain when Northern Rock and the Royal Bank of Scotland were teetering on the brink.

First Investment did not go under, it was given the backing of the Bulgarian National Bank, its deposit account holders received the full protection of their savings as guaranteed by the European Union agreement and it has already paid back half the loans it received from the National Bank.

The perpetrators of the false rumours have been convicted and jailed for their crimes; theirs was a modern take on the kinds of scams carried out by unscrupulous families in New York at the turn of the 20th Century to buy up successful banks for pennies on the dollar.

As a result of these shenanigans, the option to live off the interest from your savings has been wrecked for good but the strong pound has helped to cushion the blow. We've seen our spending power increase from what was already a good starting point by more than 10%.

As mentioned before, the UK state pension is eight times higher than the Bulgarian equivalent and in five years I can access my private pension. Chris and I are going to be able to live very, very comfortably for the rest of our lives.

The vast numbers of refugees from Syria fleeing their war torn country, desperate to reach safety and a new life have filled TV screens and newspaper headlines across the world. Millions of them have already reached Western Europe and Scandinavia and when the spring arrives who knows how many more will attempt the agonizing journey and how many will die trying. One thing is certain, they do not want to settle here, they are headed for the wealthier countries and while the vast majority of them are decent people, the tiny minority are ruining it for them by their appalling attacks on women in Cologne and Hamburg on New Year's Eve. The horrible rise of the Far Right has presented scenes resembling Germany in the run up to the Second World War and the financial parallels are there too. It is becoming a very dangerous problem for the European

Union, the Eurozone crisis has not been solved, it has been replaced in the headlines by falling oil and commodity prices.

The stock markets have had the worst beginning to a new year ever. The FTSE 100 and Dow Jones have lost over 20%, stocks on the Chinese market have plummeted by 40% and their economic activity has reached 25 year lows. The Japanese Nikkei has fared little better despite trillions of yen being pumped into the system to stimulate their economy. The Russian economy has contracted by nearly 4% in one year because of the low oil price and wages fell by 10%, the Saudis need oil at over $100 just to break even and the financiers in Abu Dhabi will be expecting to bail out their little neighbours in Dubai before very long. Dubai's situation is little better than that of Greece.

A perfect storm seems to be brewing in the global economy, Professor Steve Keen, Gerald Celente and Peter Schiff all warned of the crash of 2007/8 before it happened. They were mocked by mainstream media, Celente was never invited back on to flagship news shows in America and Schiff is often shouted down and ridiculed for his views. All of them are forecasting the next meltdown to occur this year. They point out quite correctly that all that has changed since 2007/8 is the amount of accumulated debt into an even bigger bubble. All bubbles burst eventually and this will be no different. The UK government developed the 'help to buy' scheme to entice first time buyers back into the housing market and in the last twelve months house prices have increased by 10%. See any sign of a bubble here?

The Bush administration did something similar fifteen years ago when they guaranteed to prospective home buyers that the government would pay for their down payments on their homes. It sounded great at the time, many got their shot at being part of the 'American Dream' but the long term consequences led to a vast bubble in the housing market and ultimately the Sub Prime mortgages disaster and the 07/08 collapse.

The Japanese economy has tried everything to stimulate growth, they have printed trillions of yen, had 0% interest rates for nearly twenty years, yet still the Nikkei is less than 17,000 points from its pre-collapse level of just under 39,000 points. It is common now to get 40, 50 and even 100 year mortgages. In the UK, terms are now being lengthened to 30 or 35 years. Do you see any similarities here? Do you remember Albert Einstein's definition of insanity?

January also brings the annual World Economic Forum Jamboree in Davos, Switzerland. Zurich Airport gets turned into the world's largest collection of private jets and helicopters as the members of the Bilderberg Group and a smattering of celebrities are whisked up to the glittering, alpine resort in their blacked out limousines. No expense is spared in the amount of champagne, caviar and fine wine consumed. Their excesses make the parties of King Louis XVI and Marie Antoinette look like the results of a raid on the dustbins behind Tesco and sycophants from the media will fawn over their every word. But then they do have good reasons to be cheerful up there on their lofty peak, they have been the beneficiaries of the bail out money, the number of billionaires has doubled and best of all, the worn down tax payer has picked up the tab. No wonder then that they suggested pumping $100 trillion stimulus money into the global economy in 2013 and $200 trillion a year later.

Oxfam has just produced a report revealing that sixty-two individuals have as much wealth as three and a half billion people. It's pretty unlikely that any of these individuals did their shopping at the Aldi store in Davos while they were there. Here is the sharpest and most telling contrast. The people in our village were happy to share what little they had with us when we were arrived in 2012. How many members of the glitterati would be so accommodating to complete strangers?

There is another element that has drastically changed in the last five months and that is the Schengen Agreement. It is under great strain and has been suspended in some locations across Europe as a result of the refugee crisis. This has brought long queues and delays to traffic, it is also putting a financial burden on the Eurozone economy, the Euro crisis has not been solved, far from it, the European Central Bank continues to pump €60 billion every month into the system in stimulus measures with the same results- virtually zero growth and more debt to be paid with austerity measures or Cyprus style bail-ins.

Driving south or eastbound should present no problems at all, more time for the opposite is needed, heading for the smaller border points may reduce delays but ultimately, if Schengen fails the EU goes down with it. They will find a way to solve the problem as soon as they can.

Finally, the last words of Steve Jobs have been plastered over the media, perhaps they are only allegorical but if true, they chime exactly with the results of the Care Home survey results that were reported by the Daily Mail in 2012 and one of the main reasons for me writing this book.

It took being on his death bed to realize that being a multi-billionaire now meant nothing. He couldn't pay for someone else to have his illness for him and he probably would have swapped his fortune for another day of life with his nearest and dearest. Time isn't an enemy or some monster lying in wait to attack us, that keeping ever busier, more hectic lives will somehow keep it from our door. It's the most precious gift any of us will ever have and perhaps, the greatest collective mistake we continue to make is ignoring it until it is too late. Maybe the enjoyment of time itself is the greatest achievement any of us can attain to. It doesn't matter how much our homes are worth, if we become famous or not, how many electronic gadgets we accumulate or how much money we have in the bank, we can't take those things with us so why spend our lives struggling to pay for them.

Some readers may well not care one jot about the economic reasons for leaving Britain; it might simply boil down to being sick of the bloody awful weather that has affected the country for the last five years. Who could blame them?

It matters not to me whether my book sells one copy or a million, my life here will continue as it has done since the end of 2011 with adventure, excitement, fulfilment, new challenges and best of all, sharing it with Chris. I'd love to imagine a scene where a person is reading a dog-eared copy of this book in a pub, it's throwing it down outside, as it has been for weeks on end, seeing the sun almost seems like a distant dream and another huge credit card bill awaits them at home. That person puts the book down, finishes their drink and thinks to themselves "I can do that! I want some of that, I'm a human being damn it! My life has value!" and they have, without realizing it, already started to make it happen. That is my objective behind this book, to help one person or one couple enjoy their own adventure, to change their lives forever, anything else will be a huge bonus.

…and for those of you who were wondering - Chris' painting now hangs in pride of place on our lounge wall, a permanent reminder of the power of dreams.

USEFUL INFORMATION

Topic	Website
Property Agents	
Rightmove	www.rightmove.co.uk
Rightmove Overseas	www.rightmove.co.uk/overseas-property
Bulgarian Properties	www.bulgarianproperties.com
Bower Properties	www.bower-properties.com
New Home SV	www.newhomesv.com
Angloinfo	www.property.angloinfo.com
Airlines	
Wizz Air	www.wizzair.com
easyJet	www.easyjet.com
Ryanair	www.ryanair.com
Balkan Holidays	www.balkanholidays.co.uk
Bulgaria Air	www.air.bg
Thonas Cook	www.thomascook.com
Thomson	www.thomson.co.uk
Skyscanner	www.skyscanner.net
flight comparison site	
Car Hire	
Sixt	www.sixt.com
Europcar	www.europcar.com
Avis	www.avis.bg
Bulgaria Car Rent	www.bulgariacarrent.com
Wizz Air	www.wizzair.com

Buses	
Etap Group	www.etapgroup.com
Biomet	www.biomet.bg
BGrazpisanie.com	http://www.bgrazpisanie.com
Bulgaria-AngloINFO	www.bulgaria.angloinfo.com

Trains	
BDZ-Passengers EOOD	www.bdztransportinfo.bg
BGrazpisanie.com	www.bgrazpisanie.com
Bulgaria-AngloINFO	www.bulgaria.angloinfo.com

Taxis	
OK Supertrans (Sofia)	www.oktaxi.net
Burgas Taxi	www.burgastaxi.com
Eko Taxi Burgas	www.ekotaxiburgas.com
HHB Travel	www.varnaairporttaxis.com
	NB. Taxis are safe and readily available. Never pay more than 1lev a kilometer, the price is printed on the back windows.

Transfers	
Travel Republic	www.travelrepublic.co.uk/transfers
Bourgas Airport Transfer	www.bourgas-airport-transfer.com
Sofia Airport Transfer	www.sofia-airport-transfer.com
Varna Airport Transfer	www.varna-airport-transfer.com

Hotels	
Booking.com	www.booking.com
Travel Republic	www.travelrepublic.com
Alpharooms	www.alpharooms.com

Trivago	www.trivago.com
Hotels4u	www.hotels4u.com
News	
Novinite	www.novinite.com
Pirinsko	www.pirinsko.com
Angloinfo	www.angloinfo.com
Elhovo News	www.elhovonews.com
Expat Network	www.expatnetwork.com
The Telegraph	www.telegraph.co.uk/expat
Translator Services	
Dilyana Kuzmanovo (Yambol & Elhovo region)	dillybg@yahoo.com
Maria Hristova	alexa76@abv.bg
	Property agents and expat social media sites will have contact details for translators in other regions.
Currency Transfer	
Smart Currency Index	www.smartcurrencyexchange.com
Currency Exchange	www.currencyindex.co.uk
Transferwise	www.transferwise.com
Tourism Sites	
Bansko Guide	www.bansko-guide.com
Bulgaria Travel	www.bulgariatravel.org
Travel-Bulgaria	www.travel-bulgaria.com
Travel in Bulgaria	www.travelinbulgaria.eu
Bansko Ski	www.banskoski.com

Birdwatching Bulgaria Spatia Wildlife Walking Bulgaria Alfa Riders (Horse Riding)	www.birdwatchingbulgaria.com www.spatiawildlife.com www.walkingbulgaria.com www.alfariders.com
Expat Community Rogozen Treasures Eat.Stay.Love.Bulgaria **Facebook Groups:** Living in Bulgaria The Bansko Notice Board Bulgaria 4 All What Where When around Bulgaria Buy, Sell or Swap items group British Expats in Bulgaria Bulgaria Insurance Services Homes in Bulgaria for Sale & Rent Seed Swap Bulgaria UK 2 BG Transportation Services UK Transportation	www.rogozentreasures.com www.eatstaylovebulgaria.com

Services to Bulgaria European Pet Transport Network Aztec Villa	
UK Food Supplies Freezerman Ltd Mel's British Supermarket Chocolate Box Sokoni Foods UK Food 2U	www.freezerman.co.uk www.mbcofoodstores.com www.thechocolatebox1.webs.com www.sokoni.eu www.ukfood2u.com

SOURCES & REFERENCES
Books

Manufacturing Consent – D.Herman & Noam Chomsky (Vintage Publishing 1995)
The New Few
Ferdinand Mount (Simon & Schuster UK 2012)
The Establishment
Owen Jones (Allen Lane, Penguin Books 2014)
Confessions of an Economic Hitman
John Perkins (Ebury Press 2006)
War is a Racket
General Smedley Butler (Feral House 1935, 2003 Reprint)
How the World Works
Noam Chomsky (Hamish Hamilton 2011)
63 Documents the Government Doesn't Want You To Read
Jesse Ventura with Dick Russell (Skyhorse Publishing 2011/12)
Postcapitalism: A Guide to Our Future
Paul Mason (Penguin 2016)
Capital in the 21st Century
Thomas Piketty (Harvard University Press 2014)
The Corruption of Capitalism: why Rentiers Thrive and Work Does Not Pay

Guy Standing (Bite back 2016)

How did we get into this mess?
George Monbiot (Verso 2017)

Austerity: The history of a dangerous idea
Mark Blyth (Oxford University Press 2015)

Related Links & Documentaries

The following can all be found on YouTube:
It's Just a Ride
Bill Hicks
Born Bankrupt: State of the UK economy, Part 1 & 2 – 24/08/12
Zeitgeist: The Movie 2007 – Peter Joseph
Four Horsemen – feature documentary – official version
The Story of your Enslavement
Stefan Molyneux
The Greatest Speech Ever Made
Charlie Chaplin, extract from *The Great Dictator*
Help, Help, I'm being repressed!!
Monty Python and The Holy Grail
Silly Money – Investment Bankers
Bird & Fortune
European Debt Crisis – Economic Collapse In 3 Minutes
Clarke & Dawe
The Most Honest 3 Minutes in Television History
Jeff Daniels
Spent: Looking for Change (full documentary)
Fantastic 12 yr. old Victoria Grant explains how banks commit fraud
This 12 year old girl talks without notes in front of the Public Banking Conference in Philadelphia and explains why her home country, Canada and most of the rest of the World is in debt.
The Truth about Cancer: A Global Quest   The True History of Chemo & The Pharmaceutical Monopoly- The Truth about Cancer

Keiser Report - Weekly episodes on Russia Today detailing the lastest fraudulent acts by the global banking community.

14 year old girl picks fight with bully TV Host and WINS!

George Carlin – *The American Dream*

Voices from the Gas Fields: it started with just ONE well Ian R Crane

How Big Oil Conquered The World Corbett Report

BBC Radio 4: *Brits Abroad* Episode 5 of 5

www.bbc.co.uk/programmes/b0645fz0

References

Section 1 – Joining the Dots

1.
www.dailymail.co.uk/news/article-2950206/Buoys-big-boat-s-largest-yacht-set-stand-222-metres-long-cost-800m-commissioned-one-rich-owner.html
www.superyachtfan.com

2.
https://www.washingtonpost.com/news/on-leadership/wp/2015/08/25/the-average-sp-500-ceo-makes-more-than-200-times-the-median-worker/

3.
www.ibtimes.co.uk/number-people-employed-zero-hour-contracts-rises-20-year-almost-one-million-1580323

4.
http://www.telegraph.co.uk/news/uknews/immigration/8585750/Frank-Field-Migrants-take-nine-out-of-10-jobs.html
www.theguardian.com/politics/2016/may/20/reality-check-are-eu-migrants-really-taking-british-jobs
http://www.ons.gov.uk/peoplepopulationandcommunity/populationandmigration/internationalmigration/bulletins/migrationstatisticsquarterlyreport/2015-08-27

5.
http://www.telegraph.co.uk/finance/personalfinance/pensions/8840963/Baby-boomers-are-very-privileged-human-beings.html

http://www.news.com.au/finance/generations/as-generation-y-struggles-to-stay-afloat-the-baby-boomers-have-plenty-to-answer-for/news-story/6630927d1f80c976e6702032085cb950
http://www.chinainsight.info/society-2016/1161-the-luckiest-generations-in-the-u-s-and-in-china-the-baby-boomers-and-the-generation-89-part-iv.html
compared with:
http://www.bbc.com/news/business-36391621
http://www.bbc.com/news/magazine-21302065
http://www.bbc.com/news/magazine-36396217

6.
https://www.youtube.com/watch?v=AuqemytQ5QA

7.
www.bbc.co.uk/news/business-18944097

8.
https://www.theguardian.com/uk-news/undercover-with-paul-lewis-and-rob-evans/2016/sep/09/former-undercover-police-spies-have-become-hostile-towards-scotland-yard

9.
www.dailymail.co.uk/news/article-470235
http://www.telegraph.co.uk/news/nhs/10775085/Record-numbers-on-happy-pills.html

10.
www.theguardian.com/money/2011/jan/06/credit-cards-pay-mortgage-rent

11.
www.youtube.com/watch?v=zq3OQ2QBqms
https://psmag.com/the-imf-confirms-that-trickle-down-economics-is-indeed-a-joke-207d7ca469b#.z041q2ao7
http://www.independent.co.uk/news/business/analysis-and-features/the-wealth-that-failed-to-trickle-down-report-suggests-rich-do-get-richer-while-poor-stay-poor

12.
"The younger generation are leading the way-they see sharing as a way of life and are not so keen on owning things" - Sarwant Singh from Frost and Sullivan Market Research.
Perhaps Mr Singh is correct, or are young people resigned to never becoming as affluent as their parents?
Extract taken from:
www.bbc.com/news/business-20663919

13.
http://www.dailymail.co.uk/news/article-3520047/Annuity-rates-slashed-17-year-Thousands-savers-endure-savage-cuts-retirement-incomes.html

14.
http://www.bbc.com/news/business-37307347
or not quite so subliminally...
http://www.bbc.com/capital/story/20130813-the-dark-side-of-the-golden-years

15.
http://www.japantimes.co.jp/news/2009/01/06/refere
nce/lessons-from-when-the-bubble-
burst/#.Vo5pkbZ94_5

16.
http://www.usnews.com/opinion/blogs/economic-
intelligence/2012/08/27/repeal-of-glass-steagall-
caused-the-financial-crisis

17.
www.theguardian.com/business/2016/jul/11/hsbc-us-
money-laundering-george-osborne-report
www.bbc.com/news/business-36768140

18.
http://www.forbes.com/forbes/welcome/?toURL=http
://www.forbes.com/sites/nathanlewis/2013/05/03/the
-cyprus-bank-bail-in-is-another-crony-bankster-scam
http://www.zerohedge.com/news/2015-10-28/weve-
all-been-warned-cyprus-bail-model-coming-country-
near-you

19. A regular guest on U.S. Mainstream news outlets,
Gerald Celente of the Trends Research Institute, spoke
a few too many home truths in these clips before the
2007/8 financial crisis.
https://www.youtube.com/watch?v=d0QdLkgvJwM

20. Very emotive subject however no science is 100% accurate and more research is needed.
http://yournewswire.com/wow-italian-court-rules-vaccine-caused-autism-us-media-blacks-out-story/
http://www.mothering.com/forum/47vaccinations/1489738-italian-mmr-autism-decision-overturned.html
https://www.autismspeaks.org/site-wide/mmr
https://sharylattkisson.com/cdc-scientist-we-scheduled-meeting-to-destroy-vaccine-autism-study-documents/
https://thetruthaboutcancer.com/are-vaccines-safe-survey/
http://www.nvic.org/informed-consent.aspx
https://www.theguardian.com/society/2012/sep/01/thalidomide-scandal-timeline
http://www.bbc.com/news/uk-37183873
http://www.forbes.com/forbes/welcome/?toURL=http://www.forbes.com/sites/jamestaylor/2011/11/23/climategate-2-0-new-e-mails-rock-the-global-warming-debate/

21.
https://www.propublica.org/article/how-many-die-from-medical-mistakes-in-us-hospitals

22.
https://www.theguardian.com/business/2015/feb/23/uk-finance-bonuses-to-top-100bn-since-financial-crisis
http://www.nytimes.com/2009/07/31/business/31pay.html

Current State of the World

1.
http://enenews.com/tepco-official-admits-melted-fuel-flowed-like-volcanic-lava-nuclear-expert-melt-containment-vessel-fuel-scattered-all-place-reuters-fuel-melted
http://www.cbsnews.com/news/fukushima-tepco-power-japan-nuclear-meltdown-apologizes-cover-up/
http://enenews.com/ap-officials-admit-deadly-fukushima-meltdown-coverup-unprecedented-nuclear-disaster-about-bad-tepco-president-lied-about-meltdowns

2.
http://blogs.channel4.com/factcheck/factcheck-what-else-does-the-church-of-england-invest-in/14091
https://www.theguardian.com/sustainable-business/comic-relief-panorama-cash-arms-tobacco-charities-investment

3.
http://blueandgreentomorrow.com/2013/09/09/church-of-england-under-fire-for-10m-arms-investment/

4.
http://edition.cnn.com/2014/02/18/us/chevron-pennsylvania-explosion-pizzas/
https://www.youtube.com/watch?v=3W2N-XCDsFY

5.
http://www.usatoday.com/story/money/business/2014/02/22/exxon-mobil-tillerson-ceo-fracking/5726603/

6.
www.dailymail.co.uk/news/article-2608449/Village-damned-Mysterious-suicides-Agonising-illness-And-25-years-UKs-worst-case-mass-poisoning-evidence

7.
http://www.imdb.com/title/tt0195685/?ref_=nv_sr_3

8.
https://www.youtube.com/watch?v=9HzSOrbvNUQ

9.
http://www.independent.co.uk/voices/comment/what-is-ttip-and-six-reasons-why-the-answer-should-scare-you-9779688.html
https://www.youtube.com/watch?v=Y4OQeekSD6s

10.
http://www.pambazuka.org/governance/bangladeshi-textile-factory-collapse-over-900-dead-lessons-africa
http://www.reuters.com/article/us-bangladesh-fire-idUSBRE94801T20130509

11.
http://www.bbc.com/news/world-africa-19292909

12.
http://www.eyewitnesstohistory.com/snprelief4.htm

13.
https://www.theguardian.com/world/2013/sep/26/nsa-surveillance-anti-vietnam-muhammad-ali-mlk
14.
https://en.wikipedia.org/wiki/Frank_Church

15.
https://www.washingtonpost.com/world/national-security/band-of-activists-who-burglarized-fbi-office-in-1971-come-forward/2014/01/07/898d9e0c-77b4-11e3-8963-b4b654bcc9b2_story.html

16.
http://www.nytimes.com/2014/11/16/magazine/what-an-uncensored-letter-to-mlk-reveals.html
http://www.huffingtonpost.com/2014/01/20/martin-luther-king-fbi_n_4631112.html
http://www.nytimes.com/2012/04/29/opinion/sunday/terrorist-plots-helped-along-by-the-fbi.html
https://www.theguardian.com/world/2014/jul/21/government-agents-directly-involved-us-terror-plots-report
https://www.youtube.com/watch?v=GGHXjO8wHsA
http://www.wikileaksusa.org/operation_mockingbird.html

17.
http://europe.newsweek.com/my-god-theyre-killing-us-our-1970-coverage-kent-state-326852?rm=eu
http://www.history.com/topics/vietnam-war/kent-state

18.
http://www.bbc.com/news/magazine-37517619

19.
www.youtube.com/watch?v=Z3XeuCxJCzg

20.
https://www.theguardian.com/world/2004/jun/11/dut
roux.ianblack

21.
https://www.theguardian.com/world/series/charlie-
skelton-bilderblog
http://www.goodreads.com/book/show/1790841.The
_True_Story_of_the_Bilderberg_Group
https://www.amazon.com/Shadows-Power-Council-
Relations-American/dp/0882791346
https://www.youtube.com/watch?v=CyBCFvbU--Y

Weapons of Mass Distraction.
1.
http://www.globescan.com/news_archives/bbcreut_c
ountry.html
http://www.gallup.com/poll/185927/americans-trust-
media-remains-historical-low.aspx

2.
*"In general, the art of government consists of taking as
much money as possible from one class of citizens to
give to another"* - Voltaire, 1694-1778

3.
http://www.dailymail.co.uk/property/article-3787059/Millions-working-families-cut-essentials-pay-rent-says-Shelter.html
http://www.bbc.com/news/education-36144084

4.
www.lawfulpath.com/ref/sw4qw/index.shtml

5.
http://news.bbc.co.uk/2/hi/uk/7449255.stm
http://www.telegraph.co.uk/news/politics/conservative/8826360/History-of-recent-data-blunders-by-government.html

If Voting Changes Anything It'd be Illegal
1.
http://www.bbc.com/news/business-29353907
http://www.dailymail.co.uk/travel/travel_news/article-2807555/Monarch-Airlines-agrees-125m-rescue-package-staff-suffer-30-pay-cut-hundreds-set-redundancy.html

2.
www.opendemocracy.net/ourkingdom/robin-mcalpine/whats-really-happening-at-grangemouth-and-what-it-tells-us
http://www.manchestereveningnews.co.uk/business/meet-billionaire-ineos-boss-jim-10026213

3.
https://www.youtube.com/watch?v=3we77fFdpVw

4.

http://247wallst.com/economy/2016/10/04/imf-further-downgrades-global-growth-forecasts/
http://www.latimes.com/business/la-fi-agenda-mergers-20151116-story.html
http://www.bloomberg.com/news/articles/2016-01-05/2015-was-best-ever-year-for-m-a-this-year-looks-pretty-good-too
http://www.marketwatch.com/story/us-companies-spent-record-amount-on-buybacks-over-past-12-months-2016-06-22
http://www.nasdaq.com/article/share-buybacks-rise-to-record-level-in-first-quarter-cm639356
http://www.reuters.com/investigates/special-report/usa-buybacks-pay/

5.

https://www.theguardian.com/politics/2000/nov/05/uk.oil

6.

http://ec.europa.eu/social/main.jsp?catId=1036

7.

http://www.independent.ie/irish-news/election-2016/whole-country-hopping-mad-and-talking-about-water-charges-but-not-the-dil-34661437.html

8.

http://www.koreaherald.com/view.php?ud=20141010000544

Genetically Modified Thinking
Repent & Reform
1.
http://www.sahistory.org.za/topic/truth-and-reconciliation-commission-trc

2.
http://www.nuenergy.org/nikola-tesla-radiant-energy-system/

3.
http://www.goodreads.com/book/show/30289.The_Republic

Section 2 – The Great Escape From Austerity, Conformity and the Rat Race
1.
www.amazon.co.uk/Psychic-Warrior-Paranormal-Espionage-Programme/dp/1905570384/ref=sr_1_1?s=books&ie=UTF8&qid=1475683232&sr=1-1&ke

2.
https://www.youtube.com/watch?v=K2Wl2M4yLkY
https://www.youtube.com/watch?v=IKRcKfJFr48

3.
http://www.imdb.com/title/tt0241303/?ref_=nv_sr_3

4.
The Algarve Resident, January, 2012.

5.
http://www.bbc.com/news/magazine-37411250
https://www.theguardian.com/commentisfree/2016/mar/01/proposed-snoopers-charter-shows-governments-contempt-for-privacy
"Trust is good, surveillance is better" - East German Stasi motto.

6.
http://www.dailymail.co.uk/health/article-2515508/Top-regrets-dying-revealed.html
https://www.youtube.com/watch?v=JZ2xhBQ8eGA

7.
https://www.techjuice.pk/a-data-scientist-explains-odds-of-dying-in-a-terrorist-attack/
https://www.washingtonpost.com/news/monkey-cage/wp/2015/11/23/youre-more-likely-to-be-fatally-crushed-by-furniture-than-killed-by-a-terrorist/

8.
http://www.dailymail.co.uk/travel/travel_news/article-2762021/Security-scare-JFK-Airport-New-York-luggage-logo-similar-ISIS-insignia

9.
http://www.telegraph.co.uk/news/uknews/terrorism-in-the-uk/9380536/M6-fake-cigarette-terrorism-alert-We-could-have-been-shot-say-passengers.html

10.
http://www.dailymail.co.uk/money/news/article-3788100/Cost-basic-funeral-soars-13th-year-running-costing-average-3-897.html

Further Information

Facebook Page: It's About Time. Quit the Rat Race Forever

https://www.facebook.com/Its-about-time-Quit-the-rat-race-forever-1703348223216438/